The Unofficial Commonwealth

The Story of the Commonwealth Foundation 1965–1980

The Unofficial Commonwealth

The Story of the Commonwealth Foundation 1965–1980

JOHN CHADWICK

London
GEORGE ALLEN & UNWIN
Boston   Sydney

George Allen & Unwin (Publishers) Ltd,
40 Museum Street, London WC1A 1LU, UK

George Allen & Unwin (Publishers) Ltd,
Park Lane, Hemel Hempstead, Herts HP2 4TE, UK

Allen & Unwin, Inc.,
9 Winchester Terrace, Winchester, Mass. 01890, USA

George Allen & Unwin Australia Pty Ltd,
8 Napier Street, North Sydney, NSW 2060, Australia

First published in 1982

British Library Cataloguing in Publication Data

Chadwick, John
    The unofficial Commonwealth: the story of the
Commonwealth Foundation 1965–1980.
1. Commonwealth Foundation – History
I. Title
331.7′12′0601   HD8038.G7
ISBN 0-04-341021-9

Library of Congress Cataloging in Publication Data

Chadwick, John, 1915 –
    The unofficial Commonwealth.
Bibliography: p.
Includes index.
1. Commonwealth Foundation (British Commonwealth)
2. Professions – Great Britain. 3. Professions –
Commonwealth of Nations. I. Title.
HD8038.G7C47   331.7′12′0601   82-1742
ISBN 0-04-341021-9   AACR2

Set in 11 on 12 point Baskerville by Bedford Typesetters
and printed in Great Britain
by Mackays of Chatham

To friends and former colleagues
across the Commonwealth

Contents

Foreword

Much has been written about the development of the modern Commonwealth. Others have concentrated on the Commonwealth's governmental institutions. In this book we learn something of the achievements of non-governmental organisations and individuals in the 'unofficial' Commonwealth. The accepted terminology is stiff and impersonal. I like to think that it is here, among the far-reaching informal bodies, where the people of the Commonwealth meet.

The Commonwealth as an international association of states is widely known; its influence is significant; its contribution to world affairs is increasingly recognised. Its unofficial activities spreading through many varied exchanges have been largely unpublicised; there is little on record either for the general reader or for the student.

John Chadwick's book will fill that gap in our knowledge. He traverses the professional and private Commonwealth scene as it has developed and expanded since the 1960s. The story is inevitably linked to the growth of the Commonwealth Foundation. Established by Commonwealth heads of government in 1965, with an imaginative and pragmatic brief to 'promote professional exchange within the Commonwealth', the Foundation has been a catalyst for much of the Commonwealth's work among the institutions and people of the Commonwealth. As its founding Director, for the first fourteen years to mid-1980, John Chadwick has been uniquely placed to listen, to influence and to record the achievements of those years. His account is an invaluable personal history of the development of the Foundation within the wider non-official scene.

In providing support for this publication, the Board of Trustees of the Commonwealth Foundation acknowledges and respects the author's personal views, which do not necessarily accord in all instances with their own, or the Foundation's member governments, collectively or individually.

Mr Chadwick's lucid and informative account will be widely read by those who seek knowledge of the Commonwealth, and wish to explore its example of hope to the world community.

THE RT HON. SIR ADETOKUNBO ADEMOLA,
GCON, KBE, KT CFR, PC
Chairman of the Board of Trustees
Victoria Island
Lagos, Nigeria
December 1981

Preface

The Commonwealth is still better geared to abuse than praise. In this short study I have suggested that its future lies as much, if not more, with people than with governments. To argue in short that it has now become a functional rather than a political force for good.

Lecturing in the early 1960s to a forgotten audience I had hinted that 'the further one leans under the bonnet of the Commonwealth machine, the more hitherto unnoticed parts one finds. The difficulty is as much to avoid tinkering with what other mechanics have had their hands on, as to single out the private bits and pieces to which no one as yet has added a much needed drop of oil. Committees and conferences abound and the Commonwealth has no lack of drivers (front and rear). But, if it is to survive the next perilous decade it may well be, as a distinguished Canadian put it not so long ago, "because thousands of teachers, scholars and administrators, working or studying in each others' countries . . . strengthen the fabric of an association in which people get along better than governments".'

Those words were uttered well before the Commonwealth Foundation, whose activities figure largely here, had come to life. But, given the wealth of private, learned, voluntary and professional endeavour within the Commonwealth in its various stages of development from the late 1940s onwards, it is remarkable how little attention has been paid to date to the significance of the functional relationship.

Platitudes there have been in plenty. They have done much to obscure the enduring value of the Commonwealth relationship. Kith and kin, the common language, a shared historical heritage, like educational standards – nearly all such debatable shibboleths do more harm than good to a proper understanding of the Commonwealth of the 1980s.

One may now reject the jibe of a leading British conservative who, in the late 1950s, dismissed the whole concept as 'a gigantic farce'. Far better to accept, as a former Prime Minister of New Zealand, the late Sir Keith Holyoake, put it on returning home from the stormy London Heads of Government Conference of 1966: 'The Commonwealth is changing, but it is vital, it is vigorous, and it is still very much in the formative stage. We must not close our minds and think – this is the Commonwealth and here it stops: here are the lines it has followed in the past and must follow in the future.'

Or, jumping some thirteen years ahead, better to endorse the sage reflections of an anonymous Commonwealth elder with years of practical experience behind him. As he put it at a high-level Anglo-Canadian colloquium held under the auspices of Leeds University in October 1979: 'One important strength of the [Commonwealth] association lay in its freedom from the need to advocate a response to every difficulty or crisis. That did not mean that the Commonwealth could not act usefully on particular occasions: but it did imply that there was no call to have a whole apparatus of rules or a vote, and no compulsion to reach strict or binding formulae ... The Commonwealth in short [was] an example of advanced political behaviour where there was an opportunity to discuss complicated matters in a civilised way.'*

Those privileged (as I have been over close on three decades in a strictly back-room way) to attend Commonwealth meetings of all kinds, will testify – allowance made for a few notable exceptions – to the refreshing absence of public postures struck. If then politicians can so discipline themselves, how much more may one expect by way of co-operation between those happily far removed from the stress and strain of politics. It is with them – with the private army of professionals, the academics, those involved in learned and voluntary endeavour, with the arts and the media; with, in short, all those who go to make up the 'unofficial Commonwealth' – that this book is primarily concerned.

*The Commonwealth Foundation, Occasional Paper no. 49, *Britain and Canada: A Colloquium held at Leeds University, October 1979*, p. 98.

Acknowledgements

My first debt is to the Chairman and Trustees of the Commonwealth Foundation for their encouragement of this venture, and to its Director, Mr Ric Throssell, for the access which he has given me to Foundation papers.

Secondly, I must thank the Royal Commonwealth Society and in particular its Librarian, Donald Simpson, and his staff, for the research facilities so willingly placed at my disposal and for their patience in dealing with numerous requests for enlightenment.

Thirdly, I owe a considerable debt to representatives of the many Commonwealth professional associations referred to in this book; not least to the Chairwoman of their Standing Committee, Miss Margaret Brayton, for advice and correction repeatedly received.

Fourthly, my thanks go to other friends and former colleagues, far more expert in Commonwealth affairs than I, for their kindness in commenting so patiently on my manuscript and in offering much valuable advice. At the risk of omitting some who have helped to avoid sins of both commission and omission I must single out Richard Symonds, author of that remarkable survey of 1966, *The British and Their Successors*, from whose visionary wisdom I have greatly profited. My gratitude also goes to the secretaries of the Commonwealth Associations of Surveying and Land Economy, of Architecture and of Legal Education, Robert Steel, CBE, Graham McCullough and Thomas Colchester, CMG, who, apart from stalwart co-operation during my own years as Director of the Commonwealth Foundation, have taken infinite trouble in reading, discussing and correcting the drafts of this book at various stages.

Fifthly, I am equally indebted to such scholars as Professor Richard Jolly, lately of the Institute of Development Studies, Sussex, and to Professor David Dilks of the Department of Modern History at Leeds University for their comments and encouragement.

ACKNOWLEDGEMENTS

Sixthly, my warm thanks go to the Director and Editor of the Duke University Press, Durham, North Carolina, for permission to draw extensively, in preparing this book, on a chapter which I had contributed in 1966 to that university's publication *A Decade of the Commonwealth, 1955–64.*

Finally, this book would not have seen the light of day but for the patient typing and retyping of the manuscript by my former colleague and secretary, Mrs Nancy Duncan, MBE. She, as though dealing with a more illustrious namesake of mine, has upheld her previous record for unravelling latter-day Minoan scripts.

London, September 1981

PART I

*Empire and Commonwealth –
the Unofficial Side of the Coin*

1

The Birth and Growth of the Charitable Idea

> Charity in its legal sense comprises four principal
> divisions: trusts for the relief of poverty; trusts for
> the advancement of education; trusts for the
> advancement of religion; and trusts for other
> purposes beneficial to the community, not falling
> under any of the preceding heads.
>
> Lord Macnaghten, 1891

> 'The British Government will ... take any further
> steps needed to constitute the [Commonwealth]
> Foundation as a legal charity.
>
> HM Stationery Office,
> Cmnd 2714, August 1965

From the first relevant English statute of 1601[1] to the Charities
Act of 1960[2] the church, acting through its ecclesiastical courts,
may be said to have influenced the law relating to charities.
In the Middle Ages great importance was attached to charitable
giving, both as a Christian duty and as a means of salvation.

The Church stood to gain directly through gifts for the
advancement of religion ... the Ecclesiastical Courts
singled out for special privilege gifts to charity ... they
put charitable trusts in a class by themselves. First, they

3

exempted charitable gifts from the rule against perpetuities ... They achieved this by conferring upon charity a fictitious personality, treating it as an artificial legatee. They then granted to it the right to hold property in perpetuity if it was to be used for a charitable purpose.[3]

The Reformation, however, brought many changes. By the turn of the sixteenth century uncertainties had arisen as to the very objects of charitable trusts. Many of these, with educational advancement and social welfare in view, had by then been divorced from ecclesiastical administration. A new society, entrepreneurial and adventurous, was emerging. With it, as so often at a time of major social change, came both economic distress and increasing vagrancy. It was a combination of such circumstances, coupled with a realisation that the aims of many existing charities were now outdated, which led to the first statutory definition of charitable intent.

Thus the preamble to the Act of 1601, which was intended to 'redress the Mis-employment of Lands, Goods and stocks of money heretofore given to Charitable Uses', defined purposes deemed to be charitable in the following terms:

The relief of aged, impotent and poor people: the maintenance of sick and maimed soldiers and mariners, schools of learning, free schools and scholars in universities, the repair of bridges, ports, havens, causeways, churches, sea-banks and highways: the education and preferment of orphans; the relief, stock or maintenance of houses of correction; the marriage of poor maids, the supportation aid and help of young tradesmen, handicraftsmen and persons decayed, the relief or redemption of prisoners or captives; and the aid or care of any poor inhabitants concerning payment of fifteens, setting out soldiers and other taxes.

While the preamble seems by hindsight astonishingly comprehensive, embracing as it does social welfare, education, defence of the realm, public works and trade, it was in those days seen as a guide rather than as a limiting factor. It was indeed inferred in the Act that 'many more hereafter will (hopefully) charitably give'.

The longer-term significance of the statute was fourfold. First, it recognised the increasing role of the state, as opposed to the church alone, in charitable endeavour. Secondly, it accepted that the intentions of many earlier donors had been estopped 'by reason of frauds, breaches of trust and negligence'. Thirdly, the Act provided machinery for the better control of charitable trusts. Thus the Lord Chancellor of England was now empowered to appoint commissions of bishops 'and other persons of good and sound behaviour' to inquire into suspected local cases of malfeasance and to ensure generally that all goods, chattels and moneys destined for charitable use were 'duly and faithfully thus employed'. Fourthly, the statute so fully recognised the spirit of individual and collective charitable intent, so cynically foresaw the opportunities for abuse and so well appreciated the need for an elastic interpretation of 'donor's intent' that it was not until the mid-nineteenth century that any serious attempt was made to improve the law.

By then, to quote from a Charity Commission memorandum of 1972, 'many trusts had fallen into the hands of corrupt or lazy Trustees, or had disappeared or had been misapplied, while others had become hopelessly out of date'.[4] It was this situation which, following numerous parliamentary debates and commissions of inquiry, was to lead to the creation, under the Charitable Trusts Act of 1853,[5] of a Board of Charity Commissioners. Taken with amending legislation enacted in 1855 and 1860 that statute was, in Nathan's words, to prove 'a thoroughgoing and comprehensive measure . . . a milestone in the history of the law of charitable trusts'. It was at that time that a Charity Commission was first established, with powers of investigation, including those of the scrutiny of accounts. These, trustees of charities were now required to furnish annually. The commissioners were further empowered to advise, arbitrate and generally to control the institution of legal proceedings on behalf of charitable trusts as well as their dealings in real estate. The Act also provided for the appointment of a Treasurer of Public Charities and of a Trustee of Charitable Funds. Between them these officers ensured that 'land and securities could be placed in the custody of a body

5

having perpetual succession and without prejudice to the administration of the trust by the trustees. This was an admirable means of preventing the disappearance of trust endowments.'[6]

So matters rested for close on one hundred further years.

The end of World War II was to prove the next turning point. At that juncture the rapid passage, between 1944 and 1948, of the Education, National Insurance and National Assistance Acts was, as Lord Beveridge suggested, to create a need for 'political invention to find new ways of fruitful co-operation between public authorities and voluntary agencies'.[7] In short – to borrow once more from Lord Nathan's admirable analysis of the state of charities in postwar Britain – all forms of voluntary organisation were now faced with the task of redefining their function in a changed social setting. 'The whole voluntary movement was faced with steeply rising costs at a time when the traditional type of benefactor was finding it increasingly difficult to continue to support charitable effort.' In short, as the Attlee administration agreed, the time had come to investigate the latter-day relevance of numerous existing trusts; to catalogue them comprehensively for the first time, to redefine the aims of charities and the range of investment possibilities open to them, and above all to examine the function of charity in what had now become the Welfare State. Thus it came about in January 1950 that a departmental committee of inquiry, chaired by Lord Nathan, was appointed by the Prime Minister. Its terms of reference were: 'to consider and report on the changes in the law and practice (except as regards taxation) relating to charitable trusts in England and Wales which would be necessary to enable the maximum benefit to the community to be derived from them'. Out of the deliberations of the Nathan Committee, not without much parliamentary opposition, was to emerge the Charities Act of 1960.[8]

The broad aims of the new statute were 'to modernise the machinery of administration of charity law ... to establish a statutory foundation for voluntary co-operation between charity and the statutory welfare services on a basis of equality and partnership ... to establish a central register of charities and to extend and specify the conditions which must be satisfied before the purposes of a charitable trust can be altered'.[9]

In view of what will be said later in this book on the 'adversary factor', that is, of the relationship between certain Commonwealth governments and their nationally based charitable or voluntary societies, it should at this point be emphasised that under the new statute of 1960 the Charity Commissioners were, as the bishops had been in the days of the first Elizabeth, to remain free from government control. Even though the Act itself had of necessity been piloted through the Commons by the Home Secretary of the day, neither that minister nor his successors were granted any power to direct the commissioners. Nor were the latter to be answerable to Parliament for their actions. The courts alone could challenge their decisions. All that was required of the commissioners executively was that they should report annually to the Home Secretary on their operations.

In practice the Act of 1960 was, short of invading the autonomy of charitable and voluntary bodies, designed to help them to operate with more efficiency. Thus free legal advice now became available to trustees of charities and to their advisers or employees. They could be guided as to how best the original purposes of an outdated trust could be adapted to more recent circumstances. At the same time, and this was a significant advance, Section 4 of the Act required all charities in England and Wales (Scotland as yet enjoying no such law) to be registered. This in practice meant an increasingly strict investigation of the bona fides of proposed new charitable bodies, since their admission to the register would automatically entitle them to tax privileges. At the same time the commissioners were now empowered to inquire into the activities of individual charitable bodies, to call for properly audited accounts and to encourage local authorities to review the operation of charities within their areas.

In all this the newly appointed Official Custodian for Charities, whose powers derived from Section 3 of the Act, was to play an important part. For it was he who had to act as the permanent holder of charity lands and of other property and shares vested in him and he who would collect dividends and remit them, free of tax, to relevant trustees.

If so much has been said, by way of introduction, on the

7

conduct of charitable bodies in Britain and as to the measure
of official interest in them, the excuse for doing so is threefold.
First, the development of charitable organisations in this
country, their aims and objects from the earliest days and the
restricted control exercised over their activities by the state
clearly provided a pattern by which dominions of settlement
and colonies of occupation were later to be largely guided.
Secondly, the 'charitable instinct', spreading from these
islands through church missionary societies, pioneers of
education and later traders, voluntary workers and not least
the wives of colonial administrators, had been instrumental in
creating a network of voluntary, often linked, organisations
throughout the modern Commonwealth. Prominent in such
endeavour were to be the many learned and professional
societies, founded in Britain but which, because of the growth
of Empire, were to do much to promote the concept of the
Commonwealth as a functional force for good.

The strength of the charitable ethos as a peculiarly Anglo-
Saxon (and incidentally 'exportable') phenomenon may be
appreciated from two bald figures. First: in England and Wales
alone some 2,500 new charities are added annually to the
register established under the Act of 1960. Second: that
register (to the exclusion of the so-called 'friendly societies')
now contains no less than 130,000 entries – some ten times the
number of US charities registered with the Library of Congress
in Washington.

Today the bulk of those organisations on the London register
will of course be charities with strictly domestic interests, as
often as not parochial and possessed of minute funds. A few,
chiefly involved with civil liberties, race and aspects of social
welfare, may veer increasingly towards the fringes of political
involvement and thus raise doubts in the minds of the commissioners themselves as to their proper maintenance on the
register.

One should not venture too far in this context into the
discretion of the commissioners. The 'Moonies' trial will be
fresh in many memories. But it is relevant, in passing, to draw
attention to some of the practical problems encountered by the
Charity Commission when endeavouring to decide what
constitutes the 'general public benefit'. At one extreme, as

illustrated in a recent article in *The Times*,[10] looms the dilemma resulting from Thomas Man's charitable award of 1713 of 'six chaldrons of coal' per annum to the poor (if any) of Tooting Graveny. Allowing for compound interest that gift today represents £5,885 worth of coal per year. To whom should it now be distributed in default of any traceable indigents in Tooting Graveny? At the other extreme, reverting to the Unification Church, where does denominational freedom and the right of religious sects to decide on the public interest begin and end? Given the relief from income tax which charitable status generally attracts, such questions affect the common weal not only in Britain but elsewhere in the Commonwealth.

Far more to the point, as involving this study, has been the increasing number of charities registered in the postwar years, whose concern has been international or Commonwealth-wide, as opposed to strictly local, in intent.

It is towards the latter that this study will be mainly directed. But with the legal background to charitable endeavour now briefly sketched, and with a reminder that the British concept of what is charitable covers a wide field ranging through church and educational endeavour, the activities of learned societies and the professions to social welfare, relief, the arts and sport, it is now time to examine how such efforts prospered in earlier days, not within the British Isles alone but outward from a British base. How in short did the 'unofficial Commonwealth', through an earlier Empire, come to life?

In the following chapter an effort will be made to summarise the strength and spread of non-governmental bodies throughout the Commonwealth as they existed in the 1960s. But a number of the organisations there listed had found their origins in far earlier days. While titles will often have changed to adapt to changing times, basic aims will have survived, thus underlining how well-founded the efforts of several such leading bodies have proved.

The earliest of all British-based but Empire-minded 'charities' was undoubtedly the Royal Society of London. Founded informally in or about 1645 by a group of scholars, its Second Charter, granted by Charles II in 1663, described this venerable scientific body as 'The Royal Society of London for Improving

9

Natural Knowledge'. Its influence on Empire and later Commonwealth is evident from chapter I(i) of its statutes, where it is laid down that every candidate for admission as a fellow 'must be a British subject or Commonwealth citizen or citizen of the Irish Republic or, in the opinion of the Council, ordinarily resident in a Commonwealth country'.

Less ancient, but falling within the same category of learned charitable bodies which from their earliest days influenced and spread knowledge of the Empire, were the Royal Geographical Society, founded in 1830, and the Royal Society of Arts, Manufactures and Commerce launched from a London coffee-house in 1754.

Between them the three societies truly reflected 'an age of insatiable curiosity and creative power'; this over a period when 'our fathers conquered Canada and half India, rediscovered and began to settle Australia, and traded on an ever increasing scale all over the inhabited globe'. The Royal Society of Arts had indeed been instrumental from its earliest days in encouraging scientific and agricultural research. It promoted raw silk production in the American plantations, introduced new crops to the West Indies and encouraged the cultivation of hemp in Lower Canada. The promotion of the wool trade with Australia and of imports of logwood, coconut oil, wine and potash from the dependencies were further examples of the society's pioneering scientific and commercial ventures. In a later age, stimulated by the Great Exhibition of 1851 which was to bring many colonial visitors to London, the society was inspired to form Indian and African sections. These in time were to be subsumed in what is today's Commonwealth Section. Thus through public lectures, prizes for scientific and artistic achievement and exhibitions the society was to play a notable part in keeping before the public all that the Empire signified in terms of non-governmental endeavour.

Admittedly the efforts first of the Royal Commonwealth Society and later of the Colonial (latterly Commonwealth) Institute were in time to overshadow the endeavours of the Royal Society of Arts in relation to the Commonwealth in general.[11] Indeed of all the learned societies of earlier days, that which was to have the profoundest impact on British thinking about the Empire as it was expanding in its mid-

and late-nineteenth-century heyday was undoubtedly the Royal Colonial Institute, later to become known successively as the Royal Empire and finally the Royal Commonwealth Society.

The institute was established at a moment in nineteenth-century time where political attitudes in Britain towards colonial expansion were in sharp conflict. On the one side might be chalked up Disraeli's somewhat throw-away remark of 1852: 'wretched colonies are a millstone round our necks'; and on the other Lord John Russell's appreciative remarks in 1855 apropos of the introduction of responsible government to the Australian colonies, that the latter had avowed their desire 'to assimilate their institutions as far as possible to those of the mother country'. Their imperial loyalty was 'not merely the expression of a common sentiment arising from common origin, but [was] connected with a deliberate attachment to the ancient laws of the community from which their own was sprung'.

It was such sentiments, promoted in part by opposition to Gladstone's anti-Empire administration which had swept to power in 1868, and again by a movement promoted by the Royal Society of Arts for the creation of a colonial centre in London (the latter proposal warmly embraced by the London-based Australian lobby), which led in 1869 to the foundation of the Royal Colonial Institute. In view of what follows in this book in relation to professional co-operation in the Commonwealth, it seems essential to quote the following passages from the minutes of a public meeting, held in June 1868, which was to lead by March 1870 to Queen Victoria's patronage of the institute itself. That meeting, as the historian of the later-named Royal Commonwealth Society was to put it[12] was convened under the auspices of Viscount Bury and others who 'had been taking a vigorous and sympathetic interest in colonial affairs and were distressed by the influence of the separatists on parliamentary and public opinion in Britain'. (One has only to substitute 'Commonwealth' for 'colonial' affairs to arrive at a similar condition at roughly one hundred years remove.) As Lord Bury summed up the general aspirations of those present: 'A great want has often been felt by gentlemen connected with our several colonies ... of some meeting

place . . . where they might obtain the latest intelligence from
their own part of the world . . . We want some medium by
which we may form our scattered colonies into a homogeneous
whole.' At his suggestion the meeting was unanimously to
agree that the society, once formed, should be 'entirely non-
political'. But it should – and it was this which gave it its
status as the first truly Commonwealth non-governmental
organisation – 'occupy as regards the colonies the position
filled by the Royal Society with regard to science, or the
Royal Geographical Society with regard to geography'. It
should have 'a lecture hall, a library and reading-room' . . .
and should afford facilities 'for the reading of papers and the
holding of discussions upon colonial subjects generally: and to
undertake those investigations in connection with the colonies
which were carried out in a more general field . . . by similar
bodies in Great Britain'.[13]

Such aspirations were in fact largely reflected in the constitution as put to a general meeting in 1870. The Royal
Colonial Institute then became a body favoured by royalty,
blessed as a learned society by the two political parties of the
day and accepted by colonial visitors of all persuasions as a
convenient and neutral meeting ground for 'gentlemen'. It was
in fact to prove a model around which much later Commonwealth non-governmental endeavour was to build. At the
outset, not surprisingly, membership of the institute was overwhelmingly Anglo-Saxon, although by the 1880s a number of
Indians and Africans had been elected. In 1882, with a well-
endowed library and much useful research work to its credit,
the institute was granted a royal charter, its continuing objects
being described in that document as 'to promote the increase
and diffusion of knowledge respecting as well Our Colonies,
Dependencies and Possessions, as Our Indian Empire, and the
preservation of a permanent union between the Mother
Country and the various parts of the British Empire'.

From this time on the institute was to serve as a powerful
lobby in the Empire interest, campaigning for scientific,
educational and social co-operation, for commercial enterprise,
and the creation of 'a museum for the collection and exhibition
of Colonial and Indian productions' – a venture later to bear
fruit in the Imperial (later Commonwealth) Institute in

Kensington. One early and successful enterprise – which continues to this day – was the launching of an essay competition for schoolchildren, the aim of which was to improve the younger generation's knowledge of the Empire. Starting as a purely British experiment it had by the start of the First World War grown to take in schools and universities throughout the Empire.

In the late 1920s the institute, not without much acrimonious debate, changed its title to that of Royal Empire Society; but well before that time there had come upon the London scene three further non-governmental organisations ('NGOs'), each equally intent on promoting the still Anglo-Saxon imperial concept; namely, the Victoria League, founded in 1901; the Overseas Club (later the Royal Overseas League), established by Evelyn Wrench; and the English Speaking Union, an earlier brain-child of the latter. Efforts to amalgamate the four organisations failed consistently, and in the process the premier body – the Royal Empire Society – did face the threat, as a *Times* editorial caustically put it in October 1930, of sinking into the position of being no more than 'a club to which a museum had been bequeathed'. In short, social activities were rapidly outstripping learning and discussion and were placing the Society's charitable status increasingly at risk.

While the amalgamation of what in 1958 had become the Royal Commonwealth Society with the three other like-minded bodies remains to this day a pipe-dream (from which all four in consequence suffer financially), the former remains by far the most influential, inspiring as it still does much social, learned and voluntary endeavour.

To all the bodies so far mentioned, each to some degree working outwards into the imperial world from a British base, one must add the Imperial (later Commonwealth) Institute. Founded in London in 1868, only one year after the birth of the Royal Commonwealth Society itself, the aims of the institute were rather more to serve as a permanent exhibition of the 'colonial way of life' for the edification of the parents and children of the master race itself. Unlike the societies so far described the institute was not strictly a voluntary organisation. It claimed no learned members. It relied for funding on the British Government and, as time passed, on overseas governments for the exhibits and other audio-visual aids which it today presents. From its permanent headquarters in Kensington it has now become a living museum demonstrating all aspects of the modern Commonwealth; a mecca for millions of schoolchildren and their teachers; a centre for the arts of the Commonwealth; in short a shop-window to which other member countries now contribute their wares unstintingly and from which visitors can extract a vivid and visual wealth of information.

But such developments were by no means the limit of voluntary imperial endeavour prior to the outbreak of the First World War. Educationists too had had their part to play. As has been said, the British Empire had in its day shown some of the features of a school – 'one of the most notable schools in history'. Or, as another scholar was reflectively to express it at two generations' remove:

> Commonwealth countries have been operating together now for a very long period of time. There has been accumulated, in some cases over centuries, in many cases over decades, a vast source of knowledge – knowledge of each other's special conditions of life, of each other's societies and so on. It is a knowledge which resides in people's experience, and experience that is passed on from one to another.[14]

Much sprang inevitably from the common language. That advantage in turn gave rise, consciously or otherwise, to the extension overseas of English culture and influence, not least through the educational machinery of the Anglican Church. Failures there were to be in plenty, notably in the Irish and American settlements and later in India. But the thirst for educational advancement largely overcame antipathy towards a system and a language imposed by the British Raj. So it came about that a voluntary society, the League of the Empire, founded in 1901 to encourage educational co-operation between Britain and the countries of the Empire, was able in 1907 to convene in London a first Imperial Conference. In this representatives of the educational services from most of the self-governing and dependent territories took part. From such beginnings much of the educational advancement of the colonies, sponsored by the Colonial Office and its advisers, was to spring.

Some attention should also be paid to one long-since forgotten body – the Visual Instruction Committee of the Colonial Office. Inspired by the late Queen Mary, then Princess of Wales, it took as its cue, as early as 1902, that 'the Empire can only be held together by sympathy and under-standing, based on widely diffused knowledge of its geography, history, resources, climates and races. It is obvious that if this knowledge is to be effective it must be imparted to the coming generation. In other words it must be taught in the Schools of the Empire'.[15] This early pioneering effort, based on lantern slides and lectures, hand-coloured photographs and illustrated maps, distributed *inter alia* to the 'three Eastern Colonies of Ceylon, the Straits Settlements and Hong Kong' was in a sense to prove the harbinger of today's computerised attempts to promote a modern relax-as-you-audio-view educational system.

Meanwhile, at the tertiary level, considerable progress had been made. In Canada university colleges, founded in the tradition of the older English universities, had come into being from the late eighteenth century onwards. In 1876 Fourah Bay College, Sierra Leone, was affiliated to the University of Durham. The first Indian universities had been founded in the 1850s. Leaving aside developments in other self-governing colonies the University of Hong Kong was established in 1911.

These are but scattered examples of the advancement, largely through voluntary endeavour, of higher education throughout the Empire. Inevitably views were sharply divided as to what form such education should take. But with equal inevitability the British pragmatic question was posed: 'What loose form of co-operation should we, the educationists, devise'? The upshot was the creation in 1912, not without much prior travail, of the Bureau of Information for the Universities of the Empire, precursor of one of the most powerful of the modern Commonwealth's NGOs, the Association of Common-wealth Universities. It was the Bureau which first set to work on that now invaluable publication, the *Commonwealth Universities Yearbook*. And it was the bureau again which, in the face of many difficulties, carried persistently through one major resolution from the first Congress of 1912: namely that 'the universities of the various Dominions of The King overseas should arrange for periodic meetings of their representatives'.[16] One side-effect of such deliberations were decisions later reached in Canada, Australia and India to establish national standing committees of vice-chancellors.

Thus between the two world wars links between the universities of the Commonwealth were to become as firmly and permanently established as those between the learned and other voluntary societies referred to earlier in this chapter.

While meeting regularly between 1919–39 members of the Universities Bureau were of necessity still largely representative of the self-governing dominions and of India. But their co-ordinating endeavours were greatly encouraged by the findings of a Royal Commission set up in 1943 by the British Government under the chairmanship of Mr Justice Asquith. Among its terms of reference were 'to consider the principles which should guide the promotion of higher education, learning and research and the development of universities in the Colonies', and the means by which 'universities or other appropriate bodies in the United Kingdom may be able to co-operate with institutions of higher education in the Colonies'. One significant conclusion from the Asquith Report was that 'Colonial universities should be autonomous in the sense in which the universities of Great Britain are autonomous – the colonial universities should in effect, have full freedom to manage their own affairs'.[17]

From such recommendations, backed by the imaginative stimulus offered by the Colonial Development and Welfare Act of 1940, was to spring the rapid postwar crop of university institutions throughout the newer Commonwealth and the entrenchment of the Association of Commonwealth Universities as perhaps the most influential of all non-governmental bodies in the Commonwealth today.

Notes and References

1   43 Eliz. 1, c. 4.
2   8 and 9 Eliz. 2, c. 58.
3   Lord Nathan, *The Charities Act 1960* (London, 1962), pp. 2–3. (As chairman of the interdepartmental committee appointed in 1950 to consider and report on changes in the law and practice relating to charitable trusts in England and Wales, Lord Nathan may be accepted as a unique authority on the growth of the charitable concept in the English-speaking world.)
4   On this latter point, reference is invited to Anthony Trollope's *The Warden* and to the opening chapters of *Barchester Towers* respecting the fate of an outdated trust.
5   2 Halsbury's Statute (2nd edn) 838.
6   Nathan, op. cit., p. 5.
7   Lord Beveridge, *Voluntary Action: A Report on Methods of Social Advance* (London, 1948).
8   8 and 9 Eliz. 2, c. 58.
9   Nathan, op. cit., p. 17.
10 Gerald Hill, 'When charity begins to get complicated', *The Times*, April 1981.
11 For a full description of the society's work see Derek Hudson and Kenneth W. Luckhurst, *The Royal Society of Arts 1754–1954* (London, 1954).
12 In this general context see Trevor R. Rees, *History of the Royal Commonwealth Society 1868–1968* (London, 1968).
13 Rees, ibid.
14 T. P. Soper, *The Evolving Commonwealth* (Oxford, 1965).
15 Colonial Office, Misc. Print no. 265, 1910.
16 *Report of Congress of Universities of the Empire*, 1912.
17 *Report of the Commission on Higher Education in the Colonies*, Cmnd 5647, 1945. For further information on the development of educational co-operation in the Empire and Commonwealth, the reader is invited to consult a little-known University of Rhodesia publication of 1974, Dr Norman Atkinson, *Series on Education: Occasional Paper no. 1* (Salisbury, 1972). I am indebted to the Librarian of the Royal Commonwealth Society for bringing it to my notice.

2

The Unofficial Commonwealth: the Scene in the Early 1960s

The Commonwealth is not just an association of governments. It is an association of peoples, between whom there are countless connections which need to be continuously refreshed and strengthened. There is a vast network of personal and business contacts . . . Valuable connections have grown up between us through art, sport and other activities . . . In addition there are the strong links forged by the churches. There exist also numerous bodies which bring together from different Commonwealth countries people with similar interests and experience.'

Rt Hon. Duncan Sandys,
The Modern Commonwealth (London: 1962)

'Finally, the Conference noted that the Commonwealth was an association of peoples rather than an organisation of governments. While there is much that governments can and should do, the real strength of the partnership lies in the ties of friendship that bind its peoples together. In the modern world of easy travel, the degree of personal contact between individuals in every walk of life, throughout all Commonwealth countries, is increasing rapidly . . .

The Future of the Commonwealth: A British View
(London:1963). Report of a conference held
at Ditchley Park, Oxfordshire under the
auspices of the Commonwealth Relations Office

By the early 1960s no thesis had become easier to sustain than that the Commonwealth was expanding itself to extinction. Those nostalgic for Empire could by then point to its racial and political diversity and to the collapse of the tight-knit, like-minded Anglo-Saxon club; purists to a lowering of administrative, ethical and 'Western' standards, jurists to breaches of the rule of law. The economist, pondering over changes in the traditional patterns of trade and on the fate of the £ sterling, might argue that Britain could no longer be of both the Commonwealth and Europe. It must thus suit her to sacrifice the Commonwealth relationship. Sections of the press, in part influencing and in turn partly reflecting public and parliamentary opinion, also tended to the short-term (and short-sighted) view that the Commonwealth had by now outlived its use and meaning. What, such critics asked, was the significance of a group of nations which, as its number increased, brought in its train more disputes, more antagonistic votes at the United Nations, further burdens for the British taxpayer, and no countervailing political advantages? One influential politician went so far as to comment that 'The Commonwealth has really become a gigantic farce'.[1]

Yet, as one optimist could still write: 'Those who pick the Commonwealth to pieces never examine the probable outcome if they prove themselves right. The position is not static. What will happen is not to be assessed by analysis but to be achieved by action.' Among the acts which Britain herself should take to ensure a fuller understanding of the Commonwealth, this commentator listed as 'in the long run perhaps the most important of all, the resolute development and extension of the network of educational links, exchanges and assistance programmes which are part of the very fibre of the partnership'.[2]

In those earlier years most apologists for the Commonwealth tended to explain its significance largely in terms of a special relationship between governments, based on a common language, shared administrative and judicial practices, and a political like-mindedness. From these there seemed naturally to flow habits of close and informal consultation. Such privileged exchanges took place either bilaterally or in a wide range of committees and *ad hoc* meetings, from those of the prime ministers downwards.

19

Even today that habit of consultation remains of the highest importance. Without it, and its supporting machinery, the special Commonwealth relationship could not survive. But while the official means of consultation have been often and exhaustively analysed there was still lacking as recently as the early 1960s any parallel survey in depth of the Commonwealth's unofficial links.

In its 1963 annual handbook[3] the former British Commonwealth Relations Office devoted nearly sixty pages of close type to 'organisations and societies in Britain concerned with various aspects of Commonwealth relations'. But even this list, which incidentally underlined the difficulty of differentiating official from unofficial bodies, was far from exhaustive. Reviewing the scene in retrospect all one can now do is to select, however arbitrarily, certain broad fields of human activity in an attempt to bring home the extent to which the Commonwealth of the 1960s already prospered through its unofficial relationships. If, in the upshot, the emerging pattern still seems highly Anglocentric, this must be excused by the fact, that most Commonwealth-wide non-governmental organisations had had their genesis in Britain. Yet there was by now a growing number of national and regional organisations in other Commonwealth countries, linked in various ways with their counterparts in Britain and elsewhere, as well as a constant and healthy increase in exchanges between Commonwealth members other than Britain.

Taking first non-governmental co-operation in the field of higher education, it could be said of the 1960s that despite national aspirations and the growth in the number of independent countries, demand from throughout the Commonwealth for educational and training places in Britain, far from slackening, was increasing year by year. The British could still count it their singular good fortune that their own educational system remained relatively divorced from politics and that the legacy of learning which they could offer to their Commonwealth partners was not, therefore, identified with imperialism. The record spoke for itself. In 1944 the Commonwealth student population of Britain had amounted to 2,500; by 1964 it was close on 50,000. No longer were these students predominantly the sons and daughters of rich parents from the 'old Dominions'. Close on 90 per cent now came from the newer world. They were studying not only at universities, but at teacher training and technical colleges, in business and industry, or for the liberal professions. Admittedly much of the aid offered to such students came direct from governments, but this was far from the whole story. In the non-governmental field teachers were increasingly exchanged between local education authorities in Britain and other countries of the Commonwealth. The League for the Exchange of Commonwealth Teachers arranged for upwards of 100 Commonwealth teachers to exchange their respective jobs for a period every year. At university level it was not rare for appointments to be made from outside the home country. Oxbridge was in this sense a prominent example. In 1965, to reverse the process, there were over one thousand British academics serving in universities and technical colleges elsewhere in the Commonwealth. The Association of Commonwealth Universities, by now representing 133 institutions throughout the member countries and dependencies, and the Inter-University Council for Higher Education Overseas, both independent bodies, provided contacts between their members, helped to recruit teaching staff, facilitated the interchange of teachers and students, and promoted the exchange of ideas and teaching methods. The Association of Commonwealth Universities itself published (and still happily does so, though at unavoidably high expense) an invaluable yearbook, and organised quinquennial congresses of universities throughout the Commonwealth. Between 1949–65 its Executive Council met nine times in Commonwealth countries other than Britain for discussions on matters of common interest. The association also provided the secretariat for the Commonwealth Scholarship and Fellowship Plan and for the Committee of Vice-Chancellors and Principals of Commonwealth Universities.

Some British universities, notably London, had moreover played a special part in assisting the development of sister institutions in Africa and the Caribbean, providing facilities under which such bodies could prepare their students for degrees of the British university concerned. Teachers at these overseas colleges were invited to join with their British colleagues in the examination of their students, while syllabi were gradually modified to suit local needs. Thanks to such special relationships, contacts between the academic staffs concerned were to remain particularly close.

Other examples of non-governmental co-operation were to be found in the work of examining boards, themselves largely based on British universities. Such boards conducted examinations in the overseas Commonwealth to standards strictly akin to those required in Britain. Thus (for better or, as later experience sometimes showed, for worse) close on 90,000 overseas candidates took the Cambridge local examinations each year. There were also a number of reputable British correspondence colleges which, through their work in preparing candidates for these and other examinations, formed yet a further Commonwealth link.

Even so, and as though presaging a brake on the enthusiastic drive in the older Commonwealth to supply newly independent Commonwealth countries with Western-made 'package kits' of higher learning, voices of dissent were soon faintly heard. Writing in the *East African Journal* in May 1965 Professor A. T. Porter, a distinguished Sierra Leonean, then Principal of University College, Nairobi, recalled the far-sighted comments of a president of Harvard of the 1860s. The latter had remarked, close on a hundred years earlier, that: 'A university must grow from seed. It cannot be transplanted from England or Germany in full leaf and bearing.' As for America, so for Africa. As Dr Porter himself put it:

> European scholars, with their training, their own cultural experience, have put forward the questions that have occurred to them about Africa and have answered them in their own way. We cannot continue to depend on their answers. The African interest, the African assumptions, the African questions, have now to be put and answered. This to me should be the responsibility of our university, and its attainment a sign that we have come of age as a truly African University.

Such comments, however, beg questions passing beyond the time-scale to which this review of Commonwealth non-governmental bodies in the early 1960s is restricted. Thus to conclude this survey of higher educational links within that context one may add that British church and missionary societies were also contributing men and money to educational programmes in the newer Commonwealth. A survey by the Overseas Development Institute of 85 such societies showed that in 1962 close on 900 British nationals were engaged under Protestant auspices in education elsewhere in the newer Commonwealth. A further 158 combined such work with pastoral duties.

By the mid-1960s, moreover, it had become commonplace for British school-leavers and young graduates to go overseas for a year's service in Third World countries. The main private organisation concerned, Voluntary Service Overseas, had been formed in 1958, three years before the weightier US Peace Corps itself was launched. By 1965 some 1,400 volunteers were involved annually, mostly within the Commonwealth and largely within the teaching field. The Overseas Appointments Bureau and the Catholic Institute for International Relations were further examples of non-profit-making voluntary agencies inspired by ideals of service to the developing Commonwealth. In 1961–2 the former recruited 106, and in 1962–3 the latter some 60 teachers.

British foundations and trusts were also providing financial help to educational projects in the newer Commonwealth. About half the annual income of the Dulverton Trust (£180,000) was thus spent. The Leverhulme Trust contributed over £110,000 in the three years 1959–61, and the Nuffield Foundation £254,000 in 1961–2. The Wolfson Foundation was giving considerable help to colleges and universities in Britain to which developing countries turned for help and for professional advice. There were many others helping in small ways to strengthen Commonwealth educational links.

Through enlightened self-interest British firms with overseas involvements were also spending large sums on education and training to the benefit of developing Commonwealth countries. By 1961 the number of industrial trainees in Britain from the newer world was in the region of 5,000 a year. The Federation of British Industries Overseas Scholarship Scheme, which provided industrial training for citizens of the newer Commonwealth, was financed by some 500 British firms. Two British oil companies gave Nigeria £500,000 at independence for technical education. The Indian Institute of Technology received £250,000 worth of equipment from British industry with the promise of more to come. The Centre for Educational Television Overseas and the Overseas Visual Aids Centre were further British non-governmental organisations devoted to training, advice and research in their subjects to the benefit of citizens of the newer Commonwealth.

By 1960 there had also developed a considerable interchange in the field of the arts. Many Commonwealth students came to Britain to study music and the dramatic and plastic arts. Conversely there was an outward movement of teachers from Britain, not least of examiners from the Royal School of Music, the Trinity College of Music, and the Royal Academy of Dancing. Throughout the Commonwealth appetites were stimulated by visits, often under commercial sponsorship, of artists and musicians and of dramatic companies such as the Old Vic and the Royal Ballet, or such organisations as the Stratford, Ontario, Shakespeare Company, and the Elizabethan Trust of Australia.

Even so brief a survey must include the Institutes of Commonwealth Studies of the universities of London and Oxford. Created in the immediate postwar years, each was soon to play a prominent role in encouraging collaboration at postgraduate level between research workers from Commonwealth countries engaged in studies relating particularly to the social sciences, modern history and the politics and economics of the tropical Commonwealth. In addition Queen Elizabeth House, Oxford, provided accommodation and facilities for academic work over a wide range of Commonwealth problems. The Indian School of International Studies had established a Department of Commonwealth History which encouraged postgraduate training and research. Also active in this field were the Council for Education in the Commonwealth, with headquarters at the British House of Commons, and the Africa Educational Trust. The council aimed to create an informed public opinion on the problems of education in the Commonwealth and organised discussions between visiting Commonwealth ministers of education and local experts. The trust promoted special forms of training for Africans, supported similar organisations in Africa and, in particular arranged postgraduate nursing courses in Britain for African women from what was then Southern Rhodesia.

Turning from the broad field of education to that of the law, it must once more be emphasised that what is written here relates to the extent of non-governmental co-operation in the Commonwealth as it existed in the early 1960s. Much was soon to change respecting 'received doctrine' as applying to standards and curricula then thought to be beyond reproach, and as regards the attitudes of Third World countries towards the English systems of law and government. But at that time Commonwealth links in the legal field were still largely founded on the assumption that the English judicial system and English common law would continue to serve as the basic pattern for the administration of justice throughout the Commonwealth. Thus, while many newly independent governments were rightly concerned to build up their own law schools and examination systems, intra-Commonwealth links, both official and unofficial, remained in the early 1960s strong and widespread. British universities and the Inns of Court continued to attract thousands of Commonwealth law students annually. In many Commonwealth countries there were special arrangements for admitting English barristers and solicitors to practise. Conversely barristers and solicitors from other Commonwealth countries might be exempted from examinations and certain other requirements in England in order to be admitted to practise there.

One example of Commonwealth-wide initiatives in the legal field was the launching in 1962, with assistance from the Wolfson Foundation, of a Commonwealth Legal Assistance Scheme for Law Revision. This was operated by the British Institute of International and Comparative Law. It disseminated information on new developments of special interest in law, and particularly in law revision throughout the Commonwealth; and arranged for assistance between Commonwealth countries in the preparation of legislation, and in the study of legal problems. Several newer Commonwealth countries sought and received help from the Institute, and a series of special surveys of interest to the Commonwealth and to developing countries in particular was made under the

25

scheme, the first being a survey of hire-purchase law and credit-financing. It is significant that the majority of the earlier requests put to this body were for information on legal developments in other parts of the Commonwealth connected with projects of law reform or legal reorganisation.

Legal links were also strengthened through meetings and by the continuous interchange of visits by distinguished judicial personages. The Commonwealth and Empire Law Conference, launched in 1955, had by 1965 held the third of its quinquennial meetings, on that occasion in Sydney, Australia, when no less than 3,000 delegates attended. This was a notable example of members of the same profession coming together from throughout the Commonwealth to discuss subjects of mutual interest. Mention should also be made of the Council of Legal Education, which, as the body holding examinations for the English Bar, frequently advised on problems of legal education in the newer world.

It could indeed well be said at the time – and that cliché still rings largely true – that despite all the political changes that the Commonwealth had witnessed, traditions of law and standards of justice still remained among the strongest links between all Commonwealth countries. As one observer later put it – and the comment is of wider import – 'the traditions are so strong they come welling back as soon as the tides change'.[4]

Turning next to the fields of medicine and its allied disciplines, it might well be claimed that these were (and are) the best developed of the Commonwealth's unofficial free-masonries. By 1963 the British General Medical Council recognised upwards of fifty medical qualifications granted by other Commonwealth countries. Close on 17,500 doctors appeared on that year's Commonwealth List of the British Medical Register. While no distinctions were made in the council's Home List, this too clearly contained the names of many doctors from other Commonwealth countries who had qualified in Britain itself.

While intra-Commonwealth reciprocity was later to raise some awkward human and political issues nearly all Commonwealth countries, with the exception of certain Canadian provinces, then granted reciprocal treatment to British doctors.

The General Medical Council also stood ready to guide other Commonwealth countries, which were then establishing their own medical schools, on the eventual recognition of their degrees by the council. From such moves towards mutual help had sprung the Commonwealth Medical Association, established in 1948. For its part, the British Medical Association already enjoyed wide-ranging links throughout the Commonwealth. It was affiliated with similar bodies in Canada, India, Pakistan, Ceylon and Malaya and had branches in many other then colonial territories. The College of General Practitioners in turn had faculties in Canada, Africa and Australasia, and the Royal College of Obstetricians and Gynaecologists regional councils in the older Commonwealth. The Royal College of Surgeons conducted examinations and had reciprocity of examination regulations in certain Commonwealth member states, while the Royal Society of Tropical Medicine and Hygiene maintained touch, through local secretaries, with problems of mutual concern in at least nine of the then independent Commonwealth states. The Royal College of Veterinary Surgeons had members throughout the Commonwealth, while the British Veterinary Association was in affiliation with sister organisations in a large number of other member countries.

The dental and nursing professions followed much the same co-operative path. While the Register of the British Dental Council carried names for the most part European, the various nursing councils and boards of midwives recognised any Commonwealth qualifications imposing standards similar to their own. Admittedly no detailed statistics covering the movement of qualified nurses and trainees between Commonwealth countries were then available, but all the evidence pointed to the fact that this was a constantly growing and highly mobile guild. To give but two random examples: in 1962–3 580 nurses trained in Australia and 40 trained in Nigeria were entered on the British Register. Australia and Canada in turn opened their doors to trainees from Malaysia and the Caribbean.

Among numerous voluntary bodies in the medical field were the British Red Cross Society and the British Chest and Heart Association, both of which were in touch with affiliated

27

societies in most other Commonwealth countries and which awarded scholarships to doctors, nurses, and medical workers from within the Commonwealth; the British Leprosy Relief Association, which worked within the Commonwealth through grants and loaned staff; the Royal Commonwealth Society for the Blind, whose mobile teams were active above all in Commonwealth Africa, and which operated a scholarship fund and trained teachers and welfare workers from many Commonwealth countries; and the Commonwealth Society for the Deaf, whose aims were to promote the welfare, education and employment of deaf people.

In the lay field the British Institute of Hospital Administrators arranged long courses of practical training for Commonwealth students, while the St John's Ambulance Association and Brigade operated first-aid and nursing courses and could boast, outside Britain, of a Commonwealth membership of 120,000 uniformed and disciplined workers in the brigade's many branches.

All that has been said so far designedly omits the wide-ranging co-operation which took place (and still happily does so) through continuous meetings of Commonwealth ministers and officials concerned with problems of education, the law and medicine. Nor can the preceding paragraphs claim to present a full picture of the wealth of voluntary and professional co-operation in these fields. In some areas, indeed, governments were now finding themselves increasingly obliged to shoulder financial burdens hitherto largely carried by the private sector. Scientific research was a marked case in point. Yet the learned societies of the older Commonwealth still retained their traditional function of communicating scientific knowledge. They continued to exercise a profound influence on the development of research throughout the Commonwealth. Fellows of the Royal Society of London and of other learned British societies were drawn from the whole Commonwealth.

The Journals of these Societies are open for publication of scientific work of Commonwealth scientists who also freely participate in their meetings. Many have local sections in other Commonwealth countries and local correspondents who encourage links with United Kingdom scientists. An outstanding example of Commonwealth scientific collaboration is provided by the Royal Society Empire Scientific Conference of 1946 which was attended by representatives from all Commonwealth countries.[5]

Thus the Royal Societies of Canada and of New Zealand, the Australian Academy of Science, the National Institute of Sciences of India, and the Science Association of Nigeria – to name only a few – were among those bodies maintaining close and continuous links with each other and with their counterpart societies in Britain. The Rutherford Memorial Lecture, established by the Royal Society of London, was delivered biennially in other Commonwealth countries, while meetings of the British Association for the Advancement of Science were held not only in London but elsewhere in the Commonwealth. The Royal Society of Arts for its part held examinations in commercial and industrial subjects which were taken widely throughout the Commonwealth.

The interchange of scientists, moreover, was still largely financed through non-governmental channels. Thus the Nuffield Foundation awarded fellowships and scholarships to scientists from other Commonwealth countries as well as giving direct support for research in the Commonwealth. In addition the foundation, in collaboration with the Royal Society, operated a Commonwealth-wide bursaries scheme which enabled 'investigators of proven worth' to pursue research and to learn new techniques in any country of the Commonwealth.

As to the professions generally, one can add only that a separate study would be called for if full justice were to be done to the wealth of non-official Commonwealth co-operation at that time. Here, designedly, no attempt is made to define the precise relationships existing between differing sets of professional bodies in Britain and their counterparts or associates in other Commonwealth countries. Some were exclusive, recognising only their own national qualifications; others enjoyed a thoroughgoing freemasonry. But broadly speaking all shared a common appreciation of British professional standards. Nearly all those which had grown up overseas had had widespread experience of the British educational system and training methods. Such shared experiences had two main consequences. First, many thousands of Commonwealth students continued to travel to Britain to obtain their professional qualifications, to become members of British institutions and perhaps to start their careers there. Secondly, professional bodies in one Commonwealth country would in many cases recognise the qualifications granted by another, would include holders of such non-national qualifications on their own registers and permit them to practise without their having to undergo additional prescribed national examinations. Thus the overseas Commonwealth membership of the Institute of Civil Engineers amounted by 1960 to over 4,000. Those of the Institute of Chartered Accountants, of Cost and Works Accountants, and of the Royal Institute of British Architects were of the same order. The Chartered Institute of Secretaries was another example of a body vigorous in its activities throughout the Commonwealth. In a brochure published in 1963[6] it referred to the four major overseas divisions of the Institute in Australia, Canada, New Zealand and South Africa, each with its own secretariat and local organisation. The examination syllabi set for those countries took full account of local law and practice. Consequently a student who emigrated could complete his studies under the law of the country of his adoption. Of the Institute's total membership of 28,500, over 13,000 came from these four divisions. In addition there were smaller, less formal organisations, known as associations, with a growing membership in a number of other Commonwealth territories. Twice annually over 5,000 students were examined throughout the Commonwealth.

Further examples[7] may be taken at random. For instance, trainees throughout the Commonwealth followed the syllabi of the British Institute of Radio Engineers, which also helped applicants from other Commonwealth countries over apprenticeships and trainee courses. The Chartered Insurance Institute offered correspondence courses to students in the developing world and conducted examinations in most Commonwealth countries for its diplomas. The Institution of Chemical Engineers had advisory committees in Australia and India, and its examinations were also held widely within the Commonwealth. The Institution of Mining and Metallurgy had local sections in several Commonwealth countries in Africa, as well as in Malaysia. That of Municipal Engineers allowed candidates from the Commonwealth to sit for its examinations. As a final example, the Institution of Structural Engineers held examinations twice yearly in a number of developing Commonwealth countries and in many of them had official representatives ready to advise on local problems.

But non-governmental co-operation within the Commonwealth was by no means restricted to the university world, to the professions, to learned societies or to private trusts and agencies. Parliamentarians, organisations founded on banking, commerce and industry, on the media and on sport, not to mention voluntary bodies of many kinds – all had their part to play in strengthening the functional underbelly of the Commonwealth. Thus the Commonwealth Parliamentary Association could now claim to be one of the best known and most powerful supra-national organisations of the Commonwealth. By the mid-1960s it had over eighty branches in the legislatures of the Commonwealth. Its offices at Westminster had become a regular meeting place for legislators. Similar facilities were extended by the branches overseas. The Association convened annual meetings in various capitals of the Commonwealth, while its yearly course on parliamentary practice and procedure attracted members to London from the majority of Commonwealth legislatures. The General Council of the Association, formed in 1948 and thereafter meeting annually, provided an effective link between all branches of the Association and by now performed a co-ordinating function previously undertaken by the British branch. By 1964 nine plenary conferences of the Association had been held. At each there were wide-ranging debates on such matters of mutual concern as economic relations, migration, international affairs, and defence. The American–British Group of the Congress of the United States incidentally constituted an Associated Group of the Commonwealth Parliamentary Association.

As to the business world, self-interest alone dictated that senior bankers, businessmen and industrialists throughout the Commonwealth should take a direct and personal interest in all matters likely to influence market opportunities in each others' countries.

Thus the central banks of the Commonwealth kept in constant touch. The Institute of Bankers in Britain conducted professional examinations which were widely taken elsewhere in the Commonwealth. It had centres in East Africa and Malaysia and members in many other countries. The Commonwealth Development Finance Company had as its particular aims financial assistance for development projects; the provision of ready access to British industrial, financial and commercial experience; and the investment of funds – raised principally through private sources in Britain – in projects which were unable to attract sufficient capital from governmental sources. The company was also a channel through which Commonwealth countries could seek advice and assistance on development problems.

In the business field, the Federation of Commonwealth and British Chambers of Commerce (now defunct) acted as a link between the chambers of every Commonwealth country. It was concerned in promoting trade and investment and helped in the organisation of trade missions, exhibitions and fairs. It also aimed at the introduction of a unified system of examination throughout the Commonwealth, with the long-term aim of establishing a recognised standard of commercial education. The federation convened Commonwealth congresses biennially, and was also active with the Royal Commonwealth Society in promoting the commercial education of business communities in the Commonwealth, as well as in encouraging the development of training facilities.

Regionally, the Western Hemisphere Exports Council promoted British exports to Canada and to Commonwealth countries of the Caribbean as well as to the United States. The India, Pakistan and Burma Association maintained and expanded British manufacturing and business connections in those countries, while the Ceylon and the Malayan Commercial Associations had similar aims. Comparable committees representing business interests were active in the West, East, and Central African areas and in the West Indies. Nor, in this context, could one forget the links forged between Commonwealth businessmen in the shipping, civil aviation and insurance worlds, or the personal two-way influence resulting from the presence in one Commonwealth country of a powerful business community representing another, for example, Canadians in London and Liverpool, British in Calcutta and Bombay, Australians in Singapore.

Turning now to the media it could with truth be said that the press had for long been a powerful, if increasingly rough, strand in intra-Commonwealth relationships.

Reuters, owned jointly by the British press and two Commonwealth news agencies, then served virtually the whole Commonwealth. There were sizeable British interests in newspapers publishing in a number of other Commonwealth countries. Over six hundred of the most important newspapers, periodicals, and news agencies in the Commonwealth were grouped together in the Commonwealth Press Union, which held annual conferences in London and quinquennial conferences rotating between other Commonwealth cities. The union had autonomous sections in many of the member countries. Each section nominated representatives to a central council governing the union. By the early 1960s the CPU had established committees covering such activities as the defence of press freedom, telecommunication services and the training and exchange of journalists throughout the Commonwealth. It had also established a travelling fellowship scheme to enable young journalists to study methods of journalism in other Commonwealth countries. A further organisation, the Journalists' Training Centre, founded by Roy (later the first Lord) Thomson, though not exclusive to the Commonwealth, attracted to its courses a strong and wide Commonwealth representation.

To an even more marked extent, thanks in great measure to the prewar efforts of the first Director-General of the British Broadcasting Corporation, Lord Reith, broadcasting closely linked the countries of the Commonwealth. Through its External Services and through the interchange of personnel which the Second World War greatly stimulated BBC programmes, in both English and local languages, were now beamed to all parts of the Commonwealth. The corporation maintained the closest links with its overseas counterparts. Many of the broadcasting agencies in new Commonwealth countries were indeed established with help from the BBC, which continued to second personnel and to train Commonwealth officers at its own Staff Training School. Through its transcription service the BBC made available a wide range of its own sound output. It was also common for the various organisations to extend to each other facilities in the use of studios, recording channels and the like. As a collective venture, the corporations in the independent Commonwealth had since 1945 held regular broadcasting conferences. At the fifth of these, held at Montreal in 1965, a decision was taken to establish in London a permanent conference secretariat. Thus was born the Commonwealth Broadcasting Conference, a body designed to ensure continuity in the interchange of technical information, programming, administration, and engineering.

There was also established in London in 1962 a Centre for Educational Television Overseas. Funded by the Nuffield Foundation and the British independent television companies on the one hand, and the Ministry of Overseas Development on the other, its tasks were to advise on educational programmes and on training and equipment, to the primary benefit of newly created television services in the developing Commonwealth. Finally, as a joint venture of the BBC, its Canadian and Australian counterparts and the Rank Organisation, a Commonwealth International News Film Agency was set up to provide a service of international news on film for Commonwealth subscribers.

No such survey of the unofficial Commonwealth in the early 1960s would be complete without some reference, however brief, to the contributions made by other voluntary societies and by those involved through links as varied as the arts and sport. Activities promoted, under the umbrella of the Joint Commonwealth Societies Council, through such organisations as the Royal Commonwealth Society, the Royal Overseas League, the Victoria League for Commonwealth Friendship, and the English-Speaking Union of the Commonwealth, need little introduction. Their value had for long lain as much in the fact that they had branches and committees in many parts of the Commonwealth as in the work they performed from a London base in promoting knowledge of the Commonwealth and in receiving visitors from overseas. But there was also in Britain a wide range of regional and bilateral voluntary organisations such as the British–Nigeria Association, the British Association of Malaysia, the East India Association, the Pakistan Society, the Royal African and Royal Central Asian Societies and the Women's Council. It was the general aim of all such bodies to encourage intra-Commonwealth activity and understanding in their various fields of interest and to offer facilities and hospitality to Commonwealth visitors to Britain.[8]

In the field of the arts much credit must go to the British Council. Despite the battering which that body suffered in the early postwar years at the hands of the Beaverbrook press and of other philistine lobbies within Britain, its promotion of the theatre, ballet and literature and above all of the teaching of English throughout the Commonwealth did much to maintain and indeed to enhance, in the best sense of that term, the 'British heritage'. Without such encouragement it is doubtful whether the now almost forgotten Commonwealth Arts Festival, staged in Britain in 1965, would ever have seen the light of day. But to it came African, Sinhalese and Dominican dancers: drummers from East Africa, the Australian and Winnipeg ballet companies, the folk opera of Nigeria, the National Dance Theatre Company of Jamaica and many others. From these spectacular events there emerged the beginnings of a Commonwealth Arts Association. As one writer on current Commonwealth affairs was later to put it: 'The festival lost money, but was generally adjudged a successful artistic event ... Many people in Britain were agreeably surprised at the variety and wealth of Commonwealth culture'.[9]

The same could be said of Commonwealth literature – that is, primarily, of the wealth and diversity of writing in the English language. As one delegate to the first conference on Commonwealth literature, held at Leeds University in 1964 under the inspiration of Professor Norman Jeffares, expressed it at that time:

At first sight it seems more plausible to assume diversity than unity in Commonwealth literature ... Place the settlement of Canada against the settlement of West Africa – never 'settled' in at all the same sense – and the divergence appears at its widest ... The variety of histories

35

is further complicated for the writer by the relationship between his environment and the language he uses. Here there are two broad categories. In the first, the writer brings his own language – English – to an alien environment and a fresh set of experiences – Australia, Canada, New Zealand. In the other the writer brings an alien language to his own social and cultural inheritance: India, West Africa. Yet the categories have fundamental kinship. Viewing his society, the writer constantly faces the evidence of the impact between what is native to it and what is derived from association with Britain, whatever its form.[10]

It was incidentally from the conference at Leeds that the significant *Journal of Commonwealth Literature* was born and that impetus was provided for the later creation of a Commonwealth-wide association for literature and language studies.

There were, of course, countless other examples of personal, if sometimes less tangible bonds linking individual citizens of the Commonwealth. Some such, for example, as a military career involving shared experience in the Commonwealth Brigade in Korea or Malaya, with the UN (largely Commonwealth) force in the Belgian Congo, or training and exchange courses or service with other Commonwealth forces, would on a strict interpretation have resulted from government action. But others, such as participation in the Scouting, Girl Guides or Boys' Brigade movements; in the special Commonwealth school or training courses of the Outward Bound Trust; or in a wide range of sporting activities, whose highest manifestations were the Commonwealth Games or those peculiarly Commonwealth sports, cricket and (*pace* the French and Rumanians) rugby, stemmed from wholly voluntary endeavour.

Nor should the impact of latter-day migration be ignored. While in postwar years migration within the Commonwealth had become largely controlled and financed by governments, there was still much voluntary effort, notably by bodies such as the Women's Migration and Overseas Appointment Societies, the Australian Big Brother Movement, and by various church bodies. Indeed many migrants still travelled within the Commonwealth without help from governments.[11] The sum total of their individual experiences, the links which they maintained with their homelands and the further flow of visits which their own remove encouraged from within the family circle all served to spread knowledge (if not always appreciation) of the Commonwealth connection. Even out of the heated controversy to which permanent Commonwealth immigration to Britain had already given rise, there emerged the hard fact that the British health and transport services could hardly have survived save for the injection of labour from the Caribbean, West Africa and Asia.

Nor should other initiatives involving young people throughout the Commonwealth be overlooked. First, more through accident than design the Duke of Edinburgh's Award Scheme, launched in 1956 as a challenge to the youth of Britain, soon found itself obliged to extend its operations overseas. Within ten years the project was operating in twenty-four Commonwealth countries outside the United Kingdom and upwards of ten thousand young people had played their parts in a project which was by then making a major contribution to Commonwealth cross-fertilisation.

Likewise COMEX – the Commonwealth Expedition – had, despite much cynicism (if not open opposition) from certain Whitehall quarters shown what the vision of one man, Colonel Lionel Gregory, could do to promote links between young people of the Commonwealth. Under this particular scheme, now increasingly successful, the aim was to organise, at minimum cost, overland visits from a British base to the Indian sub-continent by multi-ethnic groups selected from throughout the Commonwealth. Much the same aim was to inspire visits to and from Britain, within a Commonwealth context and under the auspices of the Royal Commonwealth Society, of small groups of young, hand-picked professionals and youth leaders. Both ventures were spontaneous. Neither derived from or was in any substantial way supported by governments. Each represented the spirit of the Commonwealth at its grass-roots best.

What deductions, then, may one draw from this brief survey of unofficial Commonwealth links in the early 1960s?

First, clearly, that as one continuing aftermath of the British heritage, Britain and the older 'Dominions' between them still enjoyed a long and solid tradition of voluntary effort and co-operation, and that each was rich in private institutions and organisations of all kinds.

Secondly, that in almost every field of human endeavour the modern Commonwealth could offer some example of co-operation on the non-governmental plane.

And thirdly, that governments had often to rely on the unofficial Commonwealth for that specialised knowledge and experience of which they themselves stood in need in furthering their own development programmes. This latter point was underlined by the British Government itself at the United Nations General Assembly of 1963 when it appealed to all non-governmental organisations 'to put their increased enthusiasm, energy and other resources into a world campaign in the basic human fields of food, health and education (including training) to start in 1965 and to continue for the remainder of the U.N. Development Decade.'[12]

At the same time some less heartening conclusions could be reached – in Commonwealth terms at least. For instance, much of what has been described above touched largely on unofficial links between the older 'settler' member countries of the Commonwealth. More newly independent countries did not all share the same attitude to non-governmental bodies. Nor, as long-serving expatriates withdrew from former colonies, often to be replaced by short-term and more technically oriented contract officers, did the ethos of voluntary service always long survive. Marching in parallel to such developments came a new breed of internationally minded rather than Commonwealth-minded philanthropists, representing such globally operating non-governmental organisations as OXFAM, Christian Aid or War on Want. To such bodies the Commonwealth was part only (though admittedly a large part) of the world-wide scene.

Furthermore, as will be mentioned later in this survey, the British heritage, with its insistence on standards, syllabi, textbooks and professional training more appropriate to the older than the newer world, was already threatening to cause the Commonwealth as a whole, as Lord Casey put it, to lose 'a series of important professional links with Britain and with each other'.[13]

Yet, to quote a Canadian diplomat with long experience in the field:

If the Commonwealth survives the difficult times ahead, it may well be because thousands of teachers, scholars and administrators working or studying in each others' countries – Australians and New Zealanders in Malaysia, or the Canadian military training mission in Ghana – strengthen the fabric of an association in which people get along better than governments.[14]

It is against that background that this book unfolds and that an effort is made to portray the strengths, actual and potential, of the functional Commonwealth as it has developed over the past twenty years.

Notes and References

1 'A party in search of a pattern: no. 2 – Patriotism based on reality not on a dream', by 'A Conservative', *The Times*, 2 April 1964.
2 C. S. Leslie, 'Has the Commonwealth a future?', *The Listener*, 6 February 1964.
3 *Commonwealth Relations Office List* (London, 1963).
4 Derek Ingram, *The Commonwealth at Work* (London, 1969).
5 Central Office of Information, *The Promotion of Science in the Commonwealth* (London, 1962).
6 Chartered Institute of Secretaries, *The Career of a Chartered Secretary* (London, 1963).
7 Much useful information on organisations in Britain which provided facilities for development activities may be found in the Overseas Development Institute *Development Guide* (London, 1962). However, with rare exceptions this publication did not make clear which of the five hundred organisations referred to worked exclusively in the Commonwealth field.
8 Fuller details of these and other bodies active at the time in question will be found in the *Commonwealth Relations Office List* (London, 1964) pp. 61–118.
9 Ingram, op. cit.
10 Professor D. E. S. Maxwell of the University of Ibadan, Nigeria, in *Commonwealth Literature: Report of the Leeds Conference* (London, 1965).
11 'A steady flow of people has been going from Britain to the Commonwealth since the war, numbering at the end of 1963 1,470,000'. R. P. Hornby, Under-Secretary for Commonwealth Relations, speaking in the House of Commons on 26 March 1964.
12 *UN General Assembly Resolution no. 1943* (XVIII), December 1963.
13 Rt Hon. Lord Casey, *The Future of the Commonwealth* (London, 1963).
14 John W. Holmes, *The Times*, 7 January 1964.

PART II

The Commonwealth Foundation

3

From Conception to Birth

I' the Commonwealth I would by contraries
Execute all things;

Gonzalo, *The Tempest*, Act 2

Had there been a paternity suit at issue, three fathers might well have claimed some share in the conception of the Commonwealth Foundation: the late Lords Casey and Patrick Gordon-Walker and the erstwhile Commonwealth Relations Office.

In his general survey[1] of the Commonwealth Lord Casey, drawing on wide practical experience of Commonwealth affairs, had emphasised the need to reduce the barriers of geography and to improve personal contacts in all fields, ranging from parliaments to sport. Referring to the 'scores of professional associations' and to the growing dilution of links between their parent bodies in Britain and the autonomous associations which had come gradually into existence elsewhere in the modern Commonwealth, he suggested that 'efforts should be made to re-create as many as possible of these links between old-established and important professional associations throughout the Commonwealth whilst, of course, maintaining the identity of each association in each Commonwealth country. This might start with such professional associations throughout the Commonwealth having their annual meetings in Commonwealth countries other than their own.' Governments, he continued, should be urged to subsidise the necessary travel costs. It was here that Britain could play a leading role.

43

As Governor-General of Australia, Lord Casey was later to prove a staunch ally of the Commonwealth Foundation, one part of whose future duties he had, if still loosely, adumbrated.

To Patrick Gordon-Walker, a former Secretary of State for Commonwealth Relations, went the credit of fleshing out the Casey bones. In his own survey he offered a succinct description of the numerous intra-Commonwealth bodies working outside the official field, concluding that without direct government aid much of the unofficial infrastructure would remain starved of its required resources. He went on, with much prescience, to propose that:

A possible solution would be the establishment of what might be called a Commonwealth Trust or Foundation. This could be controlled by a board made up of a nominee of each Commonwealth Government, the nominees to be persons of distinction not in Government service. The board would dispose of a fund that could be furnished both by governments and private contributions. The function of the board would be to stimulate and encourage at its discretion, all kinds of unofficial interchanges between Commonwealth countries it deemed to be of value. It would help to finance such undertakings as meetings of Commonwealth lawyers, doctors, local authority officials; sporting functions; conferences.[2]

As a blueprint for a new piece of Commonwealth machinery this came remarkably close to the model which Commonwealth governments were to devise some three years after Gordon-Walker's book appeared. Only the functions to be performed proved initially less ambitious.

At the same time it is of interest to note that, while favouring an unofficial 'Trust or Foundation' this same writer was scathing in his condemnation of those who might later seek to create within the Commonwealth some type of supra-national organisation. That, in his view, 'would be wholly alien to the nature of the Commonwealth, [whose] entire history has been a movement away from such a concept based upon the equality and sovereignty of its members'.[3] Ironically 1965 was to witness the emergence of both a 'supra-national' Commonwealth Secretariat, and of the Commonwealth Foundation itself.

But before tracing the Foundation's development from official conception to eventual birth it is worth considering why, after some five decades of debate, ending always with the rebuttal of the arguments advanced by the largely Australian-inspired 'supra-national' school of thought, a Commonwealth Secretariat and its smaller Foundation twin should have emerged so suddenly and, at the end, with no more than the faintest whisper of dissent.

The early 1960s had in fact brought the modern Commonwealth from the temporary euphoria of Indian independence in 1947 to a nadir of disillusion. The future of the Association, its value and continuing significance were under constant fire. While the departure of South Africa in 1961 had temporarily revived hopes that the major devil was now cast out, Rhodesia, race and remanent colonialism were soon amply to fill that vacuum. To those seemingly endless sores had to be added what Bruce Miller was later to describe as the 'growth or attrition' syndrome[4] – a sense of misgiving, above all in Britain, at the rapid emergence to independence within the Commonwealth of an increasing number of small, poor, unstable nation states. The dangerous – in Western eyes at least – flirtation of newer member countries with the Eastern bloc, the priority allegiance of many of them to the United Nations or the Bandung Pact, or both, served only to compound the feeling of the 'old Dominions' that the Commonwealth, as they had known it, was breaking up. Political like-mindedness, shared defence interests, economic co-operation had seemingly been broken on the altars of racism, regional polarisation and through abhorrence for that Aunt Sally of the 1960s and early 1970s, neo-colonialism. All that was left, as the cynics saw it, were the ghosts of 'kith and kin', combined with that arch-platitude of the 'common heritage'.

Thus, as the mid-1960s approached, one basic and unanswered question was whether a disillusioned Britain still laid any claim to moral leadership of the Commonwealth. If so what steps might British governments, to the left or right, now take to encourage their increasingly numerous fellow-members to search for areas of co-operation lying outside the strictly politico-economic field?

That such matters were preoccupying British ministers becomes clearer from a number of initiatives taken by successive Secretaries of State for Commonwealth Relations from the start of 1963. In April of that year the Commonwealth Office sponsored a conference at Ditchley Park with the aim of surveying the numerous existing links between peoples rather than governments of the Commonwealth. The upshot of that meeting was to underline, more forcefully than before, that there were indeed ways in which Britain could promote the importance of the unofficial Commonwealth and persuade her partners to accept that they formed not merely a grouping of governments, however fractious, but an association of peoples, brought continuously together through contact between individuals in all walks of life.

With an eye to a further Commonwealth heads of government meeting, already scheduled for the summer of the following year, the then Prime Minister, Harold Macmillan, decided in mid-1963 to commission an examination by officials of fresh ways of promoting Commonwealth co-operation, principally through non-governmental channels. He must clearly have had in mind that British policies – over Suez, Commonwealth immigration and entry into the European Economic Community – were creating strains within the Commonwealth greater far by now than anything that could be laid at the door of the Afro-Asian lobby in New York.

The British officials charged with this task were well aware of the obstacles they faced. The Commonwealth of the mid-1960s remained essentially an Anglocentric concept. Its very origins and growth had promoted a love–hate relationship between the centre and the rim. The more British ministers of whatever party failed to appreciate the aspirations and emotions of newer member countries, the more violent the reactions of the latter, not least on issues of race, would be. Hence two obvious conclusions: first, that with a steady increase in membership, resulting in constantly diverging interests, Commonwealth links at governmental level were likely, at least in the short term, to come under increasing stress: and second, that while any initiatives taken in the unofficial field would have no immediately dramatic effect, anything which promoted the growth of voluntary co-operation could only do good.

Having listed numerous non-governmental bodies on whose achievements the British Government might build, officials emphasised the particular importance of strengthening links and personal contacts in such fields as business, the professions, Parliament, science, education and youth in general. Ministers were thus urged to finance programmes which would *inter alia* promote voluntary service overseas; an increased supply of British teachers and of professional and technical experts for service in the newer Commonwealth; closer liaison between the Armed Services and trade unions of the Commonwealth; and the promotion of legal, cultural and sporting links. Teaching about the Commonwealth in schools in Britain should also be taken more seriously, while accommodation and other facilities open to Commonwealth students working in Britain should be improved.

It is noteworthy that while the supply of professional experts to other countries of the Commonwealth was touched on in the report by officials, no suggestion was made that Gordon-Walker's almost concurrent proposal for a Commonwealth-wide trust or foundation to promote professional co-operation should be examined.

The 1963 Report was indeed largely a victim of that very 'Anglocentricity' to whose dangers it had itself referred. Clearly, if some striking initiative was to be taken – in which case it would have to reflect the broader Commonwealth interest – then a far more imaginative approach would be required.

Two such attempts were made on the eve of the 1964 London Conference of Prime Ministers: the first on the initiative of Duncan Sandys (later Lord Duncan-Sandys), by now in charge of the Commonwealth Relations Office: the second by the Royal Commonwealth Society.

Late in April 1964 the Commonwealth Secretary convened at Marlborough House a one-day meeting of 'British professional bodies' – a somewhat loose definition since those invited also represented the churches, missionary societies and the press. But prominent among those present were professional leaders speaking for medicine, the law, architecture, engineering, surveying, nursing, higher education, dentistry, accountancy, secretaryship and public administration.

Opening this meeting Sandys stressed that it was the first of its kind. The views of so many professional leaders in Britain at a time when the Commonwealth was in a state of rapid growth and change would be of great interest to the British Government. As he put it, the Commonwealth today was a world in miniature. It was not merely an association of governments but also of peoples. Many interwoven strands together constituted the fabric of the association of Commonwealth peoples. In this, professional and business links played a very important part, for it was just these contacts which were the life-blood of Commonwealth relationships. — In a number of professional associations channels for these contacts already existed, but it was worth examining whether these could not be improved. Where they did not exist their creation should be seriously considered.

In discussion a number of professional and educational bodies gave evidence of their links with other countries of the Commonwealth. Much stress was laid on such problems as the lack of training places in Britain for overseas students; the failure to promote sufficiently high professional standards in colleges of technology in the developing world; the need for a Commonwealth programme of professional journal interchanges; and on difficulties, now coming increasingly to the fore, of retaining reciprocity and registration, particularly in the field of medicine, between the older and the newer Commonwealth. At the same time there was an encouraging recognition on the part of some British professional bodies of their duty to help their colleagues in the newer world to attain full autonomy, to recognise indigenous qualifications as and when appropriate standards had been attained, and to assist in devising syllabi relevant to the needs of the newer world.

Particular attention was drawn by the representative of the Royal Institute of British Architects, through a memorandum[5] submitted to the meeting, to the findings of a first fully representative conference of Commonwealth architectural societies. As the author of that paper wrote:

It was clear from the [July 1963] discussions, which

covered a wide range of professional problems, that there was a fund of knowledge and experience from which architects throughout the Commonwealth would benefit. In order to promote its agreed objectives of free exchange of ideas and experience, free movement of architects between countries, the establishment of high standards of service and recognition for the profession, the conference decided to recommend the formation as soon as possible of a Commonwealth Association of Architects on a professional basis, without distinction of politics, race or religion.

The fact that this proposal was unanimously ratified and that the pan-Commonwealth body came into existence in 1963, meeting for the first time formally in 1965, was later to prove of considerable significance as the Commonwealth Foundation in turn was born and began to map out its own priorities.

For the rest, the initiative taken by Duncan Sandys and the Commonwealth Office in bringing this group of British professional leaders together could not be said to have led to any specific blueprint for future action. The value of such exchanges was certainly recognised on all sides, the need for better reception arrangements for Commonwealth students working in Britain accepted and the strengthening of personal contacts between professionals throughout the Commonwealth seen as a laudable objective. But while Whitehall officials were doubtless subliminally impressed, no enthusiasm for Gordon-Walker's 'Trust' for professionals in the Commonwealth could yet be sensed.

In contrast to the Sandys initiative a one-day meeting convened on 22 June 1964 by the Royal Commonwealth Society was unashamedly propagandist in character. To it a wider spectrum of non-governmental interests was invited, including not only professional bodies but representatives of the media, voluntary societies, teachers' organisations and the like. The declared purpose was to persuade Commonwealth prime ministers, as they foregathered in London, of the existence of so 'many British organisations whose activities, cultural, educational, vocational, professional and commercial, contribute so much to the entity of the Commonwealth of today'.[6]

By the close of this second meeting a few practical, if not wholly original, proposals affecting the non-governmental sector had come to light. Among them were that increased funds should be found for the training in the older Commonwealth of senior administrators and professionals from Third World countries: that, subject to tax concessions being granted by governments more conferences of professional bodies should be organised in different countries of the Commonwealth, and finally that the prime ministers should 'give their encouragement to the setting up in each country of a Commonwealth centre as a focus for attention upon Commonwealth affairs over the widest possible field'.[7]

But again no mention of a pan-Commonwealth 'Trust' for the professions. On this all that could be hinted, as Whitehall put the finishing touches to the agenda and to its own documents for the London Conference of Prime Ministers, was that officials at last saw some attraction in a 'Commonwealth Trust or Foundation' to regulate and extend the non-official infrastructure of the Commonwealth. On the other hand it would in their view be dangerous to float any such proposals at the Conference for fear of a hostile reaction, not (curious as this may seem by hindsight) from other Commonwealth governments, but rather from the interested professionals themselves.

Yet, as if to underline the fact that ministers could occasionally, on matters of small import, brush aside the fears and hesitations of their advisers, Commonwealth prime ministers did at the eleventh hour decide to give a few moments' attention to the Gordon-Walker proposition. However, were it not for the fact that a plan to establish a Commonwealth Secretariat, first floated by President Nkrumah of Ghana was to gather unexpected and indeed surprising support as the 1964 conference drew towards its close, it is unlikely that the British Prime Minister would have produced the small Commonwealth Foundation rabbit from his sleeve.

In the upshot the final communiqué from the London Conference recorded that prime ministers, after studying other suitable areas for Commonwealth co-operation had concluded that:

it might be desirable to establish a Commonwealth
Foundation to administer a fund for increasing interchanges between Commonwealth organisations in professional fields. This Foundation could be administered
by an independent Board; and, while it could be financed
by contributions from Commonwealth Governments, it
would also welcome support from all quarters, whether
public or private.[8]

Thus it came about, as pragmatically as it had been unexpected, that the London Conference conceived two multinational embryos – a Commonwealth Secretariat and an
autonomous Foundation. To the Secretary of State for
Commonwealth Relations, as gynaecologist-in-chief, was left
the task of nurturing them to a point where, at a further heads
of government meeting, each could be brought to birth. It was
to prove a task involving much tedious draftsmanship and,
particularly in respect of the Commonwealth Secretariat,
consultations with all other Commonwealth governments of a
delicate and sometimes acrimonious nature.

As to the Foundation, the first problem facing Whitehall
was the preparation of a framework which could be considered
and embellished when next senior Commonwealth officials
met in January 1965 to present firm recommendations to prime
ministers – the latter having already agreed, somewhat
exceptionally, to hold a further conference in the summer of
that year.

Contrary to earlier pessimistic assumptions it soon became
clear, from soundings taken of leading British professional
bodies between July and December 1964, that they would
positively welcome the creation of a Commonwealth Foundation. They saw in it a means of strengthening unofficial links;
of increasing interchanges between younger professionals; of
encouraging intra-Commonwealth meetings; and of bringing
about a healthy growth of autonomous professional societies
in the newer Commonwealth.

The basic questions were thus how the Foundation was to
be financed; where its headquarters should be located; who
should staff it and to what detailed terms of reference its
chairman and board of trustees should work.

As to funding, the prime ministers at their summer meeting of 1964 had already in principle accepted an offer from the British Government to contribute half of a proposed annual income of £250,000. At the same time they had expressed the hope that contributions might be forthcoming from the private sector. Regarding a headquarters site, officials had first concluded that London must exclude itself on the grounds that prime ministers had already decided to establish the Commonwealth Secretariat in the British capital. However, later informal soundings of Commonwealth governments revealed that there were unlikely to be objections to the Foundation working alongside the Commonwealth Secretariat in London, the more so since so many professional bodies operating throughout the Commonwealth were themselves British-based.

In the upshot there were no major areas of controversy left when senior officials met in London in January 1965 to discuss, among other weightier matters, a draft blueprint for the Commonwealth Foundation. Their concern proved to be less with the proposed structure and terms of reference of the organisation than with the very need for its existence. Could not its duties in fact be subsumed within those which had been worked out in parallel for the Commonwealth Secretariat? On balance the conclusion reached was that a strong case existed for establishing an autonomous trust. It should be free from government influence and should take as its primary roles those of improving personal contacts and interchanges between professionals; encouraging the flow of scientific, technical and other types of professional information between non-governmental organisations throughout the Commonwealth; and of providing whatever assistance, financial or otherwise, as might be thought appropriate. In short, the Foundation should be seen to be a wholly independent body.

Having taken matters thus far, officials decided to recommend to their respective governments that the Foundation's headquarters might best be established in London; that its chairman should be a distinguished private citizen of a Commonwealth country other than Britain, and that the Foundation's annual income should not at the outset exceed £250,000. Should Britain still agree to contribute half that sum, the balance could be subscribed by other member governments on some basis still to be agreed. From the outset the small permanent staff should be urged to develop close links with the Commonwealth Secretariat which, once established, was likely to become the centre-piece of an immediate review of all other existing official intra-Commonwealth organisations.

By and large the immediate reactions of governments to these recommendations proved favourable although, as must always be expected in such circumstances, most national treasuries waited to learn how winds were blowing in other quarters before committing their own governments to precise annual contributions, however small. Thus, on the eve of the 1965 conference the British Prime Minister, by then Harold Wilson, felt able to report to his Commonwealth colleagues that since all had by and large accepted the views of their officials it should prove possible, subject to formal endorsement from the conference, to leave the final details leading to the creation of the Foundation to be worked out by Commonwealth high commissioners in London in association with the Secretary-General of the Commonwealth Secretariat once he in turn had been appointed.

In practice prime ministers, at a session on 24 June 1965, wasted little time in discussion of Foundation business, readily agreeing to Wilson's summation of the case. The essential conclusion from the meeting was a decision forthwith to publish an 'Agreed Memorandum'[9] setting forth terms of reference for the new organisation. This document laid down that, as an autonomous body to be accommodated with the Commonwealth Secretariat at the Commonwealth Centre, Marlborough House, London, the Foundation's broad remit would be 'to administer a fund for increasing interchanges between Commonwealth organisations in professional fields throughout the Commonwealth'. Among its stated tasks would be:

(a) To encourage and support fuller representation at conferences of professional bodies within the Commonwealth.
(b) To assist professional bodies within the Commonwealth to hold more conferences between themselves.

53

(c)   To facilitate the exchange of visits among professional people, especially the younger element.

(d)   To stimulate and increase the flow of professional information exchanged between the organisations concerned.

(e)   On request to assist with the setting up of national institutions or associations in countries where these do not at present exist.

(f)   To promote the growth of Commonwealth-wide associations or regional Commonwealth associations in order to reduce the present centralisation in Britain.

(g)   To consider exceptional requests for help from associations and individuals whose activities lie outside the strictly professional field but fall within the general ambit of the Foundation's operations as outlined above.

Thus, brick by brick, the small structure had been built. In the following chapters it will be seen how life was breathed into the organisation, and how and with what staff and financial backing it launched itself into what was to prove a large and relatively untravelled zone of darkness.

Notes and References

1   Rt Hon. Lord Casey, *The Future of the Commonwealth* (London, 1963).
2   Rt Hon. Lord Gordon-Walker, *The Commonwealth* (London, 1962).
3   ibid.
4   J. D. B. Miller, *A Survey of Commonwealth Affairs: Problems of Expansion and Attrition 1959–1969* (London, 1974).
5   'The relationship between the RIBA and Commonwealth architectural societies', note by Alister Macdonald, FRIBA, April 1964.
6   Royal Commonwealth Society press release, 2 July 1964.
7   ibid.
8   Conference of Commonwealth Prime Ministers, *Final Communiqué* (London, 1964).
9   Commonwealth Prime Ministers' Meeting 1965, *Agreed memorandum on the Commonwealth Foundation*, Cmnd 2714, 1965.
    Full text at Appendix A.

4

Birthpangs

[in the Commonwealth]
No occupation; all men idle, all;
And women too, but innocent and pure;
No sovereignty; –
                    Gonzalo, *The Tempest*, Act 2

Barely conceivable in 1963, the Commonwealth Secretariat
had two years later become not merely desirable but, in the
light of political developments, essential. Speed now being of
the essence heads of government, meeting once more in
London in 1965, had approved not only the terms of reference
for the secretariat's activities but also by acclaim appointed
their first Commonwealth Secretary-General, Arnold Smith.
Smith, a senior Canadian diplomat, had represented his
country in such key posts as the Soviet Union and Egypt. In
Cairo he had weathered the Suez crisis with distinction, at the
same time tackling the unenviable task of protecting British
interests following the Anglo-French invasion. With a reputation for vigour and imagination and with a strong belief in
the modern Commonwealth despite its many imperfections,
the Secretary-General lost no time in embarking on his uphill
task. By the close of August 1965 he had settled into his headquarters at Marlborough House and had assembled the
nucleus of a Commonwealth 'mix-manned' staff.

No such sense of urgency attached to the Commonwealth
Foundation. Its remit lay outside the political crisis area.

55

Moreover there was much yet to be settled before it could get down to business. In the first place, Commonwealth governments had still to appoint 'a distinguished private citizen' as its chairman. Secondly, as laid down in paragraph 5 of the Agreed Memorandum of 1965, nominations had to be made to a board of trustees. This was to 'consist of independent persons, each subscribing Government having the right to nominate one member of the Board', on which the Commonwealth Secretary-General would himself sit or be represented *ex officio*.

Thirdly, Commonwealth governments, acting through their high commissioners in London, had still to appoint 'a full time salaried Director – initially for a period of two years', the brevity of that term of office being justified by the need to await the outcome of a now pending review on the future of all existing intra-Commonwealth bodies, some of which might soon be merged with the Secretariat. The director in turn would have to recruit the small personal staff referred to in the memorandum. Fourthly, and not least, there was an obligation on the British Government to 'draw up the necessary documents to set up the Trust and take any further steps needed to constitute the Foundation as a legal charity'.

The worsening situation in Rhodesia and the convening of an exceptional Prime Ministers' Conference in Lagos, Nigeria, the first Commonwealth meeting at this high level ever to have been held outside Britain, was inevitably to add to the delay.

However, following a meeting of Commonwealth high commissioners in London on 14 December 1965, a press release from the Commonwealth Relations Office at last revealed that 'Commonwealth governments have agreed that Sir Macfarlane Burnet, OM, FRS, MD, ScD, FRCP, shall be the first Chairman of the Board of Trustees. This is an honorary appointment'. It was also agreed that 'Mr G. W. St. J. Chadwick, CMG, should be the first Director'.

A nominee of the late Sir Robert Menzies, Burnet was described in the press statement, with justice, as 'one of the most distinguished of living Australians'. He was indeed a world figure in the treatment of virus diseases. Jointly with Sir Peter Medawar, he had in 1960 received the Nobel Prize for Medicine.

The first director was referred to as an Assistant Under-Secretary of State in the Commonwealth Relations Office with previous diplomatic service in Ottawa, Dublin and Paris and at the time 'concerned with African affairs'. During his service with the Foundation he would, it was emphasised, 'be a servant not of the British Government but of . . . the Commonwealth as a whole'.

In a subsequent talk with the press the director was reported (correctly if in truncated form) as saying that the aims of the Foundation would be 'to reduce anglo-centricity in the professional field'. The new body would be 'concerned exclusively with contacts between countries at non-governmental level'.[1]

It now remained to appoint trustees to the Foundation Board, to assemble a small staff, and to register the organisation as a charity under English law.

The trustees, it may be recalled, were to be 'independent persons', a definition which was to cause some heart-searching in the years ahead. In practice what the draftsmen of the Agreed Memorandum of 1965 had had in mind was that, wherever national circumstances allowed, trustees, like the Foundation's chairman, should be 'unofficials' as opposed to ministers, diplomats or civil servants.

On that basis Britain was first in the field, nominating as its representative on the board Dr Leslie Farrer-Brown, CBE, JP, an economist by training, a Commonwealth man by persuasion and, until shortly before his appointment, the first director of Britain's largest trust, the Nuffield Foundation. He brought to his task a wealth of experience on the Commonwealth generally, on the professions and, not least, on the arcana of philanthropy. The Canadian Government in turn decided to nominate an 'unofficial' in the person of Escott Reid, a diplomat turned academic towards the close of a long and distinguished career. New Zealand chose a retired member of its own diplomatic service, Richard Campbell, who had conveniently settled in Britain and was thus close at hand. Nigeria selected a leading chartered accountant from the private sector, Akintola Williams. He, over a ten-year period, was so to combine his firm's overseas business with the Foundation's interests that he never failed to attend a board meeting throughout that time.

57

Trinidad and Tobago and (later) Barbados were others to appoint non-officials to the board. The former country was represented by a retired Permanent Secretary for Education and local cricketer of distinction, Robert Loinsworth: and the latter by Dr (later Sir) Hugh Springer, KCMG, CBE, who was to combine his trust duties with the secretary-generalship of the Association of Commonwealth Universities. Finally from Malta, or rather from the Inner Temple, came Dr C. J. Colombos, QC, an internationally recognised expert on the law of the sea. Already a stalwart octogenarian, he was most enchantingly to fulfil the role of the dormouse at the Mad Hatter's tea party.

All other countries were then, or as later events brought them to independence, represented on the Board of Trustees by their high commissioners in London. The problems created by this mixed-manning will be referred to more fully in the context of the Foundation's later efforts to build up a comprehensible long-term policy and orders of interest. But to sum up, there was at the outset a board representing the interests of twenty member countries,[2] seven of which had nominated 'unofficials' to act on their behalf.

By contrast the recruitment of the small personal staff required to support the first director proved simple to a point. The immediately foreseen needs were for no more than a competent personal assistant/shorthand-typist and a bookkeeper/administration officer. For the former post my already long-suffering 'CRO lady', Mrs N. I. Duncan, MBE, volunteered her services. For the latter a senior executive officer from the Foreign Office, R. N. Dawson, who no longer wished to serve abroad, was rapidly engaged. And so with a distinguished chairman, a fully constituted Board of Trustees, a permanent staff of three and the guarantee of a small suite of offices at Marlborough House, the Commonwealth Foundation had at last reached the take-off point.

During the events described to date I (as director-designate) had continued with my normal Whitehall duties. These had included a 'backroom boy' function in relation to prime ministers' conferences in general; an oversight of such forward planning studies as a department harassed with almost monthly independence negotiations could then afford; and responsibility to ministers at an 'upper-middle' level for relations generally with the Commonwealth in Africa. In prospect an appointment to take charge, however briefly, of a small, risk-laden but non-political organisation loomed like a busman's holiday along an unfrequented country route. Apart from having in the press at the time a chapter on the 'Unofficial Commonwealth' as a contribution to a book shortly to be published by an American university,[3] I knew little more about the professions and their politics than the man on the Clapham omnibus. Still less, to my shame, had I heard, prior to his appointment as my future chairman, of Burnet.

As things turned out, the date selected for the opening of the Commonwealth Foundation was 1 March 1966. Early in February of that year a further round of informal talks between British and United States officials on the problems of Tropical and Southern Africa was due to take place at the State Department in Washington. In an access of understanding my much respected Secretary of State, the Rt Hon. Arthur Bottomley agreed that, after joining in these talks, I should be authorised to travel onwards (as a first charge on the Foundation's still non-existent funds) to make contact in Melbourne with Burnet. What that distinguished scientist thought of his acolyte remains unrecorded save for an article which he subsequently presented to a learned Australian medical journal. In it a certain X was mentioned as having introduced a new strain of Asian 'flu virus to the State of Victoria, laying low in the process not only the chairman himself but the Chief Justice, Sir Garfield Barwick, and other professional notabilities whom he had gathered round his table to size me up. At least Burnet never held this against me during his three-year tenure of the chairmanship. Despite my 'flu-ridden state we established as friendly a rapport as could be expected between an eminent virologist and an amateur germ-carrier. Later I was to have cause to be grateful to him and to the late Lady Burnet for many personal kindnesses and for staunch support in the early days.

On return to London I took leave of colleagues in Whitehall with whom I had worked for many years and prepared to view St James's Park from another angle. In a farewell call on my Permanent Under-Secretary, Sir Saville (later Lord)

Garner, I sensed his mixed feelings that while I had perhaps been rash in volunteering to serve an unknown quantity, I was at least helping in small ways to ease an appalling promotion blockage with which he was then constantly at grips. But I do not think it occurred to either of us that, on the presumption of a mere two-year secondment, I was now saying goodbye for ever to the Whitehall scene.

The transition proved total in every sense: from a wholly national to a Commonwealth-wide loyalty; from a busy department of state where one was but one small cog in a quite large wheel to an organisation, minute though it might be, where one was in effect to be the boss; from an operating, well-oiled machine to an organisation boasting no more than a one-page blueprint. As I tried to summarise things fourteen years later in a retrospective article: 'March 1, 1966; Marlborough House. Three characters with open minds in search of empty rooms.'[4]

My first 'directorial' move, on the eve of taking up duty, was to invite all twenty founding members of the Board of Trustees to meet informally at Marlborough House. For this purpose I had prepared a first annual budget and a record of my talks with the chairman, who would not be visiting London until later in the year. The meeting was also designed to enable the 'private' trustees to get the measure of their future diplomatic colleagues and vice versa. This proved to be a useful initiative. The board began by taking note of some helpful contacts which I had been able to make with a number of leading American foundations while passing through New York in February. Some practical decisions were also reached: namely, that dependent territories, whether of Australia, Britain or New Zealand, must be brought within the Foundation's ambit; that in a first year of operation the board should meet thrice at least; that a bank account should forthwith be opened; and that the Foundation's financial year should run from July 1 to June 30. Funds unspent in one full year should be rolled over to the next and a reserve fund eventually built up. Above all, the Foundation should start cautiously. Aims and policies would emerge from full and uninhibited discussion at early meetings of the Board. As the record put it, the first year should be primarily one of reconnaisance, during which the director would make the widest possible contacts in the professional and philanthropic fields. Among the Foundation's primary aims should be to find gaps which needed filling, while at the same time avoiding unnecessary duplication of effort in fields better covered by other organisations. Given its limited funds the Foundation might also act as a catalyst *vis-à-vis* other trusts, industry and commerce, with the eventual objective of embarking on hand-picked joint schemes with such bodies on a 'dollar for dollar' basis. It was also conceded that the director might need to travel even more widely within the Commonwealth than had been envisaged.[5]

How such contacts were eventually established, and how the Foundation's aims were translated into action and in which priority areas of interest, will be discussed in the following chapters.

Notes and References

1 *Guardian*, 15 December 1965.
2 The original contributing member governments were Britain, Canada, Australia, New Zealand, India, Pakistan, Ceylon, Ghana, Malaysia, Nigeria, Cyprus, Sierra Leone, Jamaica, Trinidad and Tobago, Uganda, Malawi, Malta, Zambia, The Gambia and Singapore.
3 W. B. Hamilton et al. (eds), *A Decade of the Commonwealth, 1955–1964* (Durham, NC, 1965).
4 'The Commonwealth Foundation 1966–1980: a retrospection', *Round Table* no. 280, October 1980.
5 Commonwealth Foundation Papers, record of a first informal meeting of trustees, Marlborough House, London, 25 February 1966.

5

First Steps

> Give all thou canst: high heaven rejects the lore
> of nicely calculated less and more.
>
> Wordsworth, *Ecclesiastical Sonnet XLIII*

The first formal meeting of the Foundation's trustees spread
over the two days June 27 and June 29 1966, a time-scale
which would have sent shudders down the spines of latter-day
board members. But the two-part session was at least convened
in the comforting knowledge that there was to be no question
of the infant organisation being swallowed into the Commonwealth Secretariat maw even before it had learned to walk.
A Review Committee on Intra-Commonwealth Organisations,
commissioned by prime ministers at their conference in 1965
and composed of the representatives of seven Commonwealth
countries under the chairmanship of Lord Sherfield, had by
now forwarded its recommendations to governments. While
proposing that organisations such as the Commonwealth
Liaison and Economic Committees and the Commonwealth
Education Liaison Committee and Unit should forthwith be
merged with the Secretariat, the report had no more than this
to say about the Commonwealth Foundation:

> We took note . . . of the Agreed Memorandum of June
> 1965 establishing the Foundation. We note in particular
> that paragraph 5 . . . had already prescribed a form of
> liaison arrangement between the Foundation and the

Commonwealth Secretariat and that paragraph 7 had also determined the nature of the assistance to be provided to the Foundation by the Secretariat. We consider therefore that the relationship with the Commonwealth Secretariat has already been settled and the need for a further review does not arise.[1]

Not that doubts did not from time to time revive, as the secretariat itself expanded, that the camel might ultimately strain to catch the gnat. But to the small Foundation staff it was a relief that it could from the outset plan the future policies and programmes of what was now accepted as a wholly independent, autonomous body.

It was the chairman himself who set both the tone and the goals for the Foundation in his opening address to Trustees on June 27. Having, as an internationally-minded scientist, firmly declared his concern 'to foster the ideal of one world [rather] than to perpetuate the Commonwealth as a political unit', he added the rider that 'anything that we can do within the Commonwealth must also be of benefit to the world as a whole'.

There need be no excuse for quoting here the following passages from Burnet's inaugural remarks. They showed vision and have stood the test of time.

I believe that the Prime Ministers and their advisers who conceived this Foundation and its function showed a touch of genius. It is necessary to look rather carefully behind the obvious difficulties of the present time to find what is common to us all, on which we can help to build an important part of a better world. These common experiences and loyalties within the Commonwealth may be stronger than we think. There is first the use of English as a working language at the professional and technological level and second some experience of the working of English Common Law. Third, the effects of common educational and administrative processes have left a legacy which will not easily fade. At the professional level everywhere in the Commonwealth we may differ on many points but our education has given us what are by now almost instinctively shared processes of thought ... This leads to my [fourth] point which is concerned with the most important of those shared attitudes, viz., the recognition that a country can only prosper if there is a solid core of professionally trained men with the intellect, discipline and knowledge that is adequate to deal effectively with the myriad of technical problems that arise at every level in this 20th century.

Far more is necessary than the Foundation can possibly undertake but I believe that we have an important opportunity in front of us. Here we can and must forget about the problems of power and politics, of race and religion. Our task is to provide our small contribution towards ensuring that throughout the Commonwealth the people who can deal with health and education, with roads and dams and airports, who can advise on agriculture and industry – that these people shall be able to talk together; to exchange facts and opinions, and to work together for the good of their peoples.

Turning to organisational matters the chairman reminded his colleagues, and the staff, that any newly created body could only formulate practical policies within the framework of its constitution and that, with the relatively small funds available to trustees their activities, at least in the early experimental years, must be 'more catalytic than executive'. Mistakes would undoubtedly be made. Thus policy decisions must be kept flexible enough to avoid their repetition.[2]

The first paper to come before the board on that occasion was the draft of a Declaration of Trust establishing the Foundation as a charity under English law. Despite the obligation on the British Government under the Agreed Memorandum of 1965 to 'take the necessary steps' to bring about this development, their legal advisers had seemingly wilted under the strain of defining the parameters of the world of the professions. It thus fell to me to make contact with a suitable firm of solicitors and to seek advice from learned counsel familiar with the requirements and thinking of the Charity Commissioners. That done, it also proved necessary (and considerably more difficult) to convince all concerned of both the international character of this particular Foundation and of the Commonwealth's pragmatic and, to a lawyer, exasperatingly illogical way of doing business. Much patience was needed before those involved could be brought to accept that it was not the 'done thing' in Commonwealth circles for votes to be recorded. Decisions were reached by consensus. Silence was taken as assent. Almost equally daunting was the need to provide some definition of 'the professions', a matter on which the Agreed Memorandum had remained most wisely silent, but on which, quite properly from their custodial viewpoint, the Charity Commission's lawyers laid much stress. My own plea to the Foundation's legal advisers on this basic issue was for a maximum of flexibility, coupled with a reminder that the professional community was itself a child of constant change – yesteryear's barber for instance being today's respected surgeon. Happily both lawyers and trustees ended by agreeing that the Foundation should not be laced from the very start into a straitjacket of definitions. Thus the Trust Deed, as eventually registered with the Charity Commission on 15 December 1966, described the aims of the Foundation in the following catch-all phrase: 'To maintain and improve (in the interests of the public) standards of knowledge attainment and conduct in the skilled or learned professions or skilled auxiliary occupations within the Commonwealth.'[3]

A constitution annexed to the Trust Deed provided among other things for new or amended provisions; accession of further subscribing members; rates of national contributions and, an important point, for the right of the board to invest monies and to use income unexpended in one financial year in any succeeding year.

Having thus complied with the demands of the laws of England, the trustees then embarked on a first policy debate. Among the conclusions reached were that at least two years of trial and error would be needed before the Foundation could claim to have worked out precise priorities and areas of action, and that there could be no dissent from the view that the bulk of financial aid should go to developing countries of the Commonwealth. It was also agreed that dependent territories should be eligible for assistance: that trustees should not be content to sit back and wait for applications to reach them but should initiate and implement projects of their own and that the staff, in the course of making contact with professional bodies throughout the Commonwealth, should draw up a full list of these for guidance of the board, together with notes as to their grant-worthiness.

On the negative side trustees concluded that the Foundation should not concern itself with basic research or with scholarly activities unlikely to have direct impact on the immediate needs of the public, nor should they become involved in fields of primary and secondary education, or with projects which could more appropriately be financed under national and international technical aid schemes.

Understandably the number of awards made at the close of the first board meeting was minimal. Caution was the password. What could not be spent in the early months could always be invested and, under the rules applying to charities, earn tax-free interest. Rather than succumbing to the temptations of the stock market the staff, with encouragement from trustees, placed such funds as could be spared on short and longer-term deposit with a leading bank. That in fact still remains their policy – one not to be regretted since, at least until 1975, the annual tax-free interest earned proved enough to defray the bulk of the Foundation's (then still) modest administrative costs.

Once over the hurdle of the first meeting of trustees it became my task to make contact with as many professional bodies and foundations as time allowed; to travel the Commonwealth; to learn the arts of philanthropy (in the course of which one quickly found that dispensing money wisely was no easy task); and to ensure that the Foundation was not led into duplicating the work of bigger, if not necessarily better, brothers.

Already in February 1966 I had been helped, through the good offices of the Foundation Library Center in New York (an admirable research and information body, having alas no equivalent in Britain) to make contact with such leading United States trusts as Ford, Carnegie, Asia, Kellogg and Rockefeller. Their scientific, agricultural and educational efforts in the Commonwealth alone were impressive and of relatively long standing, while their disposable grant income

placed the Commonwealth Foundation well down towards
the bottom of the Third Division. Yet, as a newcomer, I
received nothing but encouragement. Small could, apparently,
be beautiful. Or, as was mentioned to me at Rockefeller, one
of its former presidents had once told the staff that 'a common
fallacy – and even some foundation executives may not be
immune from it – is that money can create ideas, and that a
great deal of money can create better ideas . . . But there is no
substitute for brains'. Subconsciously that president may have
had in mind Blake's earlier dictum that mankind can do
good and make effective change only in 'minute particulars'.
A good motto perhaps for the Commonwealth Foundation
which, through trial and error, was soon to find that the small
award offered to a well-selected individual at a crucial point
in his or her career was likelier to produce greater dividends
than might a much larger grant towards some project over
which trustees could exercise far less control.

One broad conclusion from this first and indeed from later
visits to New York, was that Americans took philanthropy
more seriously than the British did. Perhaps it was that the
opportunities for company or 'dynastic' tax evasion were
greater and that the interest of Congress in legislation affecting
private trusts, was consequently much keener than that shown
by Parliament at Westminster. Whatever the root causes,
there was certainly a greater weight of literature on the
subject on the far side of the Atlantic.

To risk one more American quotation, the source of which
can no longer be traced but which in those early months,
struck me as sage if obvious: 'Giving away money wisely is an
extraordinarily subtle and difficult task, with social and
intellectual complications that keep your conscience active
and your mind bothered.' More controversially, as the president
of this particular family trust went on: 'The philanthropoid
must never tell anyone what he ought to be interested in. He
must ask questions and listen to answers. He must not place
the answer he would like to have come back to him. He, of all
persons, must never start a question by saying "Don't you
think . .?" '

Reflecting on this effusion of wisdom I concluded, ruefully,
that if it was difficult for a family trust, occupied with some

quite restricted domestic problem, to part with money wisely, then how much more intractable must be the task facing a new and ill-financed organisation, whose oyster was the whole Commonwealth and all and every profession and sub-profession in it. As to this particular philanthropoid's concluding advice my own brief experience, after talking with visiting applicants or with those met on journeys overseas, was that listening was only half the job. A high proportion of worthy applicants proved to be genuinely embarrassed when the time came to hold out their begging bowl. If they were not to be dismissed as inarticulate, it was up to the listener to 'smoke them out'. Thus the supposedly sinful question 'Don't you think?' quite often led to the clearer formulation of a project which might otherwise have foundered.

Heartened at any rate by the readiness of those transatlantic trusts whose staffs it has been my good fortune to meet, and which had been so ready to open their files and minds and to hint at prospects for future collaboration, I had assumed, when preparing to introduce the Foundation to well-established sister organisations in Britain, whose own activities brought them in some way into contact with Commonwealth affairs, that one would receive an equally warm reception. In practice the majority of British trust directors proved somewhat conservative in outlook. As a generalisation it could be said that the higher the disposable income and the wider the geographical involvement, the warmer would be the interest shown in a newcomer to the philanthropic field. But such bodies were in a minority. Most foundations concerned with relief and rehabilitation, with the social sciences or again with medical and scientific projects seemed, above all when they were handling the funds of some individual Maecenas or his family, to be reluctant to pool knowledge or to collaborate, for economy's sake, on some joint project. Thus, the more depressing such reactions were, the more grateful one became to those few major trusts, among them the Nuffield Foundation, which were prepared to encourage, to exchange ideas, to accept or to refer project applications and eventually to agree to embark on conjoint ventures.

Happily, as the staff launched on its task of making the Foundation known to the professions in the older Commonwealth and through them to their colleagues in the newer world, few such setbacks were encountered. Here it was rather a question of finding time enough to call on so many well-known bodies and to discover how many others, hitherto unsuspected, existed. A number of the leading professions had of course already welcomed the decision of prime ministers to create the Commonwealth Foundation. Their links with sister bodies in the older countries were now a part of history. As to the newer Commonwealth they were, generally speaking, as anxious as the politicians to ensure that professional autonomy followed on national independence and that the earlier branch relationship with the parent (and generally British) body was replaced by a healthier one of equal status. There were of course exceptions, some organisations still looking to student and overseas membership fees as being of greater short-term benefit to their own domestic membership. This was a short-sighted view, held chiefly by the still imperial-minded. But by the close of its first ten years of life the Foundation could claim to have played some part in persuading certain of these 'backwoodsmen' to change their ways. As the first trustee for Canada had meanwhile put it in the early days when addressing a professional audience in Toronto: 'We of the Commonwealth Foundation certainly do not press professional associations in the Commonwealth to co-operate if they do not want to. But if professional associations want to co-operate, the Commonwealth Foundation stands ready to help them.'[4]

The experience gained from the board's original assault on such problems and from my own contact-building was to some degree summarised in a policy paper submitted to the board in the summer of 1966. It will serve as an introduction to the various types of project activities on which trustees were to embark from the start of 1967 onwards.

The necessary body of information, which must be the basis for any long-term policy, can only be slowly acquired – by making wide-ranging contacts, sifting the wheat from the chaff, and above all through patient listening, discussion and imaginative thought. By gradual degrees, the Director of a thinly staffed Foundation should, with the help of his Trustees, aim at building up an informal body of expert honorary advisers. He should not display eagerness to spend funds simply because the funds are there. He and his Board should be on guard against schemes promoted by professional fund raisers: and should not allow themselves to be impressed by the high patronage behind which applicants for money may be sheltering. In general, the Director should seek to interest his Trustees in new projects – preferably those which do not involve continuing annual commitments. He should not allow his organisation to acquire the reputation of being one to which the same body or individual can return time and again for help. In other words, a Foundation should be mentally mobile, acting now in one fresh area, now in another, as an extra engine to help a train over a stiff grade.

In two senses our Foundation is unique. It is the only Commonwealth organisation collectively financed by Member Governments and working in the unofficial field. It is probably the only Foundation in the world which, through the composition of its Board of Trustees, transcends national boundaries. If its funds are small (and its staff exiguous) it can at least lay claim from the start to a certain peculiarity.

We are, as United Kingdom law requires, a legal Charity. But our aims are practical, not eleemosynary. The large question Trustees will wish to debate is how the Foundation's somewhat vague and far-reaching terms of reference can be translated into action.

Perhaps one may start with some negatives. Our funds are not available to promote sport within the Commonwealth, to assist journalism, broadcasting or television – at least 'initially'. Nor are they at the disposal of 'Education' which, for these purposes, can presumably be defined as anything affecting formally organised systems from the primary to the post-graduate stage. Again the arts and culture are generally excluded. In all these fields other, and for the most part larger, Commonwealth and international organisations exist. It would seem senseless to duplicate their efforts.

The positives are far harder to define. As the secretary of a sister Foundation has asked – 'What do you mean by "professions"?'. No doubt we shall have to proceed pragmatically. But, judging by the wide and heart-warming response from learned societies and professional institutions in Britain to our first letters of introduction, and the increasing number of letters from elsewhere in the Commonwealth, it should not be difficult to sort out those bodies with a genuine intra-Commonwealth character from those pursuing narrower national aims.

Clearly, as was emphasised at our first informal meeting, the Board will wish to advance cautiously and to ensure that what little monies we spend in the early months are seen to be wisely spent. The art of saying 'No' will have to be cultivated. Projects need to be scrutinised with great care and in many cases views exchanged with other Foundations and agencies. The general aim should be to make applicants feel that a grant from the Commonwealth Foundation is a hall-mark on their own efficiency. The weight of applications itself will be a measure of the Foundation's effectiveness.

Many Foundations have programmes, to each of which a percentage of annual income is allocated. Programmes clearly can only emerge from priorities, and the latter from experience gained. A new foundation must discover, sometimes by hit-or-miss methods, where gaps exist and in what fields it can most helpfully operate. Once that stage is reached, priorities will begin to sort themselves out and programmes can logically follow. But for a start, the pragmatic approach seems the only possible one.

In short, the Commonwealth Foundation will best develop in the light of its own acquired experience.[5]

By the close of 1967 that experience had dictated a series of developments, first among which had been help to the individual, whether through attendance at conferences or seminars of value, or for tailor-made visits or through a variety of short-term bursary schemes. From these first and sometimes controversial efforts a Commonwealth Foundation Lectureship programme was developed. The need for a better supply of professional journals to individuals and their institutes in the developing world was uncovered and the professions themselves were gradually persuaded to collaborate in wider ventures, some of which will be described in the following chapters.

As the Foundation entered on its second year of activity and published its first Progress Report[6] it was heartening to trustees, who had already grown in number from twenty-one to twenty-five, to read in *The Times* that 'probably the most encouraging sign in recent years of the health of the Commonwealth has been the Commonwealth Foundation, formed early in 1966 to strengthen the links between professional men and women and their institutions'.[7]

Notes and References

1 *Report of the Review Committee on Intra-Commonwealth Organisations*, Marlborough House, London, August 1966.
2 Commonwealth Foundation Papers, record of the first meeting of the Board of Trustees, Marlborough House, London, 27 June 1966.
3 *Trust Deed*, registered with the Charity Commission, London, 1966. For full text see Appendix B.
4 Escott Reid, speech to centenary meeting of the Canadian Paediatric Society, Toronto, 7 September 1967.
5 'Some first thoughts on policy', extracts from a paper from the director to trustees, 27 May 1966.
6 Commonwealth Foundation, *First Progress Report, March 1966–October 1967*.
7 *The Times*, 29 August 1967.

6

Some Early Initiatives

And now, while the great ones depart to their dinner
The secretary sits, growing thinner and thinner
Racking his brains to record and report
What he thinks that they think
That they ought to have thought.

Anon.

Among the more important activities envisaged for the
Foundation under its Agreed Memorandum were to 'encourage
and support fuller representation at conferences of professional
bodies within the Commonwealth ... (and to) facilitate the
exchange of visits among professional people, especially the
younger element'.

Such dictates implied a full appreciation on the part of the
permanent staff of the professional areas within which it was
to operate, and the forging of links with the greatest possible
number of professional societies throughout the Commonwealth. By 1970 considerable progress had in fact been made
with the task of delineation and trustees were able to commission the publication of a detailed guide, the first of its kind,
which was to provide information on upwards of one thousand
professional societies active throughout the Commonwealth.[1]

In a percipient introduction the editor, Sir James Currie,
KCMG, CBE, quoted Bacon's dictum: 'I hold every man a
debtor to his profession; from the which as men of course do
seek to receive countenance and profit, so ought they of duty

73

to endeavour themselves by way of amends to be a help and ornament there-unto.' Sir James went on to offer a succinct definition of latter-day 'professional man'. As he put it:

> The first characteristic of a profession is that its terms of entry should be well defined. By this I mean that, as a result of education and training, the fitness of the professional man should be recognised by everyone, because he has, in an approved way, shown himself fit and skilled in practice. He is thus acceptable not only to his professional colleagues but to the public who employ him. The second characteristic of a profession is that it imposes a discipline on its members. This may be by a stipulated code of ethics set down as part of the constitution or by an accepted, often unwritten, way of working. This code is known, and acknowledged to be known, not only by the profession and accepted by it; it is recognised by the public, who are protected by it. The third characteristic is that a professional man may have to submit his qualifications to some statutory or authoritative body as a prelude to practice. This means that he must obtain a recognition, which, again, can be accepted as a standard, and as a protection to the public. These three characteristics are to be found in most professions – the recognition of fitness through adequate approved qualifications, the discipline and control of the organisation, and the permission to practise through some form of registration or licensing.

Armed with such definitions and emboldened by the numerous contacts made, the Foundation was now better placed to concentrate on ways of applying funds to the benefit of individual professional men and women throughout the Commonwealth. Awards of this kind were in fact to become its basic bread and butter although, as experience of the Commonwealth's major needs expanded, by no means the most costly. There were of course problems to be faced in the early days – of duplication for instance; of the time-scale of awards, or of the types of individuals who might or might not qualify for grants.

To take one random but typical example of a case likely

to raise the bogy of duplication: should a soil scientist from Southeast Asia seeking to carry out research in Canada be advised, on turning to the Foundation for funds, to re-direct his inquiries to the Food and Agricultural Organisation of the United Nations? Or to the Canadian International Development Agency? To the Agricultural Institute of Canada or perhaps to the Royal Society? Or could the request best be handled by the Commonwealth Foundation itself? Such dilemmas would never be wholly resolved. But they could be eased as the staff gradually acquired further knowledge of the limits within which other trusts and agencies performed. Meanwhile the board was soon to set its face against any action likely to confuse the Foundation with the technical aid programmes of other larger bodies. In short trustees were not to be seen as financing long-term postings; offering scholarships for postgraduate studies or financing sabbaticals. As things stood there was to be – to repeat Burnet's happy phrase – no lack of ecological niches into which they could quickly move.

Little, as soon became apparent, was being done to promote short-term refresher, study or research visits, particularly from the newer to the older world, and, more significantly, between Third World countries themselves. Nor, seemingly, had any serious attention been paid to the problems of mental and physical isolation so often faced by a Western-trained professional man or woman who had later returned to work in a remote area of his country or in some small newly independent island state. All too often, as mid-career approached, such people were to find that the world had passed them by. Modern technology had overtaken the knowledge which, as expatriate students, they had first imbibed. They met few if any of their own ilk. Journals, let alone reference libraries, were hard to come by and often quite beyond their own resources.

Such handicaps made them either ready grist to the brain-drain mill or tended to reduce them, after promising beginnings, to the status of second-class professionals.

To help the worthier of such individuals did not require vast funds. To their credit the trustees quickly saw that there was practical mileage to be gained not through the issue of cheques with numerous noughts attaching, but by the award of modest grants to enable young doctors, members of the

75

ancillary medical professions, scientists, technologists, dentists and the like to get away from their isolated places of work for periods of as little as six to eight weeks at a time.

Some would attend short, specialised updating courses, of which the British Council ran many of proved value. Others might have expressed a preference for a tailor-made study visit to university departments, laboratories and so forth in another Commonwealth country of their choice. Others again would have sought to complete a piece of collaborative research with some distant colleague, who had hitherto been no more than a paper correspondent. Such awards, made increasingly at the personal discretion of the director, were rarely to cost upwards of £1,000 per head. In many cases a grant went no further than to provide an essential airfare, the grantee and his university, organisation, or government, as appropriate, meeting the extra costs involved.

Within the first ten years many hundreds of younger, professionally qualified men and women, by no means all from the newer Commonwealth, had benefited from such awards. Only a handful failed at the last moment to travel or for some good reason cut short their studies overseas. None, to the staff's knowledge, indulged in the philanthropoid's permanent nightmare – that of playing off one Trust against another and ending up with two air tickets, one each from a brace of unsuspecting agencies. It was indeed a condition laid down in respect of any award sanctioned by the board that a grantee should submit a cogent, well-supported application and at the close of his project a report on his experiences. While a few successful applicants proved less communicative once their journeys had begun – and were harried somewhat mercilessly in consequence – the majority of reports received served only to confirm that a small travel grant, judiciously applied, could earn dividends far in excess of funds actually laid out. Nor were the resultant benefits restricted to the individual alone. By updating his knowledge and techniques, by talking over his problems with others in his field, he returned home intellectually refreshed, a better teacher or practitioner with improved skills which would in small but perhaps significant ways contribute towards the development process of his homeland. And, in travelling abroad for so short a time, he was less likely to cede to the temptation of a more sophisticated life-style, thereby adding to the brain-drain problems of the newer states.

It was another aspect of the brain-drain syndrome which led the Foundation to a further broad, if today obvious conclusion: namely that the teaching of new techniques, the introduction of revised degree and diploma courses, and the provision of managerial advice to newly formed professional societies in the developing world could better be met by exporting the professional adviser to the point of need than by importing a group of acolytes at inflated cost to a centre of excellence in some older country of the Commonwealth. Today such conclusions are self-evident. But at the time the Foundation was struggling into life there was still a marked tendency in the Western world to conclude that 'Daddy knows best' and that the finest knowledge could only be acquired by travelling from afar and climbing on his knee.

The fallacies are now all too apparent. What, for instance, is the value of removing a promising pharmacologist from Central Africa and of letting him loose on the sophisticated equipment of some advanced and well-endowed Canadian laboratory, if the only result is to be the return home of a frustrated individual to his still ill-equipped teaching hospital? Likewise how dangerous for a British or Australian pundit to hold forth *in situ* to a small visiting team from the South Pacific on the best means of introducing a local diploma course on data processing. At far less cost the guru could visit his pupils, assess the local social and economic scene, devise a course, its length and intake level, and advise on textbooks and standards suited to conditions on the spot. Such a visitor could at the same time, if so requested and at small extra expense, offer his expertise to other Commonwealth countries along his line of route.

The development of such policies relating to the movement and exchange of individuals inevitably carried trustees into the more debatable area of conference-going – debatable in the sense that after making a few relatively large awards in the early months for 'bloc' Commonwealth attendance at major conferences of seeming value, members of the board began to divide into two camps as to the likely throughput from this

77

type of activity. On the one hand stood those, strongly supported by the first Commonwealth Secretary-General, Arnold Smith, who argued that anything which helped to bring professional men and women in the Commonwealth together could but do good, and that attendance at major Commonwealth conferences was a further means of curing mental isolation and of adding to the common pool of knowledge and experience. Moreover, some newly independent governments were too poor even to be able to send their officials, let alone private sector representatives (if any), to such important recurring conferences as those of say ministers of law, health or education. As against this there were those who queried the lasting value of large-scale conferences, not least in view of the constantly rising cost of airfares. To help a representative group of, say, lawyers from the newer world to attend one of the quinquennial Commonwealth law conferences might cost as much as £15,000 (far more indeed today). For the inside of a week's attendance, was so ephemeral an event worth money of that order? Was this an effective contribution compared to the more urgent, for example, agricultural, needs of the newer world?

Even in 1980 the value of conference-going was still subject to unresolved but amicable debate. Meanwhile some compromise decisions were reached in the late 1960s and, broadly, still apply. The first was that ministers and officials, as opposed to unofficial professional delegates, would rate low in Foundation terms as potential beneficiaries; that an annual financial ceiling – originally £60,000, but later in the light of inflation raised to £100,000 – should be set for conference-going: and third, that all applications for attendance at any major conference should be processed through its organisers. In other words, Foundation staff could not be expected to deal with *ad hoc* requests from possibly unknown and unsupported individuals. Finally, in expressing a marked preference for the small well-planned meeting, preferably regional in character, as opposed to the large-scale pan-Commonwealth conference, trustees would not rule out the possibility of supporting the presence of suitably qualified Commonwealth citizens at professional meetings taking place outside the Commonwealth.

Step by step, therefore, the Foundation had by the close

of 1969 reached the point where some firm but not immutable guide-lines could be offered to individual seekers after travel grants. They were briefly that while stereotyped application forms were still eschewed in the interests of a warmer human relationship between the donor and his client, any qualified man or woman applying for a grant must produce, in addition to a succinctly argued and costed case, compact biodata and evidence from a higher authority in support of an application. Those seeking study or research awards, as opposed to grants for conference attendance, would at the same time have to satisfy the board as to the readiness of the receiving institution – university, professional society, laboratory as appropriate – to offer the required 'bench facilities' and to organise a convincing work and visit programme. With rare exceptions it was also laid down as conditions of any award first, that three months would be the outside limit of a grant, and secondly that the maximum contribution from the Foundation would cover no more than modest local living costs plus up to 75 per cent of the value of a return economy airfare.

In parallel with these programmes in support of individual travel the trustees devised three further schemes in response to the further injunction in the Agreed Memorandum of 1965 that they should 'stimulate and increase the flow of professional information'. The first was the introduction of a Commonwealth Foundation Lectureship programme; the second a decision to supply, within reasonable financial limits, books and journals to professional institutions most in need – a policy which was later to lead to the birth of several new primary journals; and the third, the creation of a steadily increasing number of regional or multinational short-term bursary schemes.

The Foundation Lectureship programme was launched, experimentally, late in 1967. Under it three individuals, eminent in their own professional fields, were to be invited in a given year to travel to a particular region of the Commonwealth; to deliver a series of public lectures in each country on a theme of their choosing and, perhaps more importantly, to run a series of one- or two-day seminars for university students and, as appropriate, post-graduates; to meet government officials and professionals for discussion of mutual

79

problems; to expose themselves to the media and generally to advise on local problems as and when requested.

Despite a rather fumbling start, due more to the difficulty of persuading receiving governments and institutions to co-operate than to any failings on the part of the eminent lecturers themselves, the project proved successful to a point where trustees were persuaded to maintain it to this day. One immediate attraction of the programme was its multi-Commonwealth nature: another the professional knowledge which it helped to disseminate throughout the Commonwealth thanks to the publication of reports from returning lecturers in the Foundation's 'Occasional Paper' series, some twelve of whose fifty-odd titles to date relate to the upshot of such travels. The subjects covered[2] have to date included such practical issues as the organisation of scientific programmes in the newer world, animal husbandry and genetics, industrial pollution, orthopaedic problems, the conservation of historic monuments in Africa, architectural research, paediatric surgery, nurse teaching and the care of burns in Asia. In many cases the lecturers themselves, to whom trustees must remain indebted for their enthusiasm (sometimes in conditions alien to expectations), were to be instrumental in making recommendations which led not only the Foundation itself but governments and other agencies to pursue some hitherto unthought of line of policy or further programme, to the lasting benefit of one or more of the countries visited. In other cases the mere visit of a Foundation lecturer to a given area was to promote lasting and fruitful contacts between his own institution or professional body and those whom he had met en route. Often, this was to lead in turn to a 'twinning' with or adoption of a local faculty or group, the introduction of a professional interchange scheme, or the supply of much needed equipment, books and journals.

Journals and books were indeed to become a continuing preoccupation. While the Foundation's income would never run to the construction of libraries, however small, nor to their wholesale stocking, experience gained by the staff, above all from widespread travel, soon revealed how voracious was the appetite for the printed word. Countries of South and Southeast Asia, because of their acute foreign exchange problems, or of the African, Caribbean and Pacific regions due to the sheer poverty of their professional and technical institutions, were desperately short of the journals they required, whether for teachers, students or practitioners. Again the isolated professional, far removed from those centres of knowledge which Western man now takes for granted, looked for information in a form less sophisticated and more suited to his immediate needs than that which say the *Lancet* or the *Accountant* could offer – should he indeed be lucky enough to lay his hands, in say Tonga or St Vincent, on an outdated seamail copy.

To overcome such difficulties, of which they were soon all too acutely aware, the Foundation's trustees were to take a number of initiatives. The first, experimentally launched, aimed to overcome the foreign exchange obstacles faced by the Institution of Engineers in India by offering both its headquarters office and its forty branches a guaranteed three-year supply of a wide range of relevant British, Canadian and Australian journals. It was heartening to find, in response to this initiative, first that a number of editors and publishers approached by the Foundation spontaneously offered to reduce their own subscription rates, and secondly that within the three-year period the institution found it possible to persuade the Indian Government to increase its foreign currency allocation. A second venture sponsored by the trustees led to the free distribution over a three-year period to a carefully devised list of teaching and mission hospitals, medical officers of health and up-country doctors throughout the newer Commonwealth of the London School of Hygiene's publications *Tropical Diseases Bulletin* and *Abstracts of Hygiene*. A similar award was later made for the distribution of *Tropical Animal Health and Production* from the Royal (Dick) School of Edinburgh. In many cases the recipients of such journals were later to find it possible to subscribe directly to them once the Foundation's pilot grants expired.

In time, and as travel overseas brought to notice the particular needs of some newly formed university faculty, institute of technology or professional society I was able, under my discretionary powers as director, to make a number of such small, gap- (and shelf-) filling awards, few of them in excess of £500. It also proved possible on occasion to resolve the dilemma facing kindly donors of intent from the older Commonwealth who were prepared to offer runs of vital professional journals or collections of books from their own libraries to some institution in the developing world where they had themselves once served. Such donors could hardly be expected to meet the additional packing and freight costs involved. These charges the Foundation was in deserving cases only too ready to absorb.

More significant, perhaps, in support of the 'printed word' was the Foundation's contribution towards the launching of three entirely new primary journals, each purposely designed to meet developing country needs. The first of these, *Tropical Doctor*, came to birth following lengthy discussion with a committee, appointed by the Royal Society of Medicine, of British doctors with long service in the newer world. Thanks to a three-year Foundation award the journal, a quarterly, was launched in 1973. This publication too was initially distributed free of charge to a carefully sifted list of recipients throughout the tropical Commonwealth. At the same time it was advertised for sale across the world. Within a short time it was to prove the contention of its original editor, Dr Hugh Clegg, that there was indeed an unfilled need for a primary journal such as this. The editorial board was subsequently expanded to include a number of eminent doctors from the newer world itself. Within four years the project had become self-supporting and was attracting a growing, paid-up membership.

A further successful venture was the launching, in co-operation with the Intermediate Technology Group of London, of a further journal, *Appropriate Technology*. Designed as a service to field workers in newer countries of the Commonwealth, this also attracted a pump-priming Foundation grant and was soon to acquire a growing list of subscribers. They saw in the journal a means either of passing on to others experience which they themselves had gained or of profiting, thanks to well-illustrated articles, from innovations and technological breakthroughs described by colleagues working in like fields.

A third initiative for which Foundation funds were voted aimed to transform a French language dental journal edited from the University of Dakar in Senegal into a bilingual Anglo–French quarterly geared to the needs of the dental profession throughout Africa. This was admittedly a risk venture. But here again, within five years of its inception the journal, in new and enlarged format, had made its mark and was beginning to attract a readership spreading well beyond the African continent itself.

From the earliest days trustees had also been instrumental in supporting or initiating a range of short-term bursary schemes many of which, for want of sufficient funds or staff, were operated in close consultation with other agencies. They were to cover such fields as the natural sciences, architecture, veterinary medicine, fire-engineering, university administration, agriculture, geography, race relations and latterly the needs of medical electives. While it would be wearisome to recite details of all such projects, a few points are worth emphasising. The first is that, with the exception of the Commonwealth Scientific Bursaries programme, run in conjunction with the Royal Society of London and for which awards to distinguished scientists in the newer Commonwealth were available for up to a full academic year, all projects were restricted to periods of three months. A second is that (with one solitary exception) each scheme attracted from the outset an impressive and constantly growing list of applicants, a fact which was to oblige trustees in many cases to forgo their mere 'pump priming' role and repeatedly to renew their funding. By 1980 there were indeed several bursary programmes which had been in operation for as long as a decade, thus bringing the Foundation up against the dilemma of whether to sacrifice success in the interests of novelty or, failing the readiness of others to pick up the torch, to 'send good money after good'. A third feature of this type of activity was the readiness of outside agencies such as the Agricultural Institute of Canada, the Ontario Veterinary College or the Association of Commonwealth Universities to administer such Foundation-sponsored bursary schemes; and, notably, of the Canadian International Development Agency to contribute towards the costs of several of them on a dollar for dollar basis – a response which both heartened the trustees and added to their prestige generally, as well as giving added weight and content to the schemes in question. Nor could one forget that, thanks to the ability of the Foundation to receive funds from the private sector the trustees were to become indebted to such donors as Guinness Overseas and to the trustees of the late George Drew, formerly Premier of Ontario, for funds which enabled the Foundation to launch and to administer two further small but successful projects. The first allowed for three senior nurse tutors from the Caribbean to attend a diploma health course annually at the Liverpool School of Tropical Medicine. The second provided travel grants to a number of young Canadians, selected on the Foundation's behalf by Canadian University Services Overseas, for brief, professionally oriented study projects in the newer Commonwealth.

One cannot conclude this review of the Foundation's role in support of individual endeavour without singling out two particular bursary schemes for special mention. By coincidence they are the first and as yet last to have been initiated. The former arose indirectly from my earlier involvement as a backroom Whitehall boy in the beginnings of Britain's first Commonwealth Immigrants Act. This had brought me, as a bearleader of ministers from Pakistan and India, into forcible contact with the problems facing both local authorities and their communities on the one hand and immigrants on the other in such areas as South London, Bedford, Birmingham and Bradford. Translated to the Foundation and finding myself in a rather better position to recommend the immediate disbursement of small sums of money it occurred to me that growing friction and gaps in comprehension between Commonwealth immigrants and those most directly concerned with them – the heads of primary and secondary schools, social workers and alas police, magistrates and probation officers might marginally be eased if some of the latter could be helped to visit the countries of origin of such immigrants. If they could get a grasp of the local environment, stay with families of origin, attend juvenile courts, talk to the police, to church leaders, schoolteachers, politicians, then they might come home with a greater understanding of West Indian mores or of the devotion of the sub-continental immigrant to family, dress and caste. There was of course nothing novel in such thoughts. However, the practical upshot was a three-year award from the Foundation to the (then) British Community Relations Commission. Under this some two dozen senior police officers, head teachers, probation and social workers were helped for short periods to visit North India, Pakistan and a number of Caribbean islands. Interestingly enough, the carefully selected senior police bursars turned out to be the star turns of this experiment which, because of its success in human terms, was eventually to be extended for a further three-year period. Later commended by a Select Committee of Parliament at Westminster it was, on that body's recommendation, transferred to the Home Office – this just at a point in time when trustees themselves were beginning to wonder whether it would be proper for them to vote yet further funds to a venture which, in the last resort, they saw as a responsibility of Britain rather than of the Commonwealth as a whole.

The latest in the bursary project series, to the benefit of medical electives, was launched only at the close of 1979. In that year the Board of Trustees, wittingly breaching that rule which excluded students from their terms of reference, voted the modest experimental sum of £30,000, spread over a three-year period, to enable a small, carefully selected number of senior medical students, usually in their fifth year of study, to undertake visits to other countries of the Commonwealth. Three conditions were imposed: first, that successful candidates from the older Commonwealth must volunteer to serve their electives in the newer world: secondly that preference, in the case of new world applicants would be given to those willing to spend their time in other Third World countries; and thirdly, that elective periods should not normally exceed six weeks. The response to this project, in which the Foundation had been able to involve the Deans of Medical Schools throughout the Commonwealth as 'pre-screeners' of applications, was such as to risk overwhelming the Foundation's slender staff resources. But a first wave of electives was nominated and sent forth well before the close of 1980. All those selected had written with enthusiasm of their desire to be of service. Many indeed, attached to small district hospitals in mini-states, were not only to gain first-hand experience of how to get by with the barest minimum of medical facilities;

85

they were also to serve virtually as already qualified doctors in situations where an extra pair of hands, for however brief a time, was to prove a godsend.

This too was a project serving to underline the faith of an ill-financed Foundation in the dividends to be earned from small grants judiciously applied – a lesson perhaps for the big-league donors, private and official, whose capital out-pourings have so often led to uncontrolled peculation and mismanagement.

By the time the earliest of such projects in support of individual professional movement and exchange were firmly under way, the time had come for the Foundation's first chairman, Sir Macfarlane Burnet, whose original appointment had already been renewed for a further two-year period, to cede his place.

At a meeting of the Board of Trustees in the summer of 1969 Burnet reminded his colleagues of the need for Commonwealth governments to nominate his successor. In a farewell address, wide-ranging though somewhat pessimistic in tone, he had this to say of the Commonwealth and of the period of his chairmanship:

> Our special niche, as I see it, is to maintain the morale and effectiveness of the middle-level people who are applying the technical and managerial skills in the developing countries . . . The efforts of both the Foundation and the (Commonwealth) Secretariat should be to use to the best advantage the tools that history has given us – the English language, a common respect for the dignity of professional work, and past associations more often cordial than corrosive, between governmental and professional personnel.

At root, as Burnet saw it, the Foundation was concerned 'with seeing that the professional-status jobs shall be done better and in so far as they are done better, the standard of living, the health and the opportunities for leisure of the peoples [of the Commonwealth] will be improved'.[3]

By the end of 1969 Commonwealth heads of government, after consultation through the usual channels, had invited a further 'distinguished private citizen', Dr Robert Gardiner of Ghana, to assume the chairmanship for the two-year period beginning January 1, 1970. A former head of his country's civil service, an economist of international repute and at that time Secretary-General of the United Nations Economic Commission for Africa (which post he was still to hold from his headquarters in Addis Ababa) Gardiner was to bring to the Foundation a deep knowledge, not only of African affairs, but of the development problems facing the Third World as a whole. He took up his office just as trustees were beginning to re-examine their own original priorities, when the importance of rural development was coming increasingly to the fore, and when the Foundation was launching what were to become its own major initiatives in the years ahead – the creation of a network of national professional centres in the newer world, and the encouragement of a growing range of pan-Commonwealth professional associations.

Both ventures will be examined in the following chapters.

Notes and References

1   Sir James Currie (ed.), *Professional Organizations in the Commonwealth* (London, 1970).
2   For a summary list of lectureships undertaken between 1967 and 1981, see Appendix G. Publications resulting from such visits are listed in the Bibliography.
3   Commonwealth Foundation Papers, record of Board of Trustees meeting, July 1969.

7

Professional Centres

> The Commonwealth is one of the great mysteries
> of the world in which we live . . . the very fact that
> it brings together such wide varieties of people at
> all sorts of levels – politicians, lawyers, civil
> servants, and above all, teachers . . . makes it a
> force in world affairs.
>
> George Thomson MP, 1963

As had been foreseen from the outset, overseas travel was to
prove one of the most effective means of introducing the
Commonwealth Foundation to its far-flung constituency; of
creating interest in professional co-operation; of discovering
people, organisations and areas most in need of help; of
stimulating projects and eventually of assessing progress.

In the early days the burden and pleasure of travelling the
Commonwealth fell solely on the director. From 1970 onwards,
when a first deputy director, U. A. Ansari of Pakistan, was
appointed, journeys could to some degree be shared, as they
were later to be with two subsequent deputies: first Paul (later
Sir Paul) Scoon, now Governor-General of Grenada, and
latterly with S. Mahendra from Sri Lanka. However, and with
the unfailing support of the trustees, the lion's share still fell
to the director. It thus became customary for me to travel for
as long as three to four months each year, rotating on longer
annual journeys between differing regions of the Commonwealth and from time to time attending conferences, not least

those of heads of government, or of other ministers which were likely to prove of direct interest to the Foundation's work.

By the close of some fourteen years in office I could lay claim to having become one of the Commonwealth's most itinerant citizens. By various means – from aircraft of all shapes, sizes and standards; by liner, schooner and canoe; by lorry, car and jeep; often on foot, and once by bare-backed elephant – I had in the end visited and often revisited every member country of the Commonwealth, the majority of its still dependent territories and, in passing, a large number of francophone and other foreign states. My lasting regrets were never to have set foot in such exotic places as St Helena, Ascension, Pitcairn, Tuvalau and Kiribati or the Falkland Islands. But the one hundred odd countries visited, thanks to an almost equal number of airlines, good, indifferent and sometimes frankly frightening, proved time and again that an organisation such as the Commonwealth Foundation could not effectively respond to its remit unless its staff, rather than sitting passively at Marlborough House, were prepared to travel, despite the costs, the wear and tear and the occasional frustrations involved.

This leads on to one of the Foundation's most satisfying achievements: an experiment which might never have been launched save for discussions on the spot – the creation across the developing Commonwealth of a growing network of national professional centres.

Bathetic though it sounds in retrospect, this brave experiment was launched, early in 1967, from a bar-stool in one of Kampala's then premier hotels. I had been invited by a local architect, during a first visit to Uganda, to meet with him and a group of professional colleagues and to explain the aims of the Foundation and how, if at all, his country could be helped. Somewhat overcome by the noise, the general discomfort and the expatriate capacity for beer, I inquired whether there was not some quiet professional society office to which we might retreat for serious talk. The answer from those present, representing some twelve disciplines, was that they perforce conducted business with stray visitors in this fashion. They could of course have hired a hotel room – an extravagance to be avoided save on the grandest of occasions. But normally

89

professional society business was handled either from their own homes, or, surreptitiously, in formal office hours. Only one of those present admitted to belonging to a professional body which boasted its own self-contained headquarters. But even these were far too small to seat the company gathered round the bar.

Further inquiries revealed that none of the professions represented had a membership of more than fifty – some of them, indeed, far less. Only one could afford to pay the salary of a part-time secretary to keep records of its membership, collect annual subscriptions, organise and take minutes of meetings and so forth. Struck by these admissions and perhaps even more by the fact that my visit had provided the first excuse for professional leaders in a relatively small community to meet together as a group, I suggested to my hosts that they might see virtue in carrying this encounter one stage further. Why, in short, should they not pool their scant resources and resolve their housing and administrative problems collectively? A steering committee could be set up with the aim of renting a small suite of offices and of employing a secretary/manager who could provide basic common services to the professions in Uganda as a whole. Should such an idea find favour, those interested would of course ultimately have to appoint a chairman and a representative council: draw up a constitution and fee structure, decide on the common services to be provided and map out a future programme of activities. If and when all these initial steps were taken and cost estimates agreed upon by a majority of the professional societies in Uganda and then forwarded to the Foundation, I had little doubt but that the trustees would favourably consider the prospects for a modest launching grant.

First reactions to these off-the-cuff remarks suggested polite interest, rather than enthusiasm. But on returning some two months later to London I found with genuine surprise that an outline project for what was to become the Professional Centre of Uganda was already on my desk. Under the vigorous leadership of my architectural host,[1] no less than fifteen professions, representing *inter alia* the law, medicine, architecture, engineering, surveying, accountancy, dentistry, pharmacy, the veterinary sciences, management, secretaryship and professional and technical elements of the Civil Service had met together; they had earmarked both a potential secretary and some inexpensive office space – this quite literally and in acceptable anti-élitist terms on the wrong side of the Kampala rail-track – and had forthwith petitioned the Foundation's trustees for a launching grant. This, to a total of £21,000, was sanctioned by the close of 1967. The centre then forged rapidly ahead, paving the way for others to follow in its wake. The Government of Uganda in turn showed interest in the venture and, but for the *coup* of 1971, would have made a substantial contribution to it from funds held in the Milton Obote Foundation. Ironically, Amin's rabble soldiery made short work of the centre's efforts, seizing all movable office furniture and equipment together with the small reference library, all of which had been supplied from this pioneering grant. Yet in three short years enough had been done by the professional group in Kampala to convince trustees that the experiment was worth repeating. Thus by the close of the Foundation's first quinquennium further centres had been established in Trinidad and Tobago, Kenya, Singapore, Jamaica and Malta. Steering committees had by then been set up in other developing countries. By 1981 the Foundation could claim that the network of centres fully established or at the planning stage now covered no less than eighteen newer countries of the Commonwealth.[2]

In fact, and notwithstanding the ensuing traumas, the Uganda centre itself managed marginally to survive the Amin interlude and by the close of 1981 was still able to offer some restricted secretarial service to its members. Equally encouraging was the fact that, soon after President Obote's return to power, his government paid over to the Commonwealth Foundation three years arrears of contributions.

It had of course never been in the minds of trustees that professional centres should develop into costly prestige projects. The aims which they had basically in view were fourfold: to promote professional co-operation at the national level; to offer practical facilities to groups of more often than not newly formed, small and poor professional societies by way of shared accommodation and secretarial services; to encourage an interdisciplinary approach to problems of education, training and relations with schools and universities generally; and

finally to foster collective professional advice to and co-operation with governments in respect of legislation, manpower and
development planning.

The Foundation could not of course be expected to cover
the full costs of any centre. Nor were the trustees prepared to
lend their support to a centre which was either backed by a
mere handful of the professions in a given country or whose
apparent aims it would be to adopt a trade union rather than a
professional attitude towards its local problems.

That said, it would clearly have been impossible to draw
up a rigid blueprint for all potential centres. While basic aims
would be broadly similar, each professional steering committee
would be working within differing social and economic
environments. Some might represent a country with a growing
entrepreneurial class and a sizeable and relatively wealthy
professional community. In such cases a committee might set
its sights on the acquisition of an existing building or on the
construction of a new one, as later proved the case in Kenya,
Malta and Guyana. Other professional groups, such as those in
Trinidad and Tobago, Singapore and Sri Lanka might be
fortunate enough in the early years to be offered by their own
governments a free plot of building land, or existing accommodation at a peppercorn rent. Others again, and they
were in the majority, might have a combined professional
strength of less than 1,000, a sizeable number of whom would
be expatriate and whose long-term interest in the country
could thus be but marginal. In such cases a centre, in the
early days at least, would barely consist of more than one or
two rooms for a manager supported by a general duty typist
and, with luck, conference facilities shared with some other
neighbouring, like-minded body.

There were thus risks involved. In the first few years no
one would have been rash enough to hazard how long it
would take for any particular centre to achieve viability. In
some countries early enthusiasm dwindled for want of support
for the newer professions by the older, such as law and medicine.
Sometimes factions or deplorable in-fighting based on personal
rivalries hampered progress. Or again the local political
situation, exacerbated by ministerial suspicion of the professions
as an élitist clique, proved weighty obstacles. Such factors,

combined with fund-raising problems or failure to obtain suitable premises, often led to the creation of a particular centre being inordinately delayed. Yet, in the long run, only four countries in which the interest of the professions had originally been aroused had by the close of 1981 virtually abandoned all hope of joining in this Commonwealth-wide endeavour. To it trustees had by that date voted funds totalling some £600,000; a small sum indeed in global aid terms, given the practical results achieved.

As has been stressed above, the basic aims of each national centre have much in common, however much local circumstances may differ. It is thus worth summarising from the constitution of one of the liveliest of all – that of Singapore – how the twenty-five professions incorporated into that body interpreted their own aims. They were:

(1) To provide a permanent office and such other facilities and amenities as might be necessary for carrying into effect the aims and objects of the centre.
(2) To provide premises for meetings of all member associations of the centre.
(3) To promote and enhance the status of professional bodies in Singapore.
(4) To encourage high standards of professional conduct and ethics.
(5) To encourage and assist national professional bodies.
(6) To encourage and assist persons desirous of acquiring professional qualifications.
(7) To encourage the interchange of ideas on and discussion of subjects of interdisciplinary or common interest.
(8) To ascertain and declare the corporate view of all member associations and to make or support representation to government and other appropriate bodies on questions affecting all member associations or the public interest.
(9) To promote and foster professionalism and professional education.
(10) To provide a library.
(11) To encourage good relations and understanding among member associations and between them and the public.

(12)   To organise regional and international conferences in Singapore.

(13)   To develop and maintain co-operation with other similar professional centres in the Commonwealth and neighbouring countries.

An experiment so diffuse in terms of geography, so fraught with risk and involving so high a percentage of disposable grant funds in time dictated some evaluation of progress. Thus in 1971 one of the Foundation's biennial seminars, of which more will be said in a later chapter, was in part designed to assess the value of the professional centre concept and, perhaps equally important, to bring together the chairmen or managers of all the then centres, actual or potential. This meeting took place at the headquarters of the Professional Centre of Singapore, housed on the first floor of a downtown government community housing estate, where the banners welcoming delegates to the seminar were almost hidden behind the poles of washing hanging out to dry from nearby flats. Among the thirty-one representatives from fourteen Commonwealth countries present, close on half were there to speak in the name of their national centre. While the meeting also discussed wider issues such as the professional brain-drain, the dangers of élitism and the relationship of professionals towards their own societies, ample time was allowed for a detailed survey of the achievements of the various centres in the light of some five years' experience. As the final communiqué from the seminar recorded:

National Professional Centres could offer their members many facilities and services, particularly to the benefit of new, small professional societies. Centres could also serve as co-ordinating points for all professions in a given country, old or new. They could stimulate environmental and other interdisciplinary studies and activities; strengthen links and improve understanding and rapport between the professional world, government, the field of education and the community at large. For this reason Centres should be located in the heart of a capital rather than on a site remote from the day-to-day life of the community.[3]

The passage quoted was but a bald summary of a debate on the centre concept which had ranged from scepticism to enthusiasm, from the difficulty of defining the limits of eligibility for centre membership to the equal difficulties inherent in fund-raising, staffing and in achieving credibility for the professions *vis-à-vis* their own governments and communities. Scepticism, it seemed, stemmed above all from those individual professional societies fortunate enough to enjoy their own permanent headquarters, staff and servicing facilities and which saw no advantage in contributing to the needs of their less well endowed colleagues. The latter, representing enthusiasm, were at the same time wary of admitting too many doubtful starters to membership.

The membership issue was indeed to prove something of a King Charles's Head. At one extreme I had found myself addressing a sophisticated Mediterranean audience of professionals on the virtues of an imaginative approach, only to be chided by one arch-conservative for assuming that professions other than the law, medicine and architecture rightly qualified for admission to his particular centre – this on the basis that they were the only professions to whom clients were obliged by tradition to send painted candles at Christmas. At the other extreme I was challenged with equal vigour for daring to assume that teachers' organisations in a particular Asian country, which at the time boasted three warring, trade-union-minded groups, should be excluded from that centre's precincts.

That parenthesis apart, it can happily be said that commonsense on the whole prevailed on the membership issue. The broad conclusion was that each centre must work out its own criteria in the light of local needs and susceptibilities. On behalf of the Foundation, whose staff continually emphasised its desire not to dictate conditions in this contentious area, it was simply urged that 'the sub-professions should be encouraged wherever possible to take up full or associate membership of all Centres. On the other hand, organizations discharging the narrower function of following sectional [i.e. trade union rule-of-thumb] interests should be excluded.' In the end the 1971 seminar's conclusion, in relation to borderline applications for membership, was that 'eligibility . . . should depend first

95

on whether a particular [professional society] was bound by a code of ethics which placed service to the community before personal gain: and second, on whether its members enjoyed training at higher than school level, both states being classified yard-sticks of "professionalism" '.

As to staffing and fund-raising it was realistically accepted that Foundation awards to centres could not continue *ad infinitum*. The centre manager would thus be a key to the success or failure of his particular organisation. Through his persuasion governments might be brought to support the venture in cash or kind. Through him and his supervising council alone could efforts be made to raise funds from the private sector. Above all it would be his responsibility to ensure that his centre's premises were fully occupied throughout and even beyond normal working hours and that adequate service fees were charged for such occupancy and other facilities.

The services which a professional centre could offer proved to be at the heart of the matter. As, once more, the report from the Singapore discussions recorded: 'to attract and to retain an adequate membership all Centres must offer an expanding range of services: adequate conference and [within reason] reception facilities: and above all a small but efficient secretariat'. To which, by hindsight, one might add first that one further duty incumbent on all centres must be to serve as a reception and inquiry point for professional visitors from other countries of the Commonwealth, and second that each centre should consider it a duty to maintain contact with its sister bodies, exchanging publications, newsletters, lists of services offered, charges and the like, to the benefit of all.

As soon as the more effective centres settled down and ventured beyond their primary administrative, financial and staffing problems, two issues at once loomed large: first, how to persuade governments to take serious account of the collective advice which the professions could offer; and secondly how to gain credence with their communities, thus breaking down the traditional view of professional man as an uncaring élitist, thinking little of the man in the street but much of the state of his own bankroll.

Many governments were at first reluctant to recognise, let

alone lend even moral support to a centre in their midst. There was a feeling among politicians in some newly independent countries that the professions were a luxury; that the standards which they sought to maintain had been imposed by the old imperial enemy; that these took no account of the priority needs of the developing world. In other words the accent should, in the early years at least, be on short-cut technology, represented by the 'barefoot' doctor, dentist or architect – a theory which, incidentally, few such politicians adopted when their own health or housing was at stake. Another more understandable fear expressed in official circles on the creation of a professional centre was that it would encourage the growth of an élitist club, whose members' chief concern would be to protect their own life-styles and to operate against the government's interest as an intellectual super-trade union.

Such suspicions died (and still die) hard. They were indeed exacerbated not only by the necessarily schizophrenic loyalties of professionals in government service (and they represent the great majority of such practitioners in the newer world) towards the ethos of their own profession on the one hand and on the other to the policies of ministers under whom they served, but also by the yawning communications gap between academic and practising professions – a gulf which still exists in countries of the highest sophistication.

The Minister of State for Foreign Affairs of Singapore, Rahim Ishak, succinctly outlined some of the dilemmas facing a newly independent (but admittedly highly developed) state when he opened the Foundation Seminar on 25 October 1971. 'Professions . . .', he said, 'tend to expect a high degree of autonomy. Concomitant with this is the expectation of service and commitment to the society to which they belong. It is expected that professionals have a broader role in society than merely self-seeking private interests. This necessitates an awareness of the greater public need and an involvement in the affairs of the nation in which the professional lives . . . skilled human resources tend to be scarce. The professionally trained are therefore at a premium as their careers imply competence based on expertise. This gives them status and authority.' But, as the minister continued: 'The tragedy has

97

been that in new countries professionals all too often have not been committed to their nations but have viewed themselves as free agents capable of moving at any time to the developed countries in the West ... Skills acquired at much cost have been used in the developed countries rather than in the modernizing societies where they are most needed. This lack of commitment and unwillingness to be involved in the rapidly changing societies in their homeland has been a critical defect in the outlook of segments of the new technocratic élite.' A multi-disciplinary approach was needed, stressed the minister, if 'we are to discover what it is that is lacking in the technically-oriented that prevents them from having an abiding commitment to their native countries'. He concluded his part-condemnation of the role of professional men in society by posing these thought-provoking questions: 'Is it because a long period of training, often in a developed country, leads to the divorce of the professional from his environment? Could it be argued that the over-training of professionals leads to an inability to absorb these skills and to provide the tools with which they are most familiar? Are the hopes and aspirations in the social, economic, political and cultural fields not being met and fulfilled?'

There will be time enough when, in a later chapter the significance of the Commonwealth-wide professional associations sponsored by the Foundation comes to be discussed, to look further into the broad role of professional man in the newer Commonwealth. But, before turning to the positive steps which the centres themselves might, and in some cases have already taken, to overcome the accusations of exclusivity levelled at their memberships, it is worth quoting one further passage from the report of the 1971 seminar. It is taken from the lead paper delivered by the Director of the Institute of Commonwealth Studies, University of London, Professor W. H. Morris-Jones.

Having, like Rahim Ishak, analysed the differing attitudes of governments and professionals towards the problems which they jointly shared in the nation-building process, and having stressed that professionally qualified man in developing states was 'a novelty in his society, his power is of a newer kind than that of the ruler as soldier: he rests on little indigenous tradition', Morris-Jones went on to draw attention to the role of individual professional centres as 'generating status . . . feeding their ideas and experience into a common pool from which others can draw'. As he saw it:

> Each Centre has to find in the end its own way of coming to terms with its government, its universities, its publics. The public relations role is vital, otherwise professional legitimacy will be lost: the professionals have to be 'sold' in new ways to their societies . . . (They) at the same time have to learn from outside, not only from London but from Bombay and Sydney. But when they do look to London, they may be well advised to study closely not the older professions in Britain but rather the new boys.

How, with all these encomia, could and did the various professional centres react? One is tempted to take that of Singapore as an example, not merely since it served as host to the seminar from whose report so many passages have been quoted but rather because from first beginnings it proved to be dynamic in development, fertile in ideas and led by a number of enthusiastic committees. The membership had from the outset accepted that, in a cost-effective capitalist–*dirigiste* society such as that in which its professions lived, there would be no hope of feather-bedding from the government. Nor would a centre, which at first blush seemed merely to perpetuate the roles and privileges of older Western-oriented societies, find even moral favour. Hence an early conclusion that membership of the Singapore centre must be the reverse of exclusive – a decision exemplified from the start through the readiness of the Centre Council, originally representing some fifteen traditional professions, to accept a widening range of bodies to its counsels. These were eventually to include the ancillary professions of nursing, physiotherapy, management training and work-study practice, together with professional groups representing – in new world terms – such barely organised activities as building, chemistry and secretaryship.

Naturally the professions of Singapore were concerned with their own interests and the centre was soon to introduce projects to the direct benefit of its membership, including comprehensive insurance cover, wholesale shopping facilities and the like. But their energies ranged far wider. Committees dealing with such varied activities as future programmes, publications, vocational guidance, transport and housing were rapidly set up. Informal links were forged by relevant interdisciplinary committees with appropriate ministries and the centre became increasingly involved in community projects supported by the government itself. Thus the Ministry of Health in turn invited doctors, nurses and other health workers to co-operate over problems of the aged. Other ministers saw the benefit of seeking advice from the centre on building development projects, on child care, the 'recycling of the retired' and so forth. Like its counterpart in Malaysia the centre also began to pioneer programmes for school-leavers and eventually for professionals in mid-career, as the result of which a series of lectures to sixth formers was launched by voluntary endeavour: career pamphlets were produced, and an ambitious directory of professions in Singapore was sponsored, the latter thanks in part to a further Foundation grant. Because of the energy displayed and its effective role in promoting regional professional consultation, the centre was eventually recognised by the government tourist board as a convention-organising 'instrument'.

Similar examples of the professions going out 'to meet the people' could soon be found elsewhere. In Jamaica, for example, members of the centre held open days for student counselling and set up a roster of volunteers ready to lecture to sixth formers on career prospects. Impressed by such initiatives the Jamaica Government in turn invited the centre to nominate delegates to sit on a number of ministerial planning committees and gradually to become more actively involved with the nation-building process. The salient point was that, contrary to the often ill-informed complaints of politicians and the public that the professions (in both the new world and the old) represented too much wealth, disloyalty to government, élitism and exclusivity, the latter were now, if still only in minor ways, being brought into the mainstream of national planning. It was indeed to the credit of these centres that professional man could now be seen by his community to be rendering a public service.

This in itself was no small achievement. It went far to explain why, despite some set-backs at the preliminary planning stage, the Foundation's trustees, throughout the first fifteen years, never lost faith in this initiative. Indeed they commissioned early in 1979 a further seminar, this time under the auspices of the Management Committee of the Malaysia Centre, a body then still despairingly in search of permanent headquarters. Invited to Kuala Lumpur to discuss problems facing 'the professional in the wider community' the representatives of nine professional centres met together with delegates from universities, pan-Commonwealth professional associations and other agencies to take stock of their own and the Foundation's efforts since 1966 and to give what guidance they could for the future.

By this time the centre network in the newer Commonwealth had considerably expanded and had been joined by three further such organisations in the older world: the Science Centre of Sydney, New South Wales; the Professional Centre of the Northern Territory, Darwin, Australia and, most recently, the London (England) Science Centre. All three bodies had attracted support from the trustees of the Commonwealth Foundation, thus underlining the fact that small professional societies in the older world were sometimes almost as much in need of financial help as those in the newer. As the Chairman of the Sydney Science Centre put it at the Kuala Lumpur seminar, there were 'problems of finance, of lack of governmental support and of communication within and without the professional community'. While many professional bodies in the older Commonwealth were 'well established, large organisations, with large offices and strong international affiliations, it had to be remembered that there were many more which were individually small in size but which collectively formed a substantial and important community: these organisations need very specific assistance of the kind associated with a Professional Centre as we know it here if, quite literally, they are to survive.'[4] That situation, added the chairman of the Sydney centre, Dr M. J. Puttock, had also been highlighted in Britain and had led to plans to create in London a similar science centre.

The latter, acting under the umbrella of the Foundation

for Science and Technology had, by the mid-1970s, attracted
the interest of close on thirty of the smaller scientific and
technological societies in Britain. All these bodies faced one
shared burden: the rapidly spiralling cost of office space in
the inner London area. That problem had been starkly
analysed in a report published in 1975 from a Joint Committee
of the Royal Society and the British Academy. It revealed
that, of close on 230 learned bodies in Britain with a collective
membership of approximately one million, 21 societies alone
contributed half that membership. In other words, some 200
societies with a combined subscription list of under half a
million were rapidly discovering, in a cold financial climate,
that small was no longer beautiful. It was in those circumstances that the Foundation for Science and Technology,
whose basic aim it had been to promote greater interdisciplinary
endeavour, decided to set up an informal Science Centre
Committee. Its task, in which the members were greatly
assisted by the founding secretary of the Clunies Ross Memorial
Foundation in Melbourne, Australia, Mr J. E. Cummins, OBE,
was to locate premises in the central London area suitable for
collective use by those smaller scientific and technological
bodies which might otherwise have been forced, under sheer
financial pressure, to abandon their toe-hold in the capital.
Supported by the Royal Society, the British Academy, the
Council of Engineering Institutions and others and under the
chairmanship of the Earl of Shannon, a spokesman in the
House of Lords on scientific issues, the committee sought
accommodation which would offer the interested societies
both conference and seminar facilities, permanent office space
and a wide range of servicing facilities. It proved an arduous
task. Not only were suitable buildings increasingly hard to
come by. By 1978 the financial climate had so far deteriorated
that an ambitious fund-raising campaign addressed to banks,
commerce and industry produced infinitely more sympathy
than cash. Meanwhile, thanks to a modest grant from the
trustees of the Commonwealth Foundation, Lord Shannon
had been able to visit the Science Centre in Sydney, Australia,
and the Professional Centres of Malaysia and Singapore. His
experiences there perhaps convinced him that in this case the
new world had something to offer to the old. However that

may be, the Foundation for Science and Technology and its Science Centre Committee accepted, towards the close of 1979, that it must lower its sights and look in the first place for premises far more modest than it had first contemplated. By a happy coincidence, just as the dream of a London centre was on the point of fading, the committee learnt that the Royal Society of Arts was looking for a tenant in part of its recently renovated premises at John Adam Street, The Strand, a historic building first acquired by the society from the Adam Brothers in 1770 at the annual rental of £200.

While far smaller than other buildings contemplated, the Adam Street premises offered several advantages. They were centrally located. They provided a sense of history in that the Society of Arts had itself been an eighteenth-century trailblazer in *inter alia* the field of the natural sciences. Modest conference and office space would be available. The rent was within the Foundation's capabilities. Above all the chance had at long last emerged of 'something being seen to be done'. In short, negotiations began in earnest: a lease was drawn up and on 1 April 1981 the London Science Centre opened its doors for business. A Management Committee, reporting to the Council of the Foundation for Science and Technology was appointed to oversee the day to day problems of the centre and an interim director and a secretary recruited. Since the directorship fell temporarily to my lot, it is barely necessary to add that, amidst the multifarious tasks of ordering everything from paper-clips to tea-bags, I lost no time in advising professional centre colleagues elsewhere in the Commonwealth of the birth of this new child. Clearly – once domestic problems had been sorted out – there was everything to be gained from the forging of links between the newest centre in the oldest member country of the Commonwealth and its more ancient peers.

By the close of 1981 the London centre, while in financial terms still precariously poised, was on the way ahead. Contact had been made with centres elsewhere in the Commonwealth. Two conference rooms had been furnished and five offices made available for use by smaller scientific and learned bodies. Service facilities were in the making, while a renewed appeal for funds was being launched in the private sector. Above all the Council of the Foundation for Science and Technology, of which the London Science Centre was increasingly the visibly active instrument, was bent on searching for inter-disciplinary forms of activity which would help to knit together the still all-too-scattered energies of a host of British learned bodies which, through lack of co-operation, would otherwise be likely to freeze to death in a cold financial climate.

Midway between the primarily science-oriented groups in London and Sydney and the broader-based centres which have been the principal subject of this chapter stood the recently created and rapidly growing Professional Centre of Darwin, Australia. That body came into existence as late as 1978, largely as the result of on-the-spot discussions between an energetic committee of Australian Northern Territory professionals and myself. It was to prove the first centre of any of those launched and financed by the Foundation to be located outside the capital city of its country. Such a precedent was, however, amply justified. As its first chairman (now Planning Vice-Chancellor of the future University of Darwin), Dr James Eedle, had explained at the Kuala Lumpur meeting:

The Northern Territory is the only tropical area in the world which forms part of a predominantly tropical land mass inhabited by people with the life style of a 'developed country' . . . its peoples live perforce in a style more akin to neighbouring countries to the north than to fellow Australians to the south, from whom they are separated by up to two thousand miles of forbidding country . . . Its peoples are sparsely scattered – 110,000 individuals spread over 1,350 million kilometers, of whom nearly half live in and around the capital city of Darwin. The population is young, mobile, multi-cultural, multi-ethnic, multilingual, modestly educated and for the most part employed in less skilled occupations . . . Against this background the Territory Government has to plan its social and economic development, providing services to its sparse and diverse population over great distances . . . This is the context in which professional groups in the Territory live and work.

The Darwin Centre was in fact soon found to be filling a felt need. Isolated groups, far removed from their various professional headquarter offices in Sydney, Melbourne or Canberra, quickly saw the virtue of pooling resources and experiences and of being able to look to the benefit of shared servicing facilities. To a three-year launching grant from the Commonwealth Foundation the newly autonomous Government of the Northern Territory added both moral and financial backing. A suitable headquarters office was rapidly obtained and staff recruited. As membership of the centre grew, so did the collective services on offer. The government announced its intention to consult the centre on all appropriate draft legislation and encouraged its membership to forge professional links with Commonwealth countries in Australia's 'Near North'. In this way contact was made between the Darwin centre and those in Fiji, Singapore, Malaysia and Sri Lanka. Looking further to the future Dr Eedle expressed the thought that, among the most useful and least costly activities of his centre could be:

> to support fellow professionals in the region by reducing their isolation and helping them to retain and reinforce their confidence as professionals working under difficulties. Small branches, small chapters, small national groups suffer from transient membership, a lack of continuity and a consequent unevenness in the enthusiasm of the group ... For the benefit of all, the Professional Centre of the Northern Territory might develop as the servicing agent for a regional association of Professional Centres of South East Asia and the Pacific.

Ambitious words, perhaps. But they did no more than echo the aspirations of the Commonwealth Foundation itself and underlined how far the centre concept had advanced since its tentative beginnings on that Kampala bar-stool only twelve years earlier.

What had in fact been achieved by the close of 1980? How many further centres might the Foundation envisage? For how long could they afford to continue support to those still unable to make ends meet? To answer such questions the trustees decided at a board meeting late in 1980 to invite the new director and his deputy to carry out, through on-the-spot inspections over the two following years, a critical evaluation. Meanwhile no further commitments extending beyond 1983 should be entered into.

Progress to date, for an overall sum of less than £1 million invested, may with some justification be described as positive. Some six professional centres are now fully self-supporting; three others are rapidly approaching that point. Funds permitting, a further nine will need support from the Foundation for some three to five further years to come. But in every case where a centre has become an established landmark in its own capital, a number of benefits have flowed. Intra-disciplinary co-operation has become a habit: the administration of individual professional bodies has improved: membership of each centre has steadily increased. The bogy of professional élitism has in part been exorcised and, through their own endeavours, the professions have gone some way towards lessening the 'comprehension gap' which had so often bedevilled relationships with both their governments and communities.

Much still remains to do. There are no grounds for complacency. Funds permitting there would still be room for the creation of centres in countries such as, say, Cyprus, Mauritius, Zimbabwe and Belize. Existing centres, moreover, will have increasingly to look to sources other than the Commonwealth Foundation for support. There is no reason why, as a generous and twice repeated donation to certain centres from Barclays International Development Fund has already shown, the interest of other donors in the private sector should not be aroused.

Meanwhile, as those attending the Foundation seminar of early 1979, concluded:

All Centres must, if the concept was still to flourish, interact increasingly between themselves. They should also be encouraged to hold 'open days', when the public could be invited to see exhibits mounted by various professional groups and to take part in debates on matters of current interest to the community. Centres must in short ensure that their activities and services were taken out to the people. It was a duty of the professions to press their respective governments to give them a greater role in the task of nation building: and to become involved from the outset in all aspects of national planning projects, large and small.

But above all – and here again the current evaluation by Foundation staff must prove the financial key – professional centres would constantly need to interact with the Commonwealth professional associations, whose origins and development are described in the pages immediately ahead.

Notes and References

1 Thomas Watson, who was later to take up office as Secretary of the Commonwealth Association of Architects.

2 A detailed list of professional centres will be found at Appendix F.

3 *The Role of the Professions in a Changing World*, report on a Foundation seminar held at the Professional Centre of Singapore, October, 1971. Commonwealth Foundation Occasional Paper no. 13.

4 *The Professional in the Wider Community*, report on a Commonwealth Foundation seminar held at the Professional Centres of Malaysia and Singapore, February 1979. Commonwealth Foundation Occasional Paper no. 46.

8

Commonwealth Professional Associations

> The Foundation will include among its aims the following objects: 'to promote the growth of Commonwealth-wide associations or regional Commonwealth Associations in order to reduce the present centralization in Britain'.
>
> Agreed Memorandum of 1965

Of all the tasks laid on trustees in the memorandum of 1965 the encouragement of pan-Commonwealth professional co-operation seemed, given the paucity of funds available, to point to the one path likeliest to lead to a maximum impact on a world-wide professional constituency. It was thus a happy omen that, as was mentioned in passing in Chapter 2, architects from a number of Commonwealth countries, old and new, had met in Malta only a few months before the Foundation's birth and had there adopted a constitution and a programme of activities for a Commonwealth Association of Architects. This was to prove a helpful prototype as the Foundation set about the uphill tasks of introducing itself to such of those older professional societies as were prepared to listen: of discussing the significance of each society's links with like bodies elsewhere in the Commonwealth: and of persuading them to co-operate yet more closely.

Initial reactions varied widely. While, through the forces of history and language every British-based professional body of any standing had long since established links with sister

organisations or with loose groupings of professionals throughout the Commonwealth and Empire, some were far from
enthusiastic about the formalisation of such contacts on a
strictly Commonwealth basis. They were inclined to cite the
lack of interest within their own membership for the 'gigantic
farce' which the Commonwealth Association was purported
to be. Or, nostalgic for Empire, they clung to the outdated
notion (one not untinged with financial selfishness) that a
parent-to-branch relationship could still with more profit be
maintained. Again, some would quote both their growing
preoccupation with the terms of the Treaty of Rome and the
lack of realism of being asked to persuade their own membership to contribute not only to some relevant international
professional organisation, to a potential European regional
body but to a Commonwealth Association to boot. There were
also a few British societies which saw in the creation of a
pan-Commonwealth organisation in their own particular field
the risks of both an open-ended financial commitment and a
lowering of standards overall. One could but accept such
views, held by a handful of British bodies to this day, short-
sighted though they seemed even in the early 1960s.

Happily there were other leading professions which valued
the Commonwealth connection. These recognised the need to
accept that, in the developing world, professional autonomy
must follow quickly on political independence. They were
thus anxious to help their less privileged overseas colleagues
along that road. Prominent among such bodies were the
British Medical Association and the Council of Engineering
Institutions, each of which had already established their own
informal groupings, restricted at the time of the Foundation's
birth in 1966 to countries of the older Commonwealth, plus
India. But other professions, notably the law, surveying, the
veterinary sciences and pharmacy, were quick to show interest
in the Foundation's aims. Nor had the architects themselves
been slow to light on the terms of the Agreed Memorandum.
Indeed, the first application for funds to reach trustees and
the very first award to be sanctioned by them in the summer
of 1966 was to the Commonwealth Association of Architects
itself – a two-year grant in the sum of £20,000 to assist in
developing its advisory services and to enable it to establish a

Commonwealth Board of Architectural Education. It is perhaps significant that that great British architect, the late Sir Robert Matthews, was at the time both arch-promoter of the Commonwealth ideal and simultaneously president of the International Union of Architects.

Thus the goodwill was there. The question facing the Foundation was how to harness it. Was the road mapped out by the architects the one to follow? If so, how best could other Commonwealth professional associations be set up? What limits, if any, should be set to their number? What structure and administrative backing should each have? Above all, what should be both the short- and long-term aims of such bodies, and by whom should the initiative be taken?

Having studied the steps taken by architectural societies throughout the Commonwealth and found them worthy of emulation, trustees concluded that it must be for the staff in the first place to make a move. Thus, following discussions late in 1966 with the British Veterinary Association, it was proposed to that body that if it should see fit to convene a meeting in London of representatives of veterinary associations throughout the Commonwealth to examine prospects for the creation of a pan-Commonwealth organisation, then the Foundation would meet the costs of such a gathering. Should this result in a broadly based recommendation to go forward, then again the trustees would in part contribute towards the cost of establishing a Commonwealth Veterinary Association. The initiative succeeded. Thanks to the co-operation of the British body, delegates from fifteen Commonwealth countries foregathered in London late in 1967. There they discussed the advantages of closer co-operation in their field and unanimously approved, *ad referendum* to their national societies, a charter for a pan-Commonwealth association. Encouraged by prospects of a three-year launching grant from the Foundation, the great majority of the societies represented quickly ratified the charter: agreed to contribute within their means to the association's funds and – a development of some significance – invited the Canadian Veterinary Medical Association to assume responsibility for establishing a small secretariat at its Ottawa headquarters. At the same time the Prime Minister (later President) of The Gambia, Sir Dawda Jawara, himself a veterinarian, was approached and agreed to accept the chairmanship.

A number of lessons were learnt from this experiment. The first was that the creation of a pan-Commonwealth professional organisation, with a small administrative headquarters staff, could be shown to be a potentially useful service to the Commonwealth as a whole and above all to the professionals concerned in the newer member states. Secondly, it was clear that, in the early stages at least, such an organisation would be a fragile plant. The more newly independent and by definition ill-financed societies it attracted, the greater would be the moral and monetary burden on professional bodies in the older states, and the heavier the obligation on the Foundation to ensure that the venture did not founder in the early years. Thirdly, the very creation of such a body implied the need for a representative council and for a committee structure based largely on the regional Commonwealth interests involved; for funds to cover the secretariat's modest overheads; the holding of occasional Commonwealth-wide conferences and regional seminars; and for the development of educational and technical programmes.

As the number of professions interested in this method of promoting Commonwealth co-operation grew, so too were the aims and objects of later associations broadened and refined. In their own charter the veterinarians had listed their objectives as being:

- To promote within the Commonwealth the interests of the veterinary and allied sciences;
- To maintain the honour and traditions of the profession;
- To effect the closest possible links between member associations;
- To facilitate the dissemination of professional knowledge and information;
- To encourage the creation of a national Veterinary Association in any Commonwealth country where none exists at present;
- To promote the interchange of veterinary surgeons and students.[1]

From experience gained other associations were to add to

their own constitutions such further objects as the fostering of appropriate standards of education; the evaluation of such standards with the aims of co-ordinating rights of professional practice and of facilitating reciprocity of qualifications; or again the fostering of a Commonwealth-wide appointments advisory service and the development of research and technical information services.

The idea had clearly taken root. By the close of 1970 – that is, within five years of the Foundation's birth – there were already in existence no less than twelve pan-Commonwealth professional associations. To those linking architects, doctors, engineers and veterinarians could now be added others representing lawyers, surveyors and land economists, pharmacists, magistrates, town planners, geographers and (somewhat marginally as it then seemed), those concerned with Commonwealth literature and, on a voluntary rather than a professional basis, with the deaf. Six further professions, moreover, were by that time showing interest in joining this rapidly expanding group, to which the Foundation had by now committed some £150,000 of its funds.[2]

It would be tedious, and to the associations themselves invidious, to single out particular professions for mention here. Individual achievements are recorded in more detail in Appendix E. On the other hand the collective impact of the professions involved on Commonwealth co-operation, and the sums invested, were such that trustees felt obliged from the outset to keep a more than usually close watch on developments and to monitor progress and performance. As a one-day 'brainstorm' session held at Marlborough House under the chairmanship of Dr Robert Gardiner in December 1970 revealed, the financing of this novel form of co-operation was already posing problems. Thus, with an eye to a heads of government conference due to take place in Singapore early in the year following, the delegates to this meeting, representing seventeen Commonwealth associations, actual or potential, adopted the following resolution:

Accepting the major financial contribution which the Commonwealth Foundation is making to our efforts to improve training and the interchange of skills and experience throughout the Commonwealth, we remain conscious of the need to make our pan-Commonwealth associations self-sustaining at the earliest possible date. Each of us is making determined efforts to obtain funds from other sources. Meanwhile, national contributions received through local membership fees to our various associations are bound in the short-term to be small. We thus express the hope that, in the interest of maintaining this valuable form of co-operation Commonwealth Heads of Government will, at their forthcoming meeting, feel able to augment the Foundation's current income so that the activities of the Commonwealth Professional Associations may continue to be sustained.[3]

The trustees were in fact able to present a convincing case at Singapore and in the upshot obtained from Commonwealth governments a small but encouraging increase in their annual income. Among the arguments advanced in favour of continuing support for the Commonwealth professional association concept and for its enlargement were the following. Architects had already pioneered new textbooks and audio-visual teaching kits suited to the needs of schools of architecture in the developing world. They had launched a scheme for the Commonwealth-wide accreditation of such schools with the aim of stimulating professional interflow, created a Commonwealth Board of Architectural Education and initiated study seminars between deans of architectural faculties, particularly in the universities of Commonwealth Africa. For their part the pharmacists had collectively devised a Commonwealth Code of Ethics and a national reception system to assist those travelling within the Commonwealth on professional business. They had also commissioned long-term studies on drug control and into the potential standard and content of a model degree course in pharmacy which might eventually be recognised throughout the Commonwealth. With equal vigour, the Commonwealth Association of Surveying and Land Economy had in its three short years of life brought seven new national surveying societies into existence in the newer Commonwealth; organised studies on manpower requirements and recruitment problems in developing countries; published a handbook on the surveying professions throughout the Commonwealth; collected and disseminated to its membership information on the form and operation of statutory and other controls regulating the practice of the professions; and set up an advisory service under which 'Commonwealth mix-manned' visiting boards could, on request, advise universities and other educational bodies.

The marked and rapid impact of these and other associations on problems of training and education and on the creation of autonomous national professional societies in the newer member states was by 1970 to bring the following not undeserved comment from two students of Commonwealth affairs:

Local needs, including those of pride, called for decentralisation which, when well managed, could preserve from elimination or even from erosion the legacy of standards as established in the United Kingdom ... In the last few years a host of new Commonwealth professional associations have come into being. This manifests the classic model of basing closer association on recognition of independence. It also has the effect of re-invigorating London's organisational role. Each of the new bodies has actively concerned itself with the question of reciprocal recognition of qualifications, aspiring explicitly or implicitly to agree a 'Commonwealth standard'.[4]

At this stage of development, not least in view of the financial encouragement which the Foundation had just received from its Commonwealth paymasters, it was only natural that much of the time of the Singapore seminar of 1971, to which reference has been made in the preceding chapter, should be devoted to a first, broad review of the professional association concept. As Morris-Jones put it in his keynote address to that meeting:

This then is the stage as it is set for us: changing sets of professions changing their situation in relation to societies in change. This is universal: no country is exempt; no profession is unaffected. Here already is one basis for the Associations and [professional] Centres alike: even if there were no developing countries or newer states, there would be a case for a coming together both of various professions within a country and of men of a single profession drawn from several countries.[5]

Morris-Jones went on to illustrate the problems on which views cried out to be exchanged: the adaptation of syllabi, training methods, extra qualifications, procedures for registration; the emergence of new professional disciplines; the changing social environment in which the professions found themselves, and the difficulties they faced in seeking to obtain a seat on one or other governmental advisory council.

There were, of course, other problems with which that seminar came to grips. One of general and obvious concern was that new states in a hurry to reach the economic take-off point tended to 'bureaucratise' the professions, to frown on the few individuals who still sought to practise privately, and to absorb the generally sparse professional manpower pool into the government machine. All this created a situation where, as Morris-Jones put it:

> Professional man becomes in some measure organisational man. The recognition he seeks is not one which will give him the right to practise but one which will put him in an appropriate salary scale . . . His professional association is for him a lobbying instrument more than a defender of a monopoly. Indeed the chartered monopoly scarcely works; professionals command a scarce resource but if government fails to pay the expected price, to whom shall they sell? Hence the ever looming braindrain bogy.

Another major issue was that of common standards. Desirable in itself as a concept; embedded in earlier imperial history insistence on the communality of standards could, if pressed too far, in turn lead via equivalence and reciprocity to the encouragement of a professional braindrain from the new world to the old. Here, yet again, Morris-Jones put his finger on it. While it was no task of a professional body to bring about a dilution of standards, and while it was easier for the professions to help each other to become the same, 'it is more worthwhile to help each other to be different . . . There can thus be mutual recognition of qualifications which in themselves are not the same.' In other words, political and social differences should be accepted, while standards remained protected. Mutual recognition of qualifications should not, as a matter of course, lead on to transferability.

Among the four leading Commonwealth professional associations represented at the seminar in Singapore there was general assent to the views expressed by their keynote speaker. Indeed discussion went far to underline the need to place still greater emphasis on the introduction in developing countries of undergraduate, graduate and postgraduate courses geared to local conditions and requirements; to respond to the growing need for mid-career training and retraining; to introduce audio-visual techniques and to extend the supranational, and thus disinterested, services which boards of education such as those promoted by the associations of Commonwealth surveyors and architects had already begun to offer to the newer member states.

At the same time the seminar accepted, and such sentiments were echoed by the Foundation itself, that the three major tasks facing the professional associations were first, that of making more widely known to the public throughout the Commonwealth the skills which each profession had to offer and on which sound economic development must be largely based; secondly, of encouraging the birth and expansion of yet more strongly based national professional societies; and thirdly, of expanding each country's manpower pool of fully trained sub-professionals and technicians.

It was of course recognised that no single Commonwealth-wide association could find all the answers to all such problems. Conditions varied widely from one developing country to another, while the professions in the older world were themselves as often as not in search of a new identity. At the same time, and despite the fragility of a venture which still depended all too heavily on the Commonwealth Foundation for support, there seemed to be grounds for optimism. Each association now had some practical achievements to its credit. Exchanges of views between them pointed to the day where, in collaboration with existing professional centres, an interdisciplinary team approach to some of the basic health and environmental problems of the newer Commonwealth could develop. The value of regional projects was becoming clearer. Moreover, in contradiction to fears that Commonwealth co-operation would do little more than duplicate the work of international agencies, events had already shown, thanks to a wealth of shared experience, that the Commonwealth often offered a more practical framework for co-operative action and for the solution of shared professional problems than did the international fraternity. This truism was the more apparent in that, even when attending an internationally sponsored professional conference the Commonwealth delegates present usually tended to find time to meet separately, thus further underlining the advantages which the functional Commonwealth enjoyed over the international community in terms of speed of action and instinctive understanding. (As a New Zealand minister once neatly put it: 'Commonwealth Education conferences begin where UNESCO conferences leave off'.)

In view of the achievements and of the wisdom pooled at this seminar the Foundation's trustees could hardly be blamed if, in preparing for a second quinquennium, they decided to keep support for existing and future pan-Commonwealth professional associations high on their order of priorities. Thus between 1971 and 1980 nine further such bodies saw the light of day – of educational administrators, legal educators, librarians, nurses, museologists, science and mathematics teachers, ecologists, journalists and, last but not least, of agricultural scientists. Somewhat marginally to these more strictly professional groupings there also emerged, with the direct backing of the Commonwealth Secretariat, a Commonwealth Association of Tax Administrators. By the close of 1980 the Foundation could thus claim to be supporting, and in the majority of cases to have been directly instrumental in conceiving, no less than twenty-one pan-Commonwealth professional associations with the prospect, funds permitting, of several yet to come. It had been no mean achievement. Yet, as the years went by, the very success of the venture was to throw up increasing problems.

The most burning, as ever, was that of overall resources. As the Foundation itself developed, so too did the many other calls upon its funds. And as the spectre of inflation grew, so in turn the potential cost of each new project rose. Each newly-formed association brought in its wake fresh liabilities. There seemed, moreover, to be few signs that the majority of the organisations formed in earlier days were yet on the road to viability. Sooner rather than later the chairman, by now Sir Hugh Springer of Barbados, and his colleagues on the Board of Trustees, would have to face up to some awkward policy decisions. First among them would be the wisdom, at a time of increasing financial stress, of going back to Commonwealth heads of government with a plea for yet further funds. Even if launched, such an appeal would be unlikely to satisfy all needs. It thus followed that some major evaluation of the performance of the associations to date would soon have to be put in hand. At that time such questions would have to be asked as to the period during which an individual association could hope to remain on the Foundation's pay-roll; what alternative funding sources could realistically be approached; whether it was equitable for Associations, after an initial period of say five years, to expect continuing grants in aid of administrative as opposed to project costs; and again whether, in view of rapidly escalating air fares across the globe, Foundation monies could any longer be spent on subsidising large-scale conferences of association office-bearers.

However, before commissioning any such evaluation, the trustees decided to promote one further interdisciplinary seminar, already referred to in the previous chapter, with the theme 'The Professional in the Wider Community'. Held under the auspices of the Professional Centres of Malaysia and of Singapore its aim was in part 'to assess the achievements and future potential of the pan-Commonwealth Professional Associations [and Centres]'.[6]

To this meeting, also attended by delegates from a number of professional centres, came the chairmen or secretaries of the Commonwealth Associations for Literature and Language Studies, of Architects, of Surveying and Land Economy, and of the newly formed Association of Scientific Agricultural Societies.

In a designedly provocative paper to this seminar I reminded delegates of the way in which the Foundation had proceeded stage by stage through four earlier 'think-tank' meetings to concentrate the minds of small groups of carefully selected professional leaders first on the broad problems facing the professions in a changing world; second on the co-operation which they, as practitioners, should seek to promote with new-world universities; third on how professions, universities and civil services could better interact; and fourth what future role professional centres and associations should play in Commonwealth development and how best they might co-ordinate their efforts. Having next drawn attention to the parlous state of the Foundation's finances, I threw out the following questions for debate:

- How, as my paper phrased it, can Commonwealth Professional Associations achieve financial independence?
- Should they now concentrate on regional as opposed to pan-Commonwealth activities?
- How can they help to promote intra-professional activity, both regionally and nationally?
- How can the 'professional image' in new-world countries be brightened *vis-à-vis* both governments and communities?
- Is the 'team approach' part at least of the answer to some of the questions raised above?

And finally, (not that any precise answers were to be expected):

- What are today's professional priorities?

In a paper commissioned for the seminar the Secretary of the Commonwealth Association of Surveying and Land Economy (and at the same time Secretary of the Royal Institution of Chartered Surveyors), Robert Steel, CBE, had clearly anticipated the majority of the questions raised. Writing from extensive knowledge of the problems facing his profession throughout the Commonwealth he went far in analysing those which his own association had faced, at the same time instancing some of the remedies which it had successfully applied. A first example of what could be achieved through well-planned pan-Commonwealth activity was the fact that, whereas at the birth in 1969 of this particular association there existed twenty societies of surveyors in fifteen Commonwealth countries, the relevant figures for 1979 were forty such societies in thirty countries. As Steel went on to say:

> Apart from the provision of local facilities for education and training, the most important need in every country is for a strong and influential society representing each profession, which can foster the development of the professions and act as a focal point for its corporate activities. In the sphere of education and training such a society must collaborate with government and universities or other teaching establishments in determining the scale of the requirements for skilled manpower, what educational facilities are required, the standards to be set, and the resources in buildings, teachers, books and other equipment required. The professional society also has an important part to play in developing the techniques of the profession, ensuring that its members are competent, establishing and administering codes of ethics, and where appropriate administering (or helping to administer) any statutory registration or regulation of the profession. It also serves as the forum for transmitting to government the corporate views of the profession on matters of public interest on which it is competent to express informed views; and the society should assume responsibility for undertaking such a programme of public relations as may be necessary to inform the public about the services which the profession provides, to encourage recruitment to the profession, and generally to promote the development of the profession for the public advantage ... In addition ... every professional society should also participate in the affairs of any professional Centre that may be formed, with a view to improving collaboration between the professions and promoting joint activities where these are in the public interest.

Having thus outlined, in terms which any of the Foundation's trustees would have found unexceptionable, the aims and objects which they had themselves looked to see implemented by the professional associations generally, Steel went on to give some further examples of the way in which his own organisation had already translated precept into practice.

In the Caribbean, for instance, a survey of manpower needs had been made, covering all Commonwealth countries in the region. Undertaken by the association at the request of the governments concerned it had revealed, *inter alia,* that the total development planning requirement for qualified surveyors in the area totalled 1,050, compared with the 400 available. Against this background it had proved possible to advise governments collectively what additional educational facilities would be needed to fill such a skilled manpower gap, how and where such facilities might best be provided and what teaching and other resources would be required. In the Pacific, where a similar survey had been carried out, the association had come up against very different circumstances. In that region, because of a minute professional base stretching across a sparsely populated ocean mass, the call was less for the highly trained professional specialist than for the Jack (and master) of all trades. Thus the prime requirement in the Pacific area was for versatility to match the many differing tasks in hand.

Among other activities to the credit of the Commonwealth Association of Surveying and Land Economy (and other of the associations could by now boast similar achievements) Steel listed the following:

● The publication of a manual on surveying and land economy, explaining the scope of its three interlinking disciplines in their fully developed state, and the problems to be dealt with in evolving to that position in developing countries;
● comprehensive studies of the state of development of surveying and land economy throughout the Commonwealth. Such studies had identified areas where improvements were necessary, either in the provision of educational facilities, in the improvement of techniques, the expansion of services, or in other ways necessary to improve the profession's services to the community;
● the creation of a Commonwealth Board of Surveying Education to promote the provision and to improve the standards of education and training in surveying and land economy throughout the Commonwealth;

- the establishment of an Educational Advisory Service from which Boards could be appointed to assess existing courses, and to advise governments, universities and other bodies on proposed new courses; and of an educational trust to award scholarships enabling young surveyors from the developing world to extend their professional education in other countries;
- the preparation of correspondence courses in surveying techniques to students for whom full-time courses of education were not available;
- the publication of guides on standards and curricula for professional and technician courses, and of lists of courses at professional level in Commonwealth countries which reached the recommended standards;
- the collection and publication of information about aid agencies able to sponsor or assist educational or other projects in which CASLE or its member societies were interested, and the fostering of inter-university links to assist the development of educational facilities in developing countries;
- publication of a model code of conduct for the guidance of member-societies; and of a report on the advantages and disadvantages of differing forms of registration of the profession;
- the holding of fourteen regional seminars in different Commonwealth countries for the discussion of regional problems, the proceedings of which had been widely disseminated;
- inauguration of a periodical 'newspaper' which both served as a vehicle for exchanging information on professional topics and provided up to date news on the activities of the profession throughout the Commonwealth;
- encouragement of the development of working relationships between indigenous professions and their national governments, with the aim of achieving input by the professions to the planning and implementation of national development programmes.

With such examples before them of the practical progress made by the surveying and other pan-Commonwealth professional associations, delegates to the Kuala Lumpur seminar of 1979 could only conclude that the Foundation must be urged to maintain and indeed to increase its support of this venture. At the same time some warning notes were sounded. By no means all Commonwealth governments were yet aware of the benefits which the associations, working where relevant in harness with national professional centres, were already bringing to the nation-building process and to each community's 'quality of life'. Thus, in seeking closer rapport with those in the seats of power, professionals would still have to exercise great patience. Again, even in limited administrative terms, financial viability remained for some associations a distant pipe-dream. At the same time annual contributions from most national societies to their pan-Commonwealth secretariats were unrealistically low. Unless strenuous efforts were made by the latter to raise them, the Foundation might soon be obliged to reassess its funding of those organisations which remained incapable of covering their basic administrative, as opposed to project, costs.

Not unexpectedly (and with some discreet prodding from the wings), the final conclusion from the seminar was couched in the following terms:

It would be useful if an across-the-board evaluation could be made of the work of the Commonwealth Professional Associations to date. This might well point the way in which certain less successful or financially unviable bodies could be helped to run their organisations with greater efficiency.

Already conscious of the need for such a survey the Board of Trustees was to lose no time in following up this recommendation.

Notes and References

1 *The Commonwealth Foundation: The First Five Years 1966–1971* (London: 1971).
2 A complete list, together with fuller details of the work of the twenty-one Commonwealth professional associations in existence at the close of 1980 will be found at Appendix E.

3 *The First Five Years*, op. cit.
4 W. H. Morris-Jones and T. Johnson, 'A Commonwealth of learning', *Round Table*, November 1970.
5 Commonwealth Foundation Occasional Paper no. 13.
6 *The Professional in the Wider Community*, Commonwealth Foundation Occasional Paper no. 46.

9

Commonwealth Professional Associations: an Evaluation

> Much devoted and often voluntary work takes place within Commonwealth Professional Associations. At the national level, professionals are often occupied with their status, although voluntary service is sometimes given to development projects. In rich countries, professional associations are sometimes unwilling to spend members' subscriptions in activities benefiting poorer countries.
>
> R. Symonds, Evaluation Report, 1980

It was at their summer meeting of 1979, held on the eve of the Commonwealth Heads of Government Conference at Lusaka in August of that year, that the Foundation's trustees finally commissioned an evaluation of the professional associations, instructing the director to look for a suitable expert to undertake the task. Most suitably, as it turned out, the choice fell on Dr Richard Symonds. Recently 'retired' to St. Antony's College and to the Institute of Commonwealth Studies at Oxford, Symonds was a man of wide administrative and academic experience. He had served the United Nations Development Programme as its Resident Representative in several countries in Asia, Africa and Eastern Europe, had made special studies of aid problems and programmes in Pakistan and – of special relevance to the Foundation – was the author of *The British and Their Successors*, a remarkable book in which he had written penetratingly of the professional heritage which, for both good and ill, Britain had left to her former colonies.

After discussion with the staff and formal endorsement from the chairman and trustees it was agreed that the evaluator should carry out his task in the winter of 1979/80, presenting his findings to the board by the close of May of the latter year. All relevant papers would be placed at his disposal; he would be provided with research assistance and, apart from inquiring into the activities of London-based professional association secretariats, would also visit those housed overseas, as well as a small number of professional centres on his line of route. To those remits Symonds added the suggestion, readily accepted, that he should also hold talks with the staffs of FAO, WHO, and UNESCO. He thus visited, in the course of his travels overseas, Canada, Jamaica, Australia, New Zealand, Singapore and Malaysia and, in the UN context, Geneva, Rome and Paris.

By the time Symonds began, late in 1979, to immerse himself in the relevant files, with generous research assistance from Barclays Bank International Development Fund in the person of Miss Linda Lewis, yet more had developed on the professional association front. By now the Foundation had committed close on £1.8 million to this cause – or some 32 per cent of grants sanctioned to that date. There were twenty-one organisations now waiting to be reviewed, six of them with their secretariats outside Britain. There had also come into being an informal but highly active London-based Professional Association Committee, chaired by the Executive Secretary of the Commonwealth Nurses' Federation, Miss Margaret Brayton. This body, formed in 1972, was by now in the habit of meeting quarterly. Foundation staff attended and spoke without commitment at its gatherings. The committee proved to be an increasingly useful forum for the exchange of ideas, publications, problems and experiments. Gradually it had developed the pattern of inviting outside experts to address its meetings on Commonwealth problems relating to such areas as education, university co-operation or the role of international aid agencies. Even more encouragingly, groups of like-minded professions began, under the committee's stimulus, to form small working groups for the study of such matters as legislation affecting the professions; problems facing professional man in small island states; reciprocity and recognition; and the role of Commonwealth non-governmental organisations lying beyond the strictly professional field. To the Foundation itself the committee increasingly provided a means both of keeping the staff abreast of developments which might otherwise have gone unnoticed, and of testing out possible new initiatives. To the evaluator it was to provide valuable guidance as he took up the somewhat complicated skein which it was now his task to unravel.

There had meanwhile been further developments, some of them encouraging, others less so, affecting certain professional associations which up to this point have barely received a mention. Both the Commonwealth Library Association, from its Jamaican-based headquarters, and the Commonwealth Nurses' Federation had for instance vigorously expanded their national memberships and now embraced some thirty-five and forty-five countries respectively. The Commonwealth Council for Educational Administration, housed at the University of Armidale, Australia, was proving how administrative costs could be kept to a minimum, thanks to generous support from an association's 'host'. Both this body and the Association for Commonwealth Literature and Language Studies fell outside the normal organisational pattern in that their respective memberships were made up more of individuals than of national societies. The Association for Commonwealth Literature had, moreover, adopted the unusual course of switching its headquarters triennially from one Commonwealth university to another. Starting from Leeds its secretariat had by 1970 moved on to Carlton University, Ottawa, and thence via Makerere, Uganda and Mysore, India, to the University of Queensland, Brisbane. By the close of 1979 it had moved back to Canada, coming temporarily to rest at the University of Guelph, Ontario. Rather than breaking the rhythm of activity this constant shift of secretariat, which in practice amounted to little more than handing over the association's files and such monies as it held from one willing group of volunteers to the next, positively stimulated regional interest in the association's work and brought about a number of interesting innovations. Not least among these were small seminars of distinguished writers drawn from throughout the Commonwealth; the improvement of the association's journal, *Commonwealth Literature*, and the unexpected blossoming of studies on Commonwealth writing, not only within the Commonwealth, as might rightly be expected, but at universities as far removed as Texas, Dakar, Tübingen, Aarhus in Denmark, Lille and Nice.

Yet, contrary to these and other encouraging signs of progress and self-help, there were disturbing reports from some associations that the goal of viability was still not so much distant as invisible. There was a growing risk that a number of paid secretaries of associations might now begin to consider themselves permanent 'pensioners' of the Foundation. A few association leaders, lulled by the regular renewal of Foundation grants, had perhaps developed too comfortable a sense of security. This in turn dampened their ardour for seeking alternative funding sources. In some quarters, too, there was a tendency to forget that the Foundation itself was not immune from the inroads of inflation and that the professional associations, while still high in its 'order of priorities', were not the only clients clamouring for help.

These, in brief, were some of the problems, aspirations and illusions which the evaluator was to face. To them were added the last-minute emergence of three further pan-Commonwealth organisations representing agricultural scientists, practising journalists and artists – each of which had yet to win its spurs – and the prospect that the Foundation might shortly be asked to recognise prospective Commonwealth-wide groupings of dentists and insurance institutes.

Against this background the terms of reference within which Symonds was invited to work were these: to evaluate the work of the associations which had been assisted by the Commonwealth Foundation to date; to give particular attention to their cost-effectiveness, to the prospects of their achieving viability and to the crucial question of continuing financial support, if any. He was also to examine the desirability of the Foundation helping to create further pan-Commonwealth Associations and to comment as he saw fit on other non-governmental bodies, such as the Commonwealth Parliamentary, Broadcasting and Forestry Associations, and the Commonwealth Press Union, all of which had received Foundation support from time to time.

The evaluator worked quickly and with a minimum of fuss. In the main his report, presented well within the time-limit set, was favourable to both the Foundation and to the associations themselves. Symonds had clearly been impressed by the devotion of those working, often on a voluntary basis, for the associations. The majority of them, as he saw it, had with remarkably small resources achieved considerable results, not least in areas such as educational administration, human ecology and science and mathematics teaching, areas in which no comparable non-governmental bodies yet existed on the broader international plane. On the other hand, as he emphasised, a growing shortage of financial resources was now leading to two disturbing developments: first to an over-great dependence by some associations on the Commonwealth Foundation for both leadership and 'rations'; and second to a decline in practical co-operation between the professional bodies at national level, due largely to rising airfare and postal charges. Inability to organise as many pan-Commonwealth conferences as before was, in his view, leading to a serious weakening of the links in the chains of professional solidarity.

While accepting the concern of trustees lest they should be faced with apparently unending commitments to general budgetary support, Symonds emphasised that if such aid was now withdrawn, many associations would have to be wound up. In the light of its terms of reference, which were markedly different from those of most other trusts, the Foundation was thus urged to take a sympathetic attitude in deserving cases for on-going financial help towards staff and general administrative costs, for travel to pan-Commonwealth and regional meetings and for project activities, with which should be included research into educational and training problems and for publications. However, no rigid formulae could be devised since the budgets of the various associations and the way in which Foundation grants were allocated to such items as headquarters costs, meetings, standard-setting, educational research and publications varied markedly. So too did the accent placed by individual organisations on such basic aims as the formation of new national professional societies; the status of the fully-trained professional; regional as opposed to Commonwealth-wide co-operation; the improvement of the image of professional man, or the encouragement of inter-disciplinary programmes.

In summing up his broad approach to the remit and anticipating his detailed recommendations, Symonds remarked that one basic question had to be faced, namely: 'Does the Commonwealth need the professions or do the professions need the Commonwealth?' He saw no facile answer. Some professions, as he judged the situation, had needed the Commonwealth framework far more in 1966 than they did at the start of the 1980s. The same might hold good for those developing countries whose regional affiliations were now stronger than their pan-Commonwealth ties. But there were those to which, because of their overriding educational and cultural interests, the broader Commonwealth connection was still paramount.

Having thus broadly accepted the value of the Common-wealth professional association concept and its need for continuing support, Symonds went on to consider what form future assistance might most usefully take – given the known limits on the Foundation's powers of generosity. His first recommendation was that those associations still standing in need of long-term budgetary support must be prepared to make some positive contribution in kind. This could best take the form of each such organisation so restructuring its secretariat as to attach itself, under what he described as the 'limpet formula', to an existing body, for example, a national pro-fessional society, university, museum or library, which would prove ready to provide premises and other servicing facilities. In this way Foundation grants-in-aid for administration could be restricted to covering part only of headquarters costs.

These points made, he went on, in frank opposition to the more cynical attitude of the permanent staff as to the value of conference activities, to propose that trustees should continue to support regional and pan-Commonwealth professional meetings: this on the understanding that such gatherings would concentrate on professional rather than constitutional and administrative problems, and that every effort was made to ensure that those national delegates in a position to do so would pay their own way to such meetings.

As to the problems of individual associations, Symonds saw no reason to suppose that those concerned with the agricultural and veterinary sciences, with architecture, engineering, surveying and pharmacy should not soon reach a state of administrative viability. In such cases any further Foundation support might be limited to travel, educational and other project activities. But there was another group, made up of librarians, museologists, educational administrators, law teachers and magistrates, for which no viability was in sight but which clearly deserved continuing help in view of the proven contributions of each to Commonwealth co-operation. As regards the Nurses' Federation, which would otherwise have fallen into the category of the non-viable, Symonds interestingly recommended that 'in order to broaden and intensify the Foundation's activities in the health field a consultant, who should be an experienced person in the world of health, should be appointed to examine the desirability and feasibility of the establishment of a Commonwealth Health Professional Association'. If implemented, such a proposal would of course sound the death-knell of one of the older pan-Commonwealth bodies, the Commonwealth Medical Association, as a separate entity.

There followed a number of further recommendations: namely, that the Foundation – much understaffed in the evaluator's judgement – might, in co-operation with some generously minded Commonwealth government, obtain the services on secondment terms of a junior programme officer, and further that trustees should make occasional use of consultants to assist the existing staff to examine particular professional problems affecting various regions of the Commonwealth. At the same time the professional associations might be urged to strengthen their links with existing professional centres, whose activities the author commended, while the informal London-based Professional Association Committee, whose work was seen to serve a valuable purpose, might bring within its ambit those British bodies which were not directly in receipt of Foundation aid. The evaluator also favoured continuing *ad hoc* support for organisations falling outside strict, non-governmental professional association definitions, for example, of broadcasters, parliamentarians and the press. He equally favoured the encouragement by trustees of other professions likely to qualify for professional association status. Finally, taking up an earlier proposal from the director, he urged the Foundation to meet the expense of a visit to Zimbabwe by a small team representing the broad Commonwealth Professional Association interest to assist in restoring links between the professions in that country and colleagues elsewhere in the Commonwealth.

Many other points of value to trustees emerged from Symonds's report. They owed much to his long experience of the workings of the United Nations Organisation and its specialised agencies. First, to the relief of the staff which had long since reached the same conclusion, Symonds found 'little duplication between the work of the Commonwealth Professional Associations and international non-governmental organisations'. Secondly, he foresaw prospects of co-operation between existing professional centres and country offices of the UN Development Programme. And thirdly, he recommended a renewed effort by Foundation staff to interest such agencies as UNESCO, FAO and WHO in the programmes of relevant professional associations.

Two conclusions from the Symonds Report deserve to be quoted as they stand. The first was that

Many Commonwealth Professional Associations have been transformed into organizations which mainly benefit the poorest countries. The Foundation has to recognize its responsibility for bringing about this transformation, which in some cases has lessened the enthusiasm of richer countries. Too much insistence on viability may lead to disintegration of Commonwealth Professional Associations. In some cases financial constraints may cause activity of CPAs to fall below a useful level. Secretaries of CPAs need to travel in order to stimulate projects which may generate funds. If the Foundation had more funds it might make an injection into some CPAs which could help them to move towards viability.

and the second that

> [Commonwealth] governments need to recognize, in relation to the Foundation's budget, that it is in the interest of the Commonwealth for certain CPAs to be subsidized for the foreseeable future.

Finally, even at the risk of inflating staff egos, past and present, this comment from the evaluator in a letter covering his report:

> I have been grateful for the complete freedom which I have been given in undertaking the study ... may I say how much I have enjoyed working with the Foundation and express my admiration for the quality of its work, despite the volume and variety of the questions which it has to handle with such a small staff. ...

The Symonds Report was presented only two months before my own retirement. The most I could do in the circumstances, without unduly committing my successor, was to advise trustees which of the recommendations seemed of the greatest urgency, how much it would cost to implement them, and how best, at a plenary meeting of the board only ten days prior to my own departure, the whole business could be furthered without undue loss of momentum. Meanwhile I suggested, and this was accepted at the board meeting of July 1980, a series of further modest bridging grants to those professional associations whose activities would otherwise have been brought to an inequitable and sudden halt.

As anticipated the trustees, who could barely have done justice at a single sitting to so voluminous and significant a review, remitted the report to a small committee for further study.

The committee met in the autumn of 1980 against the background of a steadily worsening financial situation, and finally recommended to the board that while it should continue to encourage the broad aims of all CPAs the latter could no longer expect the Foundation to subsidise their efforts indefinitely. Thus, with a few exceptions, all associations must very shortly find means of covering their own administrative costs. The committee advised that from 1981 onwards trustees should rather concentrate on support for collaborative project ventures involving groupings of the associations. Further financial backing should at the same time be made dependent on prospects for future viability, on evidence of efforts to raise funds from other sources and on the continuing effectiveness of an association's organisational structure. At the same time any new guidelines must be flexibly interpreted. Foundation support to individual associations should be withdrawn, not overnight, but over a 'phasing-out' period which could last several years.

Meeting in December 1980, the board broadly endorsed their committee's findings, instructing the new director to convey them to the CPAs.

This then was the state of the CPA 'army' as 1981 began. Out of its membership of twenty-one perhaps one-third could now be said to be administratively viable. Another five might reach that goal before too long. But there would remain a hard core of those whose national components would always remain too small or too poor (or both) for viability to be seen as realistic. It was they which would be the likeliest to round on the Foundation and to say in so many words: 'It was you who encouraged us into existence; you who preached the gospel of Commonwealth co-operation; and you who urged us to bring new national societies into being in the newer world. All these things we have now done. We have numerous achievements to our credit. Is it at this point in time that you choose to abandon us?' Happily the situation is still not so stark as this. But unless more funds can be diverted to the Foundation many of these promising ventures, through no fault of the trustees themselves, will face an anxious future.

10

Further Progress 1970–80

> Our differences in religion, language, in politics,
> even in our theories as to how countries should be
> governed, will persist. Somehow these differences
> must on no account separate us. One thing that
> holds us together is our common acceptance of the
> ideas of scholarship. Upon that, I think, will
> depend the future of cohesion in this Common-
> wealth.
>
> Sir Eric Ashby, 1963

From the three preceding chapters it might be assumed that professional centres and associations had by the close of the 1970s become the be-all and end-all of the Commonwealth Foundation. But, while the bulk of grant income was still going towards such ventures, the trustees continued constantly to review both policies and procedures and to search for new ecological niches to occupy.

At the same time there was a growing risk that too much might be attempted with too small an income, and that the Foundation's efforts would prove to have been spread ineffectively over too wide a front. In an attempt to draw attention to these dangers and to suggest some re-drawing of professional boundaries for action I had submitted to trustees as far back as 1970 a number of policy proposals. They were designed in part to stem the rapidly rising tide of individual grant applications which was by then pouring into Marlborough House, and in part to point the way to better co-ordinated and programmed activities in certain selected professional fields. In preparing this paper I had assumed three obvious propositions: first, that the trustees, as promoters of 'Commonwealth mutuality', would judge each request submitted to them by the yardstick of that project's potential contribution to the strengthening of Commonwealth links; secondly, that the Foundation should always be at pains to consult with other like-minded agencies – in other words 'initiating' and 'complementing' should be its watchwords and 'duplication' its bad word – and thirdly, that there should be no attempt to establish rigid orders of priority or programmes tending to limit future freedom of choice and action.

While suggesting that support for Commonwealth professional centres and associations should continue to be looked on as of high priority, I threw out the hint that seven years might be taken as the outside limit for continuing awards. As to conferences, it was clear that applications for travel grants were now threatening to outstrip the Foundation's resources. Some annual limits on expenditure in this area were thus called for. Finally, as to the increasing flood of individual requests for travel grants, the board might wish to consider a new approach. Under this, in close consultation with other agencies and professional institutions, trustees might introduce a number of small-scale bursary programmes in place of the growing number of *ad hoc* study and research visits which they now found themselves driven, often at short notice and in far too unco-ordinated a fashion, to sanction.

I also took up (if only to criticise) a point made by one particular trustee at an earlier date, namely that professional experts should be invited to sit with committees of trustees to advise on the development of Foundation policies generally: a suggestion which I saw as likelier to hinder rather than help the board's freedom of action and decision. In fact Foundation staff were already in constant touch with such experts and had built up a Commonwealth-wide network of unpaid honorary advisers who stood ready to offer confidential guidance as the need arose. Some trustees, moreover, held professional qualifications; while those from the newer Commonwealth would often, from local knowledge, be better judges of the value of a project to their own country than some outside expert, however competent.

When such proposals were put to a board meeting in the summer of 1971 there was for the first time some blunt speech. In a carefully prepared extempore statement one trustee took the director severely to task. As he put it: 'the poverty and paucity of ideas in this policy paper alone is proof of the mistaken claim to omniscience in all fields of knowledge and professional activity which has been asserted again and again'. We want, he added, 'to be flexible and selective in picking the brains we want to pick and we want no potions mixed for us and administered to us'. The trustee in question was particularly scathing in his condemnation of the director's alleged desire to keep professional experts at arms' length from the Foundation. He found this attitude amazing, above all in Britain where 'before the advance of British science and scholarship one preserve after another of layman's exclusive competence is falling. And yet', he concluded, 'in the use of the ... money contributed by Commonwealth Governments we can have the benefit of no minds save the mind of Mr Chadwick.'

I was beginning by now to think wryly of the old adage about setting out to please all and ending by pleasing none. But, as the discussion developed, it became clear that this impassioned outburst was attracting little sympathy. The paper which had brought such withering comments on my head was, to my secret relief, judged to reflect a common-sense approach. General doubt was expressed as to the wisdom of inviting groups of distinguished outsiders to sit with the trustees as of right to deliberate on Foundation policies. As another trustee put it: 'Such people could be and were indeed approached for advice through their separate organisations. The Foundation had not after all lightly embarked upon its existing policies and orders of interest. It should not now lightly yield to the temptation of placing its responsibilities in other hands.'

Summing up this lively and on the whole useful debate the then chairman, Robert Gardiner, with his unrivalled capacity for pouring oil on troubled waters, concluded that the basic questions which trustees should constantly be asking were, first, whether they were spending the Foundation's money as wisely and as widely as its terms of reference allowed and, secondly, whether the Foundation could always be sure of complementing rather than duplicating the efforts of the Commonwealth Secretariat. For the time being the board would be wise to be guided by the order of priorities outlined by the director, at the same time keeping in mind the possibility of promoting new projects in the fields of youth leadership, journalism and in relation to the Commonwealth Parliamentary Association. At a later date an informal meeting between a group of professional experts and members of the board might usefully be called. Meanwhile flexibility should be preserved as to any time limit on long-term awards and, in the light of what had been said of the rapid growth in the number of applications for conference attendance, the Foundation should now experimentally set a limit of £60,000 per annum to expenditure in that area.

Of greater interest at this stage of development perhaps was the concern expressed by trustees at the danger of duplication of effort between the Foundation and the Commonwealth Secretariat. It is thus worth paying some attention to the relationship between these bodies.

The Secretariat, it may be recalled, came into existence in August 1965. By 1970 its staff had grown from thirty to close on two hundred. When the three Foundation staff members in turn took up their duties at Marlborough House early in 1966, they were reminded of the statement in the Agreed Memorandum of 1965 that 'general office services will be provided by the Commonwealth Secretariat'. At the outset every effort was made to conform to that pious statement of intent. But in view of the marked divergence in the size and activities of each body, it soon became clear that no effective savings would result from a pooling of typing, accounting, machine aids and other services. Yet, thanks to the personal interest shown in the Foundation's welfare by the first Commonwealth Secretary-General, Arnold Smith, and to his regular attendance at board meetings in his capacity as a trustee *ex officio*, links between the two bodies were from the start close and, as they should be, cordial.

The Foundation of course was in no way concerned with the Commonwealth Secretariat's activities on the broad political front, nor with the co-ordinating role which the latter rapidly assumed in relation to trade and economic problems. But as the Secretariat gradually took over the preparation and handling of Commonwealth conferences of Health, Law, Education, Science and Agricultural Ministers and officials, so the Secretary-General found a need to appoint advisers and ultimately larger or smaller divisions covering these areas of expertise. Thus, from a very early stage of its development, the Foundation was in the fortunate position of being able to take advice from and to exchange views and ultimately project applications with his various advisers. By such means virtually all risks of duplication were avoided. Each side knew the other's limitations. Moreover, since at the outset the Commonwealth Secretariat budget provided little by way of grant as opposed to headquarters income, it often proved possible for the Foundation to contribute to some professional meeting or project, the inspiration for which had come from the Secretariat itself. In practice, and allowing for differences in size and significance, the spheres of responsibility of the two organisations could be simply put. The Commonwealth Secretariat worked through and with governments; the Commonwealth Foundation with non-governmental bodies.

It was only in 1971, when the Commonwealth Fund for Technical Co-operation (CFTC) was created as a branch of the Secretariat, that the distinction became a trifle blurred. From the outset CFTC was, in financial and staff terms, a far weightier organisation than the Foundation could ever hope to be. While its launching income was no more than £400,000 per annum, this had by 1980 risen to over £12 million. Even by that latter date the Foundation was still struggling to attain the £1 million per annum mark. By no means all the Fund's activities impinged on those of the Foundation. But its Education and Training Division did have terms of reference which, unless care was taken, might well lead to duplication. It was, for instance, required to assist Commonwealth governments in meeting priority manpower needs, and to offer awards for attendance at courses in universities, technical, professional and vocational institutions. But in practice the risks of duplication proved more apparent than real.

Applications for CFTC education and training awards had in fact to be backed by the Commonwealth governments concerned and were normally to the benefit of government employees. Such awards, moreover, were available only to candidates from developing countries and were normally tenable only in another Third World country. Nor could the Fund make capital awards or grants for the provision of books, journals or equipment. Nor again could a grantee from the newer world undertake studies in the older Commonwealth. In essence the two major differences between CFTC and the Foundation were, first, that the former was a multilateral technical aid arm of governments, while the latter helped individuals, whether in the public or the private sector; and secondly, that the Foundation could finance short-term study and professional travel on a multilateral Commonwealth basis whereas the Fund was restricted to movements from the old to the new Commonwealth, or between Third World countries alone.

All this said, the creation of the CFTC was in several ways to prove an additional bonus to the professions in the Commonwealth. First, through pooling of collective experience the Commonwealth Secretariat and Foundation were now in a better position to concentrate individually or jointly on development and gap-filling projects of real worth. Secondly, CFTC found itself increasingly in a position to come to the aid of regional educational and training projects which various of the professional associations and centres were anxious to promote, but for which Commonwealth Foundation funds were lacking. Thirdly, and contrariwise, the Foundation's trustees were in turn able to find modest funds to supplement Commonwealth attendance at training seminars planned by CFTC, but for which essential funds were lacking. It was due largely to the presence of a senior representative of the Fund on the Foundation's Grants Committee – a latter-day offshoot of the plenary board – that day-to-day problems of this kind were continuously discussed and practical results achieved. There also developed a habit of consultation on grant applications received by either side, as the result of which there was soon to be little likelihood either of fruitless duplication of effort, or of some luckless seeker after funds suffering the all too familiar fate of falling between two bureaucratic stools. Through pragmatic trial and error liaison between the two organisations came in fact to epitomise how rapidly and smoothly Commonwealth co-operation could produce results. By the close of the 1970s staff on both sides had come to know their limits and their capabilities. Each stood ready to supplement the other's needs within the confines of their respective incomes. The 'grey areas' of potential overlap had all but vanished. Rarely, if at all, could anyone now accuse either body of wasteful duplication.

But, even before CFTC had come upon the scene, the Foundation's trustees had been considering ways in which they could expand or diversify their own efforts to the benefit of the professions. Aid to pan-Commonwealth associations and centres had clearly highlighted the value of world-wide and national activity. Now perhaps the time had come to experiment more vigorously on the regional front; to promote intra-disciplinary endeavour, and to broaden the professional base itself. On the latter score trustees recalled a passage in the Foundation's Agreed Memorandum which had stated that, while informal contacts could usefully be developed with the Commonwealth Parliamentary Association, the Foundation should not, for fear of duplication of the activities of other bodies, 'initially seek to assume any functions in relation to cultural activities and the Press'.

In practice trustees had already tested the cultural waters in so far as they had supported the efforts of the Association for Commonwealth Literature and Language studies. And if, in 'the Press' one could subsume broadcasting, they had by the mid-1970s also provided substantial support towards attendance at conferences of the Commonwealth Broadcasting Association. But journalism had as yet been seen as lying beyond any definition, however elastically drawn, of the professions. How was the term 'initially', as expressed in the Agreed Memorandum, to be interpreted? The Commonwealth Press Union was largely funded by newspaper proprietors throughout the Commonwealth and much concerned with the training of journalists in the newer Commonwealth, and with the ethics of press freedom. This powerful and persuasive body was, in a sense, to prove instrumental in convincing trustees that a first quinquennium was time enough for the Foundation to have made up its mind to treat journalism as falling within its own elastic interpretation of the professional world. Indeed by 1971 a fruitful partnership with the Commonwealth Press Union was in the making, the Foundation providing funds to expand the union's visiting scholarship and training programmes for journalists from the newer world and to help in building up a series of short-term consultancy visits to newspapers in the developing Commonwealth by experts from the older world. From small but encouraging beginnings such support continued into the early 1980s, by which time it had been complemented through the creation of a Commonwealth Journalists' Association, whose small secretariat was set up in London late in 1979. Lest it be thought that the latter body did no more than reflect the aims of the former the answer, as accepted by both sides, was that the Commonwealth Press Union, backed by the more affluent newspaper proprietors, concentrated its funds on bursary and training programmes whereas the Journalists' Association aimed to create a representative pan-Commonwealth grouping of practising journalists concerned with the ethics, standards and technical problems of the profession, and with the welfare of its members generally.

Meanwhile, and in the midst of these developments which were marked by growing concern at the declining value of the Foundation's income in real money terms, trustees had not forgotten the strong plea from one among their number that advice should be sought on Foundation priorities and policies from experts from the outside world. Late in 1971 a further one-day 'brainstorm' session was thus convened at Marlborough House under the chairmanship of Robert Gardiner. On this occasion the accent was on medicine, science and technology. Ten eminent experts, all with extensive first-hand experience of the newer Commonwealth, accepted invitations to this meeting, as did eleven of the Foundation's trustees, and a small number of observers from other learned bodies. Before the discussion opened Gardiner posed a number of leading questions: given the small income available and the fact that the Foundation was in no sense a technical aid agency, to what degree had its attention to medical problems achieved the right emphasis? What was thought of its policy in regard to conferences? What obvious gaps had Trustees still to fill under their existing terms of reference? And finally, how should the Foundation set its sights at the start of a second quinquennium?

One senior professor of medicine with African experience set the ball rolling with the bald assertion that 'the priorities of the last decade now proved quite outdated. Yesterday the emphasis had been on the training of the specialist. Today the technologist was the man in need.'[1] The role of the technologist and of the medical auxiliary proved in fact to be at the heart of the day-long exchange of views. As another leading doctor put it, few auxiliaries were ever helped to attend a conference or seminar. Yet in the newer world 90 per cent of the population lived in villages where the doctor rarely went and where the brunt of responsibility fell on the nurse or the dispenser. To this a further delegate added that anything which the Commonwealth Foundation could do to increase the respectability of the auxiliary would be very welcome. Over the next decade the main priorities would lie in the agricultural and nutrition fields, in the training of auxiliary personnel and in population control. The standards and curricula of nursing training should be consonant with local needs, and not necessarily determined by the desire to achieve reciprocity with western-oriented nursing schools.

There was in short general agreement that technologists, whether working in the field of medicine or in such related areas as rural housing, co-operatives, engineering or the provision of clean water, were still far from receiving the training and recognition which they generally deserved. All too much had been said by countless visiting experts about what needed to be done. The Foundation could play a useful role by financing practical demonstrations to show how things could be done. Without such encouragement the fully qualified professional man, whether expatriate or indigenous, working in the newer world, would still, more often than not, continue to operate without the benefit of the skills of those auxiliaries whose collaboration would have been automatically available to him in the older Commonwealth.

The meeting went on to make some interesting suggestions as to how the status and training of auxiliaries could be improved. One proposal, which seemed to command general

143

support, was that small regional meetings and training seminars should be organised at which ideas and skills could be interchanged and where an interdisciplinary approach to problems of food, agriculture and health could be encouraged. Developing country governments should also be urged to create auxiliary grades within their administrative hierarchies and generally to recognise the vital importance of the sub-professional in the order of society.

Interestingly, the trend of the discussions relating to the training and role of the auxiliary (and here the word is used as embracing the professions generally) developed into a somewhat critical assessment of the Foundation's activities over the financing of conferences. It seemed to be the general view that 'conference-going was now overdone'. Thus the Foundation might well become more selective in that area, tailoring such aid as it continued to offer to the needs of younger professionals and sub-professionals; favouring the small rather than the large-scale meeting; and concentrating above all on conferences which were interdisciplinary in aim or content. But when money was scarce and a choice had to be made between support for attendance at a conference and the training, largely through short-term lecture and seminar visits by distinguished experts on the problems facing auxiliaries, then the latter type of activity should take precedence. There was at the same time general acceptance that, if it was to prove of lasting value, such training must be carried out *in situ*. All too often the well-intentioned had subsequently witnessed 'the difficulties which the grass-roots man who had been trained abroad met on returning home as he endeavoured to break through barriers of distrust or apathy'.

Undoubtedly this brief experimental 'brainstorm' session had proved useful, as much perhaps to those distinguished outside experts who attended as to the trustees themselves. Both sides now understood more clearly the catalytic role which the Foundation could play to the benefit of the professions in general. The visitors had concluded, a little to their own surprise perhaps, that the organisation was already working much along the lines they would themselves have wished to see it take. At the same time the trustees were fortified to have the endorsement of such an expert group for a number of policy decisions which they had taken or were on the point of initiating.

For the board had, towards the close of its first quinquennium, already come to recognise the role which the Foundation could play in assisting the sub-professions even if this had consciously to be done at some sacrifice to the claims of the higher echelons. Trustees had foreseen the need to place the growing range of rural development problems in the newer Commonwealth far higher on their list of priorities for action. They had begun to look for ways of promoting short, on-the-spot training and re-training courses for auxiliaries. There were already a number of practical examples of this shift of emphasis towards the sub-professions. Foremost among them was the increasing support offered to the regionally-based activities of the Commonwealth Nurses' Federation; the encouragement of co-operation between groups of medical laboratory technicians throughout the Commonwealth; and the financing of seminars, with an educational and training content, of radiographers, physiotherapists, speech therapists, mental health and orthopaedic technicians, medical records officers and hospital administrators. Only in the increasingly multidisciplinary area of rural development had the Foundation been a little slow to act – chiefly on the understandable grounds that this field, a vast and forbidding one, was already occupied by numerous far wealthier agencies. It was indeed difficult to see what useful impact an organisation whose annual income was not to reach the £500,000 mark until 1974 could possibly make.

It was in fact at this time, when the Foundation's original if still meagre income had virtually doubled, that the trustees took leave of their second chairman. Robert Gardiner's original two-year term of appointment had, with the assent of all Commonwealth governments, been extended until the close of 1973. During his tenure he had seen the number of trustees grow from 26 to 31. While the value of the increased income had been largely offset by the inroads of inflation, the scale of awards made had risen year by year and the Foundation could now claim to be far better known and appreciated in government, educational and professional circles throughout the Commonwealth.

Gardiner's leave-taking coincided with that of another stalwart supporter, the High Commissioner and Trustee for Jamaica, of whom the retiring chairman himself said that 'the coming departure of our respected friend and ally, Sir Laurence Lindo from the London scene will leave a grievous gap, not only in the Diplomatic Corps which he has so successfully graced as its Doyen but also as the Senior Trustee and on many occasions Acting Chairman of our Foundation'. The tribute was as sincere as it was deserved. Even at this remove I would add my own tribute and that of all who served with me during those first seven years to Laurence Lindo's unfailing courtesy, for his encouragement at times of stress, his belief in the Foundation's aims and his readiness to advise or to chair a meeting at the shortest notice. Now sadly no more, he was a Commonwealth man in the best sense of that term and proof of the dictum that a truly busy man can always find time to help his friends.

Happily the gloom felt by the staff on the simultaneous departure of both Gardiner and Lindo was largely dispelled when it became known that Commonwealth heads of government had decided to appoint as third chairman of the Foundation Sir Hugh Springer, KCMG, CBE, of Barbados. Springer was a man of many parts: barrister, trade union leader, Visiting Fellow of All Souls, and for a time Acting Governor and Commander-in-Chief of the colony from which he came. The new chairman had migrated to London at the time the Commonwealth Secretariat was formed and had then taken charge of its Education Division. By the time of his appointment to the Foundation he had become Secretary-General of the Association of Commonwealth Universities, a post which he continued to hold with distinction until his retirement towards the close of 1980. Now, for the first time, the Trustees and staff could call on the services of a London-based chairman. Not that Sir Hugh showed any desire to control the Foundation's affairs from day to day. The reassuring features of his appointment were that he brought to his task a wide knowledge of university affairs, great administrative experience, numerous professional contacts, particularly in the newer world, and a technique for bringing meetings over which he presided to practical (and speedy) conclusions. Taking a Whitehall analogy, he was the civil servant's 'dream minister': master of his brief, practising the arts of the possible, confident of the ability of his staff to muddle through but always ready to defend and guide. During his four-year tenure, which lasted until the close of 1977, the Foundation faced many problems – of expanding activities coinciding with steady growth in membership, of finance, of interpretation and finally of a widened remit.

By now the work-load falling on a staff which still numbered no more than eight – a director and his deputy, each with his personal assistant, two administrative officers-cum-bookkeepers and two stenographers – was creating serious strains. The sheer growth in the number of trustees – by 1980 they totalled 40 – involved the circulation of a great weight of paper in advance of the bi-annual meetings of the board, which had themselves become increasingly difficult to organise. In addition the staff now had to prepare documents for and service twice-yearly meetings of the Foundation's Finance Committee and to process lesser grant applications through another body, known first as the Conference and Minor Grants Committee and later as the Grants Committee *tout court*. Some ten trustees volunteered to serve in rotation on these bodies. Each helped to relieve the plenary board, which would otherwise have had to meet far more frequently, of much routine work. Indeed the Grants Committee had, well before the close of the 1970s, accepted the need for its members to meet at least six times annually. By 1979 it had been empowered to make awards, without reference to the full board and within limits of £10,000 per grant, of up to £200,000 per annum.

The preparation of annual estimates and of accounts for the visiting auditors, the latter including a massive schedule of awards sanctioned in the previous year, were other duties which consumed a great deal of junior staff time. There was also a steady stream of visitors to be seen, a constantly growing mail-bag of applications to be handled, meetings to be attended and travel to be undertaken overseas. Throughout these preoccupations the director and his deputy had to keep a constant watch on the Foundation's bank balances, persuade contributing governments to pay their annual dues in time; advise trustees on the level of expenditure which could be sanctioned in relation to annual contributions received; submit thoughts on future policy; follow through the value of grants already made and be on the constant look-out for innovative schemes which could take the Foundation into new but still practical fields of operation. It is a tribute to the staff as a whole that they accepted the need to keep their numbers small, if only to avoid unkindly accusations that the ratio between headquarters costs and grant expenditure was getting out of hand, a danger to which all trusts are vulnerable.

One of the first steps taken by the new chairman was to convene a London meeting, late in 1974, of the representatives of the by now eighteen Commonwealth professional associations. As he explained to them, the Foundation itself now stood in need of further funding. If its case to Commonwealth heads of government, next due to meet in Jamaica in April, 1975, was to stand any chance of succeeding, then the associations on which so much grant money had already been expended would soon have to convince trustees of the need for such support to be continued.

As on an earlier occasion all delegates drew attention to the need for continuing Foundation help. Try as they might, each had encountered the greatest difficulty in raising funds from the private sector: or in obtaining the agreement of their national member societies to increase their annual contributions. A few associations had by now become administratively self-supporting and regional co-operation had markedly improved. But projects in the fields of education and training, which became more and more essential as the number of professional societies in the newer Commonwealth increased, could not be put in hand unless Foundation support continued. In the words of one delegate, trustees and Commonwealth governments should be urged to continue 'to throw good money after good'. As against which the trustee for Britain, Dr Farrer Brown, inquired whether enough had yet been done to convince heads of government that the 'viability of influence' of the associations was sufficient to justify an expansion in the Foundation's income. There were perhaps better ways through which it might achieve its basic aims. Was there not a growing danger of the proliferation of such bodies, leading to the creation of yet further watertight professional compartments?

148

And might not this in turn lead to accusations of continuing élitism? In general the meeting accepted the existence of such dangers. On the other hand 'élitism' was seen to be an inescapable condition of professional life and a far lesser evil than any deliberate acceptance of a lowering of professional standards. In short, and while Commonwealth associations should beware of the danger of directing their missionising zeal only at the converted, the broad conclusions from the meeting were that such Commonwealth organisations ordered their affairs more effectively and economically than their international counterparts and that, in the words of one senior representative, 'the Associations were indeed the best agents of the Commonwealth Foundation and would remain so provided that each operated from a strong professional base and that all kept constantly in mind their collective role in the field of education'.[2]

Unhappily, despite a strongly argued case, the trustees were unable at the 1975 Jamaica Conference to persuade Commonwealth heads of government to supplement the Foundation's income to the extent required. Nothing dismayed, but with a warning to his colleagues that 'on the eve of the organisation's tenth birthday the time had come for a period of consolidation and reflection', Springer proposed that a small policy review committee of Trustees should be set up under his chairmanship. It would have, among other things, to consider whether Commonwealth professional associations rather than national professional centres should now remain at the top of the Foundation's order of interests; how best governments could be persuaded – despite so much talk about 'élitism' and 'status groups' – of the contribution which the professions could and indeed did make to their societies; how the Foundation could better contribute at grass-roots levels to the solution of rural problems, to professional-community relationships, and to the transfer of technology and management skills; and whether in the light of more often than not ill-illumined accusations directed at the Foundation for its alleged failure to concern itself with such problems, there was need for the original terms of reference to be revised.

The Review Committee met twice: in December 1975 and May 1976. Its first broad conclusions were that the Foundation had performed well to date within the existing remit and that its original terms of reference had been sufficiently wide 'to allow for substantial shifts of policy and emphasis without recourse to radical amendment of its basic terms'.[3] Thus the committee felt that it should frame its recommendations to the full board not by way of criticism of past activities 'but in a constructive spirit which would take full account of the growing desire of our respective governments to further inter-Commonwealth functional co-operation'.

Members of the committee at the same time concluded that much of the activity already in train should be retained in any future order of Foundation interests. There should be no mystical cut-off date for schemes in hand simply because they had not achieved viability within some stated short-term period. On the other hand both trustees and staff should be constantly on the look-out for fresh initiatives. In short, and in order to maintain its credibility, 'the Foundation must be seen ... to be continually adapting itself and vigorously responding as a conscious gap-filler to economic and social needs, not least in areas of appropriate technology and the sub-professions'.

Before turning to such fresh initiatives and to a revised order of interests, the committee found time to commend the way in which the Foundation had already moved in the direction of singling out a number of the sub-professions for individual and project support. At the same time its members emphasised that far more now needed to be done in respect of food technology and other rural, forestry and fisheries problems. Greater efforts must also be made to promote an inter-disciplinary team approach to the basic health, rural and urban planning problems of the tropical Commonwealth.

Next the committee recommended – and these proposals were later broadly endorsed by the board – that, without lacing themselves into a strait-jacket, trustees should take as their guide for the years remaining up to 1980 the following areas as now standing most in need of aid:

(1) Food technology and rural development;
(2) Basic medicine, dentistry and pharmacy, and professions ancillary thereto;

(3) The veterinary sciences, fisheries and forestry and those at technician level;

(4) Surveying, land economy and architecture, including technicians;

(5) Basic engineering, again including technicians;

(6) Education, relating primarily to adult education and educational administration;

(7) Management, public administration and related activities;

(8) Accountancy;

(9) Librarianship;

(10) Specialist medicine (with a primary bias towards paediatrics, orthopaedics, gastro-enterology, ophthalmology, malariology and other widespread tropical diseases);

(11) The law, with particular reference to legal aid and legal education.

Finally the committee, harking back to the original terms of reference, asked themselves whether the Foundation should continue to deploy funds supplied by so many Commonwealth governments to enhance the professional skills of 'the few' when, in many developing areas 'the many' were starving – even dying – for lack of basic human services. To this their answer, based on some ten years' experience, was an emphatic 'yes', in that any improvement of professional and sub-professional skills must in the longer term improve the quality of life. What was needed above all was a careful and continuing assessment of the differing and often shifting priority needs of each separate country, from which more effective regional and pan-Commonwealth co-operation could stem. To make this a reality civil servants, academics and professionals throughout the newer countries of the Commonwealth would have to co-operate even more closely for the public good. Only by becoming increasingly exposed to each others' needs and problems could they help to bring about that better inter-communication between the 'many' and the 'few' which Kenyatta had summed up in the one word 'Harambee'.

Notes and References

1   Commonwealth Foundation, record of a 'brainstorm session' held at Marlborough House, London, 7 October 1971.
2   Commonwealth Foundation, record of a meeting held at Marlborough House, London, 15 October 1974.
3   Commonwealth Foundation, *Report of the Policy Review Committee, 1976*.

11

The Commonwealth Foundation:
Weaknesses and Strengths

> The Commonwealth – a very lively corpse –
> the Author, c. 1966

In a retrospective article[1] written on the eve of retirement in mid-1980, I had summarised the Commonwealth Foundation's three main weaknesses as undercapitalisation from the very start, undermanning, and virtual anonymity. To such drawbacks might by inference be added the nature of the beast itself. Unique in many ways as the Foundation was as an internationally financed and governed charity, it also ran the risk of proving, through the very weight of its membership, ungovernable. The greater the number of countries joining in its work, the more that danger grew. And as the original hard core of non-official, locally domiciled trustees gradually diminished, the more difficult it became to maintain a semblance of cohesion. Constant changes in the membership of the board and of its committees – and to a lesser degree in the chairmanship itself – all tended to deprive the organisation of that continuity and built-in memory for procedure and precedent which strictly national trusts would take for granted.

To some degree such structural defects could be overcome, or at least palliated, thanks to the greater permanency of the staff itself. More serious was the financial situation.

In 1966 an annual income of £250,000, coupled with the

Foundation's right to go fund-raising in the private sector, was perhaps a not ungenerous encouragement to a body with scant life expectancy. With hindsight, however, that sum was to prove a pittance when related to the vast field of human endeavour with which, if ultimately successful, the trustees would be bound to come to grips. Nor, paradoxically, was the British government's original offer to meet half the income collectively pledged in the early years as generously helpful as might at first blush appear. In practice this 50 per cent contribution to the total annual fund at once distorted the *pro rata* subscriptions required of the twenty other founding member governments. It also gave the latter a false impression of the potential significance of the Foundation, given the artificially low contributions that they were asked to pay. Further confusion was caused when, at the close of the Foundation's first quinquennium, Britain quite understandably announced an intention to reduce her share of the annual income from 50 per cent to 30 per cent, thus leaving to trustees and staff the task of working out a radically revised fee structure which had in turn to be 'sold' to what were by then upward of thirty governments, nearly all of which had by now become used to contributing at 'bargain basement' rates.

Nor in practice had two other difficulties been foreseen. The first was the likely indifference, or outright opposition, of banks, industry and commerce to appeals for funds from an organisation which in their eyes was a child of governments, which might thus properly be expected to foster their own foundling. The second was that, having no strictly national base, and professing interests covering rather more the newer than the older Commonwealth, the Foundation would be unlikely to attract sympathy from those in the latter countries from which alone substantial donations could be expected.

Leaving aside the worsening financial climate into which the Foundation was born and the effects of inflation on its grant activities, many of them turning on the vital sector of travel, there was a third handicap, which was in time to absorb an inordinate amount of time and paper. It was simply that of gathering in, from a constantly growing number of contributing governments, sums actually pledged across the years.

During the late 1960s and early 1970s the Foundation enjoyed a record of paid-up contributions which any larger international agency might well have envied. But, as the annual income was adjusted upwards and those governments subscribing to it grew from 20 to 30 and ultimately to over 40, that proud record slipped. Unlike the Commonwealth Secretariat, which faced similar problems, the Foundation had no permanent representative of the stature of the secretary-general who could confront heads of government in person. Its appeals had to be channelled through trustees who, however sympathetic, also had their problems of distance communication. The result was an increasingly time-consuming flow each year of 'reminding' letters from the staff, accompanied in the last resort by the threat, happily only once resorted to, that the Foundation's Trust Deed debarred any trustee whose government was more than one year in arrears with its contributions from attending meetings of the board.

It was, moreover, no easy matter to present a case to Commonwealth governments in general for an increased income. By the nature of things the arguments to be advanced had first to be debated and approved by trustees as a whole. (This in turn begged the question whether they were then acting as private individuals or as representatives of their governments.) Then an agreed document had to be circulated through the good offices of the Commonwealth Secretary-General to Commonwealth senior officials. They, when meeting to prepare for a further heads of government conference, would consider the strengths and weaknesses of the case made out and then forward their own comments to their ministers. Eventually the heads of state in turn would find the Foundation document buried among the lesser papers on the agenda for their forthcoming conference and once assembled, whether in Singapore, Jamaica, Ottawa, London or Lusaka, promptly remit it back to officials meeting in the so-called 'Committee of the Whole' for what would be virtually a final view.

It was the luck of the draw whether or not Foundation officers would have the opportunity to speak again once such a document had passed from their own hands into those of the Commonwealth Secretariat. At the London Commonwealth

Conference of 1967 I had had the somewhat rare privilege, at the invitation of the then British Prime Minister, Harold Wilson, of reporting direct to the meeting on the progress of the Foundation during its first eighteen months. But when heads of government next met two years later in Singapore and a case was presented to them for raising the annual income from £250,000 to £350,000 I was merely one of the background army of functionaries admitted for their own items only to what had now become – inevitably so in view of the rapid growth in Commonwealth membership – a series of restricted conference sessions. But at Singapore there was at least the satisfaction of witnessing the heads of government give sanction to this modest claim for increased funds. In its final communiqué the conference 'noted the progress of the Commonwealth Foundation and agreed to its proposed expansion'. Two years later, in Jamaica, the income rose again to £450,000, while at Ottawa in 1975 it reached the level of £670,000 per annum.

But, as the evaluator of Commonwealth professional associations, Richard Symonds, was to say at the close of his report, already referred to in some detail in Chapter 9, the time spent by trustees and staff in arguing the case for an increased income was out of all proportion to the sums involved. As he bluntly put it:

There is a case for continuing to support many of the Commonwealth Professional Associations. To an outside consultant the sums at stake seem almost pitifully small. The whole amount awarded between 1966 and 1979 to all twenty-one CPAs, £1,788,800, is less for example than the UNDP programme in a medium sized country in a single year – or one tenth of the annual amount spent by one Commonwealth bilateral aid agency in its NGO programme. If the Commonwealth Foundation's budget were better related to the needs, much more could be done to further the work of CPAs, particularly in developing countries; and in some cases a financial injection now might enable them to become viable later. If there is any general criticism, it is that the sights have been set too low, not too high, and that heads of government, in determining the resources available, have not altogether faced the fact that the Commonwealth needs the professions as much as the professions need the Commonwealth.

In practice three handicaps constantly dogged the trustees and staff in their search for increased funds. First, the very smallness of the original income proved a formidable barrier to all efforts to achieve a once-and-for-all imaginative target figure. As those familiar with the mental processes of Treasury officials will know, it is far easier to get approval for the doubling of a figure which already has six noughts behind it than it is to do so with one which has not yet reached that mark. The smaller the increase sought to an already small amount, the greater the detailed criticism levelled at that proposed increase will be. Secondly, in so far as the Foundation was in a position to present evidence at heads of government conferences, those officials advising their ministers on the spot, and before whom one appeared as witness, had as often as not only the vaguest knowledge of the Foundation. This, with their many other preoccupations, they frequently took to be some obscure offshoot of the Commonwealth Secretariat. Thirdly, there were, as always, many other justifiable and competing claims on the time, financial capabilities and sympathy of Commonwealth governments collectively: for instance, the growing needs of the Commonwealth Fund for Technical Co-operation; of the Secretariat itself; of its Youth Programme and numerous other *ad hoc* preoccupations. By hindsight one might perhaps count it fortunate that so small and unknown an organisation had, within its first ten years, seen its income almost triple.

To turn back, however briefly, to the second of the Foundation's main structural weaknesses – that of undermanning. Any failure on that score can be levelled only at the first director. I had, perhaps to excess, the notion that a charitable body should so order its affairs that the greatest possible proportion of its funds (often contributed by governments on the razor edge of poverty) should go to the aims for which the trust had been established rather than towards headquarters and administrative costs. Thus the smaller the staff and overheads the likelier it would be that accusations of disproportionate feather-bedding might be avoided. In the first few years, thanks in part to the tax-free interest earned on various reserve accounts, it proved possible to limit head-quarters costs to some 8 per cent of annual income. That this was achieved was due also to the readiness of the small staff to work long hours and to eschew all thoughts of demarcation disputes.

At the same time the trustees were obliged to accept certain Commonwealth facts of life. The Foundation remained a small bedfellow of the far larger Commonwealth Secretariat, whose staff had by 1980 grown to well over 300. Both worked in the same building. But since the latter enjoyed diplomatic privileges, it proved impossible to escape a situation where, as members of a Commonwealth mix-manned body the staff, and particularly those recruited from overseas, must enjoy the same basic salaries and allowances, grade for grade, as their Secretariat colleagues. The Foundation in short was tied to a juggernaut and could only travel in its wake. As Secretariat conditions of service improved, so too did those of the Founda-tion, with a disproportionate effect on the latter. Thus as inflation bit increasingly deep from the mid-1970s onwards, so the ratio between headquarters costs and disposable grant income worsened.

One further weakness was mentioned at the start of this chapter, that of the Foundation's failure to publicise itself. It could of course be argued that a philanthropic body should be content to do good work by stealth and that over-much publicity would lead only to an undesirable torrent of irrelevant project applications; or, worse still, of desirable ones for which the necessary funds were simply not available. There was of course much truth in this. On the other hand it had to be remembered that the Commonwealth Foundation had been set up with the object not only of promoting professional co-operation but of underlining the importance of the Common-wealth itself as a functional force for good. There were thus political reasons for ensuring that the existence of the bush from which came the rare good wine was made widely known. Despite the distaste of the press generally for wasting paper on good news, it was not difficult to bring the Foundation's efforts to the notice of the 'ruling few' in Britain. But it was an uphill task to achieve this elsewhere in the Commonwealth.

Despite continuous travel, during which the same country or group of countries might be visited time and time again, there seemed almost always to be communication gaps, above all on the governmental plane. A minister whom one had persuaded to take some interest would have gone by the time one next visited his country. A key head of department, with whom a first-name relationship had been built up, would suddenly have been transferred. Indeed a second visit to the same area only two years after the first could well uncover blank incomprehension as to the Foundation's aims. All too often, in some African or Asian capital, I would find myself involved in a time-consuming paper-chase from ministry to ministry in search of the individual officer charged with the Foundation file. As the number of governments involved grew larger, so this problem of keeping the organisation on the map increased.

With the professional and academic worlds there was happily more continuity. At the same time the media in countries outside Britain seemed, whether from a scarcity of other news material or because of a greater appreciation of the benefits which the Commonwealth could bring them, more inclined to lend a helping hand. I thus found myself (sometimes in hilarious circumstances) learning the arts of press and television interviews and began the better to appreciate some of the pitfalls facing jet-lagged politicians confronted, at the close of a long and wearing flight, with airport lounge interrogations.

Heads of government conferences too provided useful means of promoting the Foundation's image, if not always its financial fortunes. In the long hours during which armies of senior officials were excluded from the restricted sessions of their heads of state, there was often the opportunity to draw attention to what had already been achieved by trustees in a particular country or to discuss the value of some potential project.

Turning then from weaknesses to strengths it can be said that, scant and short though their references to the Foundation were, extracts from the final communiqués of heads of government from the early 1970s onwards proved on the whole encouraging (even though the relevant paragraphs always came so close to the end of those now seemingly endless documents that most sub-editors blue-pencilled them for want of space). Thus, as the Jamaican communiqué of 1975 recorded: 'Heads of Government expressed appreciation at the progress of the Commonwealth Foundation which they regarded as having an important role to play in strengthening professional co-operation throughout the Commonwealth and noted the increased budgetary requirements for 1976–79.'[2] Or, as the London communiqué of 1977 put it, at the same time raising issues which will be dealt with in ensuing chapters:

Heads of Government acknowledged the valuable contribution made by Commonwealth non-governmental organisations and requested the (Commonwealth) Secretary-General to establish an Advisory Committee which would report on concrete steps to promote mutually beneficial ties between the official and unofficial Commonwealth. Recognising that the Commonwealth Foundation had proved its value in the professional field they considered that there might be further specific areas in which, in close consultation with non-governmental bodies, it could usefully be active on a regional or Commonwealth-wide basis. The meeting noted that increased contributions would be necessary in order to assure the income for such an extension of the Foundation's activities.[3]

Taking up the expansion of the Foundation's remit the Lusaka communiqué of 1979 struck an even more heartening note. On that occasion heads of government

commended the cost-effectiveness and imaginative work of the Commonwealth Foundation in developing and strengthening professional co-operation throughout the Commonwealth. They agreed that the Foundation's mandate should, subject to a review of its priorities, be expanded as recommended by the [already mentioned] Advisory Committee on Relationships between the official and unofficial Commonwealth in the areas of culture, information, social welfare and rural development. In order to make good the erosive effects of inflation and to permit the envisaged expansion of the Foundation's activities, the target for the Foundation's income was set at £1.1 m., although it was recognized that realisable resources were unlikely to exceed £900,000 in 1979/80.[4]

In fact the financial year 1979/80 brought in barely £800,000 despite those pious hopes. Even in the year following the target of £1.1 million was disappointingly unreached. But the recommendations emanating from two successive summit meetings that the Foundation should now expand its efforts into further fields seemed proof enough that, even without the provision of further tools to do the job, the organisation was now seen to have more strengths than weaknesses.

In retrospect it could be said that, with little money, much had been achieved. Even if the financial future of many of them was still uncertain the growing networks of pan-Commonwealth professional associations and national professional centres had between them brought to birth a sizeable number of new, independent professional societies in the still developing states. Their very existence had encouraged small, isolated professional groups in the newer world and had given them a greater consciousness of their status in their own societies. By the same token the older professional associations had been made more aware of their moral obligations to their younger brethren and had been brought to undertake a widening range of services to the latter. The existence of centres in so many new world capitals had done much – although still more remained to be done – to break down barriers of suspicion between the professions on the one hand and governments and universities on the other. Professional man, so often and often so unjustly looked on as élitist was now going out of his way to volunteer his services not merely to his clients but to his own community. Above all perhaps the professions were being tempted out of their watertight compartments and were at long last beginning to tackle national, regional and Commonwealth-wide problems of development in a team spirit. And governments in turn were increasingly recognising the need to bring professional bodies on to their planning councils.

Many such shifts of opinion, many such changes in attitude would in time have come. But to the credit of the Foundation and of those Commonwealth governments which first put faith in its creation, it could be claimed that such achievements were now taking place far earlier than might have been the case had there been no such organisation.

Meanwhile as the third chairman, Sir Hugh Springer, gave way at the close of 1977, after a highly successful four-year term of office to his successor from Nigeria, the Rt Hon. Sir Adetokunbo Ademola, GCON, KBE, Kt CFR, PC, the search for fresh initiatives, combined with a continuing review of policies and priorities, continued unabated. To Sir Adetokunbo, a lawyer of high distinction whose career had ended as Chief Justice of the Federal Republic, fell the somewhat unenviable task of presiding over the Foundation's fortunes at a time when the organisation was being urged on the one hand to do more and on the other to do so with unexpanded funds. Yet he was inheriting a by now well-organised machine. The Board of Trustees, although alarmingly large compared to the size of the permanent structure, had levelled out at a little over forty members. The accounts were in good shape. While income had not grown *pari passu* with inflation and the ever increasing calls on the Foundation's resources, a reserve fund still stood available against contingencies. And the Foundation's various committees were working with marked efficiency. The staff had become fully involved in the studies of the Advisory Committee on links between the official and the unofficial Commonwealth and, before its report was completed, had been instrumental in launching a number of initiatives in the cultural and media fields, the most striking of these being a contribution to the Commonwealth Festival held in conjunction with the Commonwealth Games, 1978, at Edmonton. This particular award, which might well have been condemned by the Trust Deed's original draftsmen as *ultra vires*, was instrumental in bringing a number of artists, musicians, dancers and singers from the poorer countries of the Commonwealth to Canada. It also acted as a stimulant to other donors. The upshot, witnessed by those fortunate enough to find themselves at the time in Edmonton, was a manifestation on a scale never before witnessed of the wealth and diversity of the cultures of the Commonwealth. At times the artists, performing in the streets and shopping areas of the city, almost outshone the athletes themselves. The final performance in the stadium, on the closing day of the games, when groups from some

162

thirty countries combined in a barely rehearsed but brilliant pageant, was witnessed by a huge and appreciative audience and was later seen on film and television by many millions of viewers throughout and well beyond the Commonwealth.

Meanwhile other less spectacular activities had continued and further initiatives were launched. The Commonwealth Foundation Lectureship Programme had grown in strength and ambit, embracing such subjects as the training of librarians and ancillary health personnel in the newer world; the delivery of dental health care; the treatment of burns; paediatric surgery; and the promotion of an interdisciplinary approach to environmental problems. From all these lectureship tours worthwhile and widely distributed reports resulted. The trustees had also authorised a second, updated edition of *Professional Organizations in the Commonwealth*, which appeared in 1976.[5] With the board's agreement I had also commissioned the preparation of three regional guides to trusts and other agencies active in varying areas of the Commonwealth. The first, covering the Commonwealth Caribbean, was printed in 1978; the second, dealing with the Commonwealth countries of Africa, in the following year; and the third, relating to South-east Asia and Oceania, early in 1981. The aim of all three guides, produced at low cost and at a reasonable price to the subscriber, was above all to provide a further service to the professional world and in particular to those living far from comprehensive reference sources. Judging by the number of appreciative comments received, this venture clearly met a need: for within something less than one hundred sheets those in quest of funds could now find details of all trusts and agencies, Commonwealth or foreign, active in their own countries and in their own particular professional and sub-professional fields of interest.

Two other ventures merit some brief mention. The first was a decision to fund, in co-operation with the University of Leeds, the Government of Canada and other local charities, a somewhat novel 'rotating' chair in modern Commonwealth studies at that university. Originally the idea encountered opposition from certain members of the board, less because of its intrinsic value than for fear that the project fell marginally outside the Foundation's terms of reference. But eventually it

163

was agreed that the chair should be held on an annual basis by a succession of eminent Commonwealth citizens from countries *outside* Britain. Those invited to hold the appointment would not necessarily come from academic walks of life. What would weigh in the selection process would be the ability of the individual, from his store of practical experience, to spread knowledge of the functional Commonwealth in one or more of its modern aspects and to teach and discuss at both undergraduate and postgraduate levels.

The first holder of the Commonwealth chair at Leeds was Professor J. J. Auchmuty, formerly Vice-Chancellor of the University of Newcastle, New South Wales, a historian with an unexampled experience of Commonwealth functional co-opera- tion, and at the time of his appointment in 1976 a Fellow of the Humanities Research Centre of the Australian National University. He was followed by the eminent Kenyan political scientist Professor Mazrui, a temporary exile to Michigan whose tenure of the chair led, not indirectly, to an invitation to him to deliver the BBC Reith Lectures of 1980. There followed two Canadians, Emeritus Professor John Holmes from Toronto, a former senior diplomat, and Dr Norman Hillmer, official Historian to the Canadian Department of National Defence. The success of this venture proved such that a highly respected teacher from the Nehru University, New Delhi – Professor Bimal Prasad – later accepted an invitation to hold the Leeds chair during the academic year 1981/2.

The second, somewhat unexpected, initiative resulted from my own travels in Africa, not to Commonwealth countries alone but to a number of francophone states. Such visits, which had included brief stays in Réunion, Gabon, Cameroon, the Ivory Coast, Benin, Togo and Senegal ended on one occasion in attendance at an anglo-francophone scientific conference at Dakar. This, partly financed from Foundation funds, was to lead to a decision to create a pan-African Association of Scientific Organisations. The trustees had incidentally become involved at an earlier date in support of similar meetings in the field of agriculture, following which a successful Association of Faculties of Agriculture in the Universities of Africa had been established.

The experience gained from such journeys and conferences,

which had brought me into direct contact with scientific and agricultural research organisations on both sides of the ex-colonial divide, could but lead to the conclusion that the growing nuclei of scientists and agronomists and their nascent professional groupings, faculties and research stations could no longer afford to work in isolation, extending the rivalries and secrecies which had for so long dogged progress, above all between the artificially created West African states. The fact that telephone calls between, say, Benin and Ghana or between Nigeria and Gabon had still, long after independence, to pass through the international switchboards in London or Paris or that surface communications between neighbouring states were still notoriously poor, might be temporarily accepted as a sad and lingering political legacy. But it was particularly dis-heartening to witness on the spot agricultural research stations, almost within an African estate agent's stone's throw of each other, where pioneering work was going on in expensive duplicate on, for instance, cocoa diseases or new strains of coffee, and experience gained was kept jealously within one or other of the former imperial folds.

To an outsider such attitudes seemed indefensible. Develop-ing Africa could not afford them. Moreover, much as previous regional scientific and other committees had promoted research co-operation in anglophone Africa, it now emerged that, under the more generous impulse of l'Organisation scientifique et technique d'outre-mer in Paris, the still more cohesive francophone states had stolen a scientific march. It thus seemed time for the Foundation to forgo, at least in the West African context, its dictum that travel and research awards to citizens of the Commonwealth could be made only within the confines of the Commonwealth itself. Hence the creation, in 1976, of an experimental three-year fund in the sum of £50,000 to promote professional co-operation between the former anglophone and francophone states of Tropical Africa. This venture could not of course be of direct financial benefit to citizens of *la francophonie*. But it was to enable the Foundation to help professionals in Commonwealth African countries to attend conferences or to pursue research and other collaborative schemes with colleagues in neighbouring francophone states. By 1980 some projects had already been sanctioned to the benefit of scientists, mathematicians, teachers and para-medicals.

In short an effort, however small, was now being made to break down yet further professional barriers and to pave the way towards regional co-operation between two superficially alien ways of life.

Meanwhile regional professional co-operation had been markedly strengthened in other areas of the Commonwealth. In the South Pacific, for instance, building on experience available at the universities in Suva, Port Moresby and Lae, and assured of the sympathy of numerous professional leaders in New Zealand and Australia, modest co-ordinating pro-grammes had been launched in the fields of medicine and dentistry. Inspectors of schools, heads of teacher training colleges, youth leaders, librarians and others had been brought together to discuss and often to find solutions to commonly shared problems. Accountants, surveyors and engineers had benefited from grants for attendance at area seminars. Inter-university links were being strengthened and the creation, thanks to the efforts of various of the Commonwealth-wide professional associations, of a number of new national pro-fessional societies was helping to lay the foundations of a new-style functional edifice. These were but small beginnings. But in areas so vast and so sparsely populated, a relatively large grouping of small states could only hope to face the coming century with confidence through a deliberate pooling of experience and resources.

In East and Central Africa the habit of functional co-opera-tion, while temporarily upset by political antagonisms, had proved more deeply rooted. Thus trustees were able to build with some success on inter-university relationships and to promote worthwhile links between surgeons, physicians, librarians, adult educators, veterinarians, architects, laboratory technologists and others. Professionally speaking there was now a growing trend towards pan-African co-operation, not least in the fields of administration, management and the natural sciences. Here too the Foundation was playing its part, welcoming the attendance at conferences and seminars which it had helped to sponsor of delegates from countries outside the Commonwealth in Africa.

But it was in the Caribbean above all that regional co-operation was most successfully pursued, thanks not only to the work of CARICOM and to the enthusiasm shown by a number of professions in the area, but also to the enlightened policies of, among others, WHO and the Canadian International Development Agency. As part brain-children of the Foundation itself there now existed the lively Organisation of Commonwealth Caribbean Bar Associations, which was to enjoy close links with the Canadian Bar; the Commonwealth Caribbean Nurses' Association, whose many island delegates met together regularly; and similar, if loose, groupings representing engineers, surveyors, architects, dentists, magistrates and others. Through such initiatives public servants, academics, practising professionals and researchers had all been brought together. Mental and geographical distances had shrunk and a number of practical projects set in train.

Two testimonials from grantees writing to the Foundation of their personal experiences are worth quoting since they sum up in simple terms how much a small award could count in and influence an individual's life. Thus an ancillary health worker in East Africa wrote (*sic*):

This was my first time to attend such an international get together. We people who are so isolated as I am here do not have get-togethers, even local, let alone international seminars of this calibre. We miss them quite a lot. I did benefit quite a lot from the seminar. I heard quite a lot and learnt quite a lot. I got a lot of practical advice from people of great experience from Australia, Singapore, Nigeria, etc., I am putting forward most of these pieces of advice given to my Government. There is one thing I hope for, from now on, and which I also pray you make true, which is, that, this assistance should be but the first of several more to come. It is quite evident to you, I am sure, that if you do not help us in this manner, nobody will.

And from a very different angle, a younger scientist from the West wrote of her first exposure to the developing world as follows:

I hope very much that this is but the first of a series of exchanges with your Foundation and that I shall be able in future to repay this kindness at least in part. Before the meeting I . . . was not sufficiently aware of the very real, though perhaps not always clearly expressed, value which the younger nations of the Commonwealth find in the Commonwealth connection. My experiences in Lusaka were certainly gratifying and I shall hope to offer some service to Commonwealth institutions in future.

A further last-minute initiative also deserves some mention. It relates to Anglo-Australian contacts in the seemingly unrelated fields of the law and sport and turns on the interest of the late Sir Robert Menzies in both fields. Following Menzies's death – and no one would dare question his role as a Commonwealth upholder – many of his friends began to ask themselves how best a practical memorial could be established in his name. Large sums were raised in Australia to promote legal research within the Commonwealth. But one subsidiary proposal, relating to medicine in sport, captured the imagination of the Foundation's trustees. They were thus persuaded to contribute towards an exchange bursary scheme in this field, the first fruits of which have happily been plucked on the eve of the Commonwealth Games at Brisbane in 1982. Funds have in short been provided to enable a British sports injury surgeon to visit Australia in the coming months and for an Australian doctor, a graduate of the University of Queensland, to work at the Institute of Sports Medicine in London.

This chapter has in short reviewed the Foundation's weaknesses and strengths. By the close of its third quinquennium 1966 already seems far distant. At that earlier date there were many cynics, pall-bearers from Westminster and Fleet Street not least among them, eager to attend the Commonwealth's funeral rites. Yet the Commonwealth had continued to confound its critics, overcoming the traumas of growth and indeed finding new strengths through growth itself. All too much is still awry. Even though well into its second decade the Commonwealth Foundation remains too restricted in its remit and in the funds available to it to be able to do more than give an occasional nudge in the right direction. But by the start of the 1980s it could be said that there had been one heartening and constant accompaniment to what trustees had to date achieved. That was the readiness of professionals throughout the Commonwealth to appreciate the value of co-operation and of the need for those more fortunately placed to help their newer colleagues. Whether as individuals in private practice, as qualified men and women scattered around the universities, government departments, research institutes, hospitals, schools, laboratories, farms or factories throughout the world, increasing numbers of them had come to realise the durable, practical value of the Commonwealth connection.

One might thus with some justification conclude that, had the Commonwealth Foundation not in 1966 been brought to life, then someone would by now have had to be commissioned to invent it. Its record, its growing cloud of witnesses and its actual and potential army of grant applicants suggest, even from one restricted angle, that the Commonwealth is still 'a very lively corpse'.

Thus, before turning to the wider issues of the significance of non-governmental organisations generally within the Commonwealth and of the Foundation's growing involvement with those of them lying beyond the strictly professional field, one is justified in concluding this general account of the Foundation itself with the thought that, to this day, the Commonwealth remains 'an association of peoples, of individuals who, at professional and other levels still have much in common: much to build on: much to conserve'.[6]

Even now I personally would share the conclusion reached by Bruce Miller at the close of his masterly, if often pessimistic, survey of the Commonwealth as it stood at the close of the 1960s. As he summarised his thoughts:

The Commonwealth of the 1970s would be one in which bodies such as the Secretariat and the Foundation strove to reinforce the non-political relations which drew Commonwealth members together. They would do so in full realization of political realities and through political means, since governments were the bodies through which co-operation would most obviously and readily be arranged . . . It would be an irony, but a reasonable and humane irony, if the Commonwealth and la Francophonie existed amicably side by side as primarily cultural bodies flourishing on what had been taught in the schools of Empire.[7]

Notes and References

1 'The Commonwealth Foundation, 1966–1980: a retrospection', *Round Table*, October 1980.
2 *The Kingston Communiqué*, May 1975.
3 *The London Communiqué*, June 1977.
4 *The Lusaka Communiqué*, August 1979.
5 Norman Tett and John Chadwick, *Professional Organizations in the Commonwealth*, 2nd edn. (London, 1976).
6 Commonwealth Foundation, *First Progress Report, 1967*.
7 J. D. B. Miller, *Survey of Commonwealth Affairs: Problems of Expansion and Attrition, 1959–1969* (London, 1974), p. 525.

PART III

The Unofficial Commonwealth Today

12

The Spirit of Dalhousie

> Voluntary organisations are independent organisations, both by inclination and constitution. The work of . . . any voluntary organisation is not conditioned by or dependent on the policies of the government in power . . . But a degree of interaction – some might call it creative friction – is inevitable and desirable.
>
> National Council for Voluntary
> Organisations (UK),
> Annual Report 1979/80

The introductory chapters to this book have in part described the extent to which the official Commonwealth, the visible portion of the iceberg, was supported by its larger underbelly – by those bodies which, in United Nations parlance, were now cumbrously described as 'non-governmental organisations' (NGOs). Some of these bodies, while operating from a British base, remained strictly Commonwealth inclined. But there were others whose creation had been inspired by the needs of the postwar world and which operated primarily in areas of relief, rehabilitation, natural disasters, population control and so forth on an international scale. Even so, and largely because of the British heritage, many of the latter were still in practice to concentrate the bulk of their endeavours on the newer countries of the Commonwealth.

To a considerable degree the creation of the Commonwealth Secretariat and Foundation, to which must be added the

173

catalytic efforts of the Royal Commonwealth Society, had by the early 1970s helped markedly to strengthen links between Commonwealth governments and their relevant voluntary societies. By the very nature of their work, officers of the former organisations were brought into increasingly close touch with the world of NGOs. Many of them were quick to realise that the latter were often better placed, and possessed greater on-the-spot experience, to carry out projects which had the support of officialdom but which officials themselves felt debarred from undertaking.

At the same time it had to be accepted that all was not sweetness and light, either between individual governments and their home-based voluntary bodies, or between ministers in developing countries and pan-Commonwealth or inter-nationally operating NGOs which sought to give advice and aid. Any honest civil servant will admit that news of an approaching NGO delegation would often create 'that sinking feeling'. Equally, the unbiased secretary of a voluntary society would (or should) privately confess to a tendency on the part of his council or committee to assume that it knew best. Such intellectual antagonism has been well described by the second Commonwealth Secretary-General, Sridath Ramphal as the 'adversary factor'. It was no novel situation, as students of the earlier relationship between church missionary societies and colonial administrations will readily recall. But it was a luxury which the postwar world could ill afford. Thus, towards the middle of the 1970s, the first serious efforts were made to break through such barriers of suspicion and to bring the official and unofficial sides together in the broader Common-wealth interest.

In small ways the Commonwealth Foundation had itself been working towards that goal. As an autonomous body it could indeed lay some claim to being the Commonwealth's 'leading NGO'. At least it had been instrumental in supporting or creating some twenty bodies entitled to describe themselves (and in some cases so to be recognised by the Economic and Social Council of the United Nations) as NGOs, namely the Commonwealth professional associations. The Commonwealth Secretariat too, through its youth, rural, social and women's programmes could be seen to be working towards closer and more practical links with the unofficial world.

As so often happens when ideas are in ferment, two apparently unrelated developments were to inspire a third and somewhat unexpected party to take the lead. Thus a one-day meeting on 'The Official and the Unofficial Commonwealth', convened in London by the Royal Commonwealth Society in June 1975, and a seminar sponsored by the Commonwealth Foundation that same year in Jamaica on links between professions, governments and universities within the Commonwealth were to pave the way for what later was to become known as the 'Spirit of Dalhousie'.

At the gateway to Canada, Dalhousie University could lay claim to being the oldest seat of higher learning in the whole of North America. Nova Scotia had always been outward-looking. Postwar developments had made Dalhousie itself even more Commonwealth-minded. The university had many students from developing countries on its campus and the staff had numerous contacts and projects in the newer world. It was from this quarter, with warm encouragement from the Government of Canada, that there tentatively emerged in the course of 1974 the idea of a major conference which would bring together officers of NGOs from all regions of the Commonwealth, together with a representative spread of delegates from various UN and official Commonwealth agencies, from other universities and from the media. The convener and general inspirer of this meeting, wholeheartedly supported by his then president, Senator Henry D. Hicks, was Professor Bala Pillay, head of the Department of History at Dalhousie. A naturalised Canadian citizen, whose early years had been lived as a Cape Coloured in South Africa, Pillay brought to his task that sense of conviction and enthusiasm without which the achievement of assembling, controlling and bringing to debate a highly disparate group of over sixty hand-picked delegates might well have failed.

As things turned out the five-day meeting, held at Dalhousie in the autumn of 1976, proved to be not only an inspiration to all those taking part but a notable stepping stone on the road to the closer involvement of Commonwealth governments with the comity of NGOs. As was later recorded in the con-

ference report, delegates had 'aimed at producing recommendations on closer co-operation within the unofficial Commonwealth, on the machinery for a continuing dialogue between
the official and the unofficial Commonwealth and on increasing
public understanding of the Commonwealth'.[1]

Papers presented to the meeting by a number of distinguished
contributors covered such subjects as the range and scope of
NGOs, economic and social development, professional work,
non-professional functional work, NGOs in the developing
Commonwealth, the media, education and the role of legislators.
Once these contributions had been debated in plenary session,
the conference divided into three commissions. Each accepted,
as a basis for submitting recommendations on the particular
subjects which it fell to them to examine, that the 'unofficial
Commonwealth' had already developed pragmatically in six
broad areas: namely,

(1) the professions, with the support of the Commonwealth
    Foundation,
(2) fields relating to development,
(3) public information and education,
(4) parliamentary government,
(5) the arts,
(6) sport.

The broad conclusions from the meeting were that, while
governments and their publics were still insufficiently informed
about NGOs in general, the latters' operations were both
economical and cost-effective. They were seen as fundamental
to the further utilisation of professional resources, relevant to
local needs in the development field and of great importance
to a better public understanding of the nature and achievements
of the Commonwealth. In short, 'the creative, flexible and
responsible capacity of NGOs needs to be more positively
recognised by Commonwealth Governments'.

The conference thus urged that further steps should be
taken by the official Commonwealth to stimulate and sustain
the growth of NGOs and to strengthen co-operation between
them. Such aims could largely be achieved by a better use of
existing Commonwealth machinery. As an autonomous

organisation the Commonwealth Foundation had, for instance, 'shown its ability to promote NGOs in the professional field and manifestly could be equally successful and economical in a wider sphere'. As regards the Commonwealth Secretariat, 'the development of closer collaboration and consultation with NGOs would fortify the growth in the relations already formed by its various departments'.

Such conclusions brought the Dalhousie meeting to recommend that Commonwealth heads of government should endorse a plan of action on the following lines:

- Issuing a declaration giving encouragement and continued support to the work of NGOs;
- Making possible at an early date the broadening of the scope – with the necessary increased income – of the Commonwealth Foundation to enable it to promote the development and to support the work of not only the professional associations, but other NGOs which have a contribution to make to Commonwealth objectives;
- Inviting the Commonwealth Secretary-General to promote collaboration with NGOs in functional activities related to the work of the Secretariat, especially in the areas of economic and social development, using CFTC funds as appropriate;
- Inviting the Commonwealth Secretary-General to make proposals for developing more fruitful consultative relationships between the Secretariat and Commonwealth NGOs;
- Making a fresh assessment of the Commonwealth's information, cultural and education programmes. In this regard, we suggest that the Secretariat should assemble relevant background papers – covering the official and unofficial Commonwealth – for consideration in detail by the senior officials' committee that meets concurrently with the Heads of Government Meeting;
- The suggestion that some 2 per cent to 3 per cent of official development assistance resources be directed through multi-lateral Commonwealth channels.

Finally, the conference urged the Commonwealth Secretary-General to support another meeting of NGOs in the course of 1978 so that further impetus could be given to these re-commendations.

Even though the suggestion that 2–3 per cent of additional development assistance resources should be directed to NGOs through multilateral channels was judged by some observers to be politically unrealistic, there was no doubting the significance of the Dalhousie meeting, a number of whose proposals were soon to be translated into action. Nor should future historians ignore the fact that this had been the first occasion on which a serious multinational effort had been made to bring the official and non-official sides of the Common-wealth together to explore possibilities for closer co-operation and to attempt to break down existing barriers of ignorance and animosity. As one of the deputy secretaries-general in the Commonwealth Secretariat summed up the basic dilemmas which the conference faced:

> Although government leaders have evidenced a stronger commitment and a deeper recognition of the Common-wealth potential, this has not been fully matched by similar perceptions on the part of the Commonwealth at large . . . A primary cause for this situation must be inadequate knowledge and appreciation of what today's Common-wealth is, what it stands for and what it seeks to do. While the Commonwealth has moved away from anglocentricity to a true multilateralism and thus has left the shadow of empire to become a community of sovereign and equal states, past memory and present ignorance have impeded wider recognition of its new role. As the people of the Commonwealth are the final arbiters of Commonwealth destiny, it is necessary that awareness of the modern Commonwealth should be made more pervasive. This is not a task for the Secretariat alone. It is a task for which should be enlisted the potential of non-governmental Commonwealth organisations to contribute to a wider understanding of the association and the development of the member states.[2]

It was left to Roy Manley, Secretary of the (British) National Social Science Council, itself affiliated to the International

Council on Social Welfare, to put some flesh on the statistics presented to the meeting on NGOs active in the Commonwealth. In a paper ranging from the value and significance of such organisations, internationally and at regional and national levels, to their numbers on the ground and the main areas within which they operated, Manley began by suggesting that NGOs could be 'pioneers, opinion formers, catalysts, co-ordinators or service agencies'. They could, he continued, 'supplement official action or . . . influence that action'. More radically, they could provide 'a lateral dimension to democracy'. While perhaps lacking the muscle of associations of employers and trade unions they were often asked to devote more time, resources and expertise to specific subjects of social concern. But, as Manley himself put it: 'the poorer countries of the Commonwealth may well regard those NGOs which criticise government policy as irritating and expensive luxuries. Even in the United Kingdom, where there is a long tradition of partnership between the public and private sectors the government is haphazard in its methods of consulting voluntary agencies'.

What in fact, as relating to the Commonwealth itself, did the spread and significance of such organisations amount to? Various guide books had attempted to list them: some writers on Commonwealth affairs had made arbitrary reference to a number of them. But on Manley's analysis (which predated a guide first published by the Commonwealth Secretariat in 1977 and to which later reference will be made), there were some one hundred recognised national, regional and Commonwealth NGOs. The only coherent group among them, as he saw it, was that of the professional associations which, while differing in aims and influence, had in common the 'furthering of their interests in a pan-Commonwealth context'. As he continued: 'It is appropriate here to acknowledge the unique contribution made by the Commonwealth Foundation to the development of these associations . . . In any discussion of Commonwealth NGOs the central role of the Foundation, which is itself an autonomous body and a legal charity, cannot be overestimated.'

From the Foundation's role in encouraging NGOs within the Commonwealth to that of the Commonwealth Secretariat itself was but a step and it was this short stride that took Manley on to more controversial ground. Having rightly referred to Sridath Ramphal's desire, expressed in a speech to the Royal Commonwealth Society on 24 June 1976, to build on the contributions which such bodies had already made to the official Commonwealth he went on to challenge the assumption that the relationship between the official and unofficial sides should remain unformalised.

The arguments in favour of the informal *status quo* were briefly that there would always be difficulty in identifying NGOs of true Commonwealth significance; that the Secretary-General's authority would be eroded if decisions as to what bodies he should or should not consult were taken out of his hands; and that political problems would arise if, as in the case of the United Nations, the Secretariat was to be empowered to confer formal consultative status on selected NGOs. Rebutting such objections, Manley proposed that the Secretary-General should be enabled, in consultation with, *inter alia*, the Commonwealth Foundation, to confer or withdraw 'Commonwealth consultative status' on or from an NGO. Those granted such status would have to be specifically related to some functional aspect of the Secretariat's work and should be authorised both to receive for comment papers touching on their fields of interest and to attend appropriate Commonwealth meetings as observers. Furthermore, biennial conferences should be held between officials of the Commonwealth Secretariat and of those Commonwealth NGOs to which consultative status had been granted.

While such propositions failed to find favour with the majority of delegates at Dalhousie, more was to be heard between 1977 and 1980 of the Manley arguments in favour of a formal Commonwealth status for deserving NGOs. Meanwhile the conference itself was overwhelmingly of the view that greater recognition of the unofficial Commonwealth by governments was urgently required. As two other paper-writers jointly put it in a discussion of the role of NGOs in economic and social development: 'By ignoring the NGOs, the people are ignored. By ignoring the people we ignore those whose consent is necessary if the transformation [of outdated economic relationships] is to take place without conflict.'[3]

While the authors of this paper expressed no opinion as to the status which NGOs should enjoy *vis-à-vis* Commonwealth governments, and indeed underlined the pride with which the former guarded their independence, they argued that such bodies could play a useful role for the Commonwealth as interpreters of current public attitudes, as a collective sounding board for new ideas and as channels of communication to a wider public. Admittedly, as many NGOs moved closer to the reality of poverty and came more critically to evaluate its causes and solutions, they might well be viewed by some in the official world as dangerous allies to have around. They would, indeed, be critical friends and would not 'sit happily in anybody's pocket' – the 'adversary factor' once again. Yet in the joint authors' view they were, for all that, 'a growing and significant force, whose resources and commitment have so far not been tapped by the Commonwealth to any significant extent'. Their efforts should indeed be recognised through the early creation, under the aegis of the Commonwealth Secretariat, of a special fund, similar to the CFTC, which would be geared to the promotion of project activities in the areas of social and economic development.

Many further examples were given at Dalhousie of the role which leading NGOs were or should be playing in furtherance of the Commonwealth concept and reality. Much, for instance, was said of contributions made by the Royal Commonwealth Society, the Association of Commonwealth Universities, the Commonwealth Parliamentary Association and Press Union, the Commonwealth Associations of Architects and of Surveyors and by the Commonwealth Human Ecology Council towards an improved public understanding of the Commonwealth in all its functional aspects. But, while sometimes verging on the euphoric, the mood of the conference was also tinged with regret for opportunities long since lost. Britain, for instance, was seen as having virtually abandoned all hope of discharging its national responsibility for informing its own public about the Commonwealth. The information programmes of the Commonwealth Secretariat were too slenderly financed to make any deep impact on public opinion overall. And, with a few notable exceptions, few governments had yet seized on the value to themselves and to their communities of working in harness with the unofficial Commonwealth. One was driven back to Sridath Ramphal's address to the Royal Commonwealth Society only a few months before the Dalhousie Conference opened. As he had then emphasised,

> Governments alone do not bear the burden of sustained commitment. The people of the Commonwealth are, in the last resort, the custodians of its future. Without their understanding of its contemporary reality, and their support for its dynamic character the capacity of governments to sustain that reality and to develop the potential of its dynamic will be severely diminished. This [Royal Commonwealth] Society, and the innumerable counterpart organs of the unofficial Commonwealth, have an immensely important contribution to make in enlarging the resources of public awareness of the realities of the contemporary Commonwealth and of commitment to its future.[4]

Clearly much remained to be done. But at long last, thanks to the promoters of the Dalhousie conference and to the support, both moral and financial, which they in turn had received from the Canadian government and from the trustees of the Commonwealth Foundation, the potential of NGOs within the Commonwealth had for once been frankly faced. By no means all the proposals aired would in the short term prove possible of achievement. Political obtuseness and financial constraints alone would temper the enthusiasm raised. But the 'Spirit of Dalhousie', diluted though it might be by suspicious politicians and their hard-headed acolytes in treasuries of the older and newer worlds alike, was now to haunt the scene. Even in May 1976, Commonwealth senior officials, meeting in Canberra to pave the way for a further heads of government conference due to be held in London in the summer of the year following, had shown some inkling of what was in the wind. An advance recommendation to their respective governments had indeed been that the report from Dalhousie should figure on the agenda for the London meeting.

However cautiously governments might in future move, one could only look back on Dalhousie as a breakthrough. It had still to be seen whether the inert counterforces of political suspicion and financial cynicism could be persuaded to go at least half-way to meet the unofficial world. For all that, the functional Commonwealth had at long last been openly recognised as a force to reckon with.

Notes and References

1 *The Commonwealth and Non-governmental Organisations*, report on the Dalhousie Conference, Halifax, Nova Scotia, October 1976.
2 Emeka Anyaoku, 'The Commonwealth Secretariat', *Dalhousie Report*.
3 P. Burns and H. Nangle, *Economic and Social Development*, paper presented at the Dalhousie Conference, 1976.
4 HE Mr S. S. Ramphal, Commonwealth Secretary-General, address to the Royal Commonwealth Society, 22 June 1976.

13

The Post-Dalhousie Scene

> The links between the official and the unofficial
> Commonwealth vary greatly: at one extreme
> N.G.O.s work entirely separately from govern-
> ments: at the other, funds and even administrative
> back-up come from governments, though in all
> cases the people are the 'doers'.
>
> Commonwealth Secretariat,
> 'Notes on the Commonwealth', 1980

One of the main recommendations from the Dalhousie
Conference had been that the Commonwealth Foundation's
mandate – and in consequence its income – should be expanded
to enable it to promote the activities of Commonwealth
NGOs lying outside the strictly professional field. Looking
ahead to the London conference of heads of government of
1977 the Foundation's trustees thus lost no time in preparing
a further detailed submission for that gathering. Once more
past achievements were listed and the case restated for a larger
annual income. For the first time reference was made to
prospective activities in the fields of culture, rural development,
the social sciences and to the particular role which women
could play in the two latter areas.

However, when senior officials met at the outset of the
London Conference in their so-called 'Committee of the
Whole', it at once became clear that the Foundation's star was
far from in the ascendant. By now inflation had bitten deep.
The problems of Southern Africa, the world economic order,

racialism in sport, competing initiatives relating to the expansion of the CFTC, regional economic co-operation and the extension of the Commonwealth youth programme all combined to thrust the modest financial ambitions of the Foundation to the bottom of the begging bowl. In any case, it was clear from the brief (and sadly mismanaged) discussions between officials, few if any of whom had had firsthand experience of the new spirit engendered at Dalhousie, that they had scant time to spare for a serious examination of the recommendations emerging from that meeting. Disappointing though the atmosphere was a Canadian proposal, first seen as a deflective tactic, that an advisory committee should be set up to examine and, as the final conference communiqué put it, to 'report on concrete steps to promote mutually beneficial ties between the official and unofficial Commonwealth',[1] turned out to be a blessing in disguise. Certainly the Foundation's short-term hopes were dashed in that no firm decisions were taken at the London Conference. But since heads of state duly instructed the Commonwealth Secretary-General to establish the proposed committee, there was at least some hope that a thorough survey, involving officials, of the role of NGOs within the Commonwealth would now be set in train.

Like the Foundation itself the 'Advisory Committee on relationships between the Official and Unofficial Commonwealth', to give it its full title, proved to be a somewhat unique body. As its eventual report,[2] forwarded to heads of government through the Commonwealth Secretary-General, made clear, the membership had been made up of fourteen individuals drawn both from governments and from non-governmental organisations. All were so selected, in a strictly personal capacity, as to ensure adequate representation of different regions and interests of the Commonwealth. Thus, under the chairmanship of Sir Geoffrey Wilson, KCMG, Chairman of OXFAM and previously Permanent Secretary of the Ministry of Overseas Development and, for a brief while, one of the Deputy Secretaries-General of the Commonwealth Secretariat itself, the members of the committee were drawn from Australia, Barbados, Britain, Canada, Ghana, India, Jamaica, Malaysia, Nigeria, Western Samoa and Zambia. Only in two cases

(Ghana and Zambia) were governments directly represented, through their present or former high commissioners in London. Other members contributed their experience through such disparate organisations as the World Council of Churches, the University of the South Pacific, the Commonwealth professional associations concerned with architecture, surveying and nursing, the Royal Commonwealth Society, the Professional Centre of Malaysia and – bridging the official and unofficial worlds – the Canadian International Development Agency and the Federal Liberal Party of Australia. One odd man out, as representative of a leading foundation elsewhere in the Commonwealth – and a most welcome one – was the Director of the Tata Endowment of India. The committee met twice in London; between 9 and 13 January and 10 and 14 July 1978. On each occasion the Commonwealth Secretariat and Foundation were represented and submitted evidence.

What, as the chairman and members of the committee asked themselves at their opening session, was 'the nature of the unofficial Commonwealth'? To this question they found no real or tidy answer. There were indeed many thousands of NGOs at work nationally, regionally or on a world-wide basis. They varied greatly in geographical scope, organisational structure and type of activity. On the other hand, all had some obvious points in common. Each was a non-profit-making body, capable of acting independently of governments. As such they could be loosely described as voluntary agencies, both secular and religious, as institutions for research and higher education, as professional associations, or indeed as any other uncategorised bodies whose aim it was to promote public information and education on issues relevant to the contemporary Commonwealth. Put more briefly, as the rapporteurs to the Dalhousie conference had expressed it, the unofficial Commonwealth could be described as 'the totality of non-governmental relations among the peoples of the Commonwealth'.

But if, as the committee itself soon recognised, its members were to report to governments within a reasonable time-scale, then some further restrictions on its own parameters would have to be devised. Thus, for practical purposes, the committee decided to limit its examination of the unofficial Commonwealth 'to those NGOs which could be seen to be contributing towards the quality of life and international understanding within the Commonwealth through for example, their help towards the development process, the eradication of poverty, the improvement of health, the creation of employment, the promotion of education, the dissemination of information, the furtherance of professional and technical know-how, and the encouragement of cultural and sporting links'.

This alone was a sufficiently daunting remit. But the committee had also to accept that the existing network of relationships between the official and unofficial sides was complex in itself. While national NGOs tended naturally to relate to the governments of the countries in which they operated, and those regional in character to establish their closest links with appropriate official regional agencies, pan-Commonwealth and internationally operating NGOs had a more complicated relationship with the official world. They tended to be in contact not only with the Commonwealth Secretariat or Foundation (or both) but also with the governments of all those countries in which they worked. The latter in turn found themselves in contact not only with their own national NGOs but also with those of a pan-Commonwealth, international and regional character. Such complex relationships, combined with the diversity among Commonwealth NGOs themselves in geographical spread, numbers and breadth of activity, naturally hampered Commonwealth-wide co-ordination and served to reduce the impact of the unofficial on the official world.

Although, as one member of the Committee saw the overall picture, some NGOs had shown 'neither the ability nor the inclination to adapt to the needs and circumstances of the modern Commonwealth', the broad conclusion was that the combined efforts and resources of NGOs represented 'a massive human and financial capital which can be invested to the mutual advantage of both official and unofficial sectors and more importantly, to the benefit of the peoples of the Commonwealth who make up a quarter of the world's population'. In short the unofficial Commonwealth, which had grown at random in response to the need for co-operative action in many fields, was seen to provide 'a network of human contacts, a bank of expertise and an independence of action which can complement official policies and programmes'.

At the same time, wise in their ways from past experience, some committee members were quick to note that that independence of action by NGOs must, if conflicts were to be avoided, take full account of the sovereign rights of governments. If the latter, in so far as they were guilty of lack of understanding, could help to overcome the adversary factor, then they would often find the unofficial world in a position to mobilise expert support and assistance on a much wider and more cost-effective basis than official agencies and to act quickly to meet urgent needs. Lack of funds would of course always remain a handicap. Indeed, as the committee's report emphasised, the relative strength and coherence of the Commonwealth professional associations had resulted largely from the extent of financial support offered by the Commonwealth Foundation. But finance was not the sole criterion of success. The unofficial network, already widespread, could be strengthened not merely by reliance on governments but through closer links and improved co-operation between the NGOs of the Commonwealth themselves.

Having thus set the stage, the committee next considered what further steps the official Commonwealth could take to improve relations with its NGOs. Its first conclusion was that communications between governments and the unofficial side were still inadequate. Thus official Commonwealth bodies at all levels, national, international and regional, should make 'a conscious drive to establish regular exchanges with the unofficial sectors'. One positive step in that direction might be a decision (often adumbrated in earlier years) by each Commonwealth government which had not already done so to create 'a specific unit or liaison centre for the purposes of establishing and maintaining contact with national NGOs, channelling information to them on appropriate government plans and material to official bodies on activities of relevant NGOs'. Recognising that the maintenance of the integrity of personality of NGOs was essential to a healthy society, the report further invited governments to think of including NGO representatives in their delegations to ministerial meetings and (controversially indeed) to those of heads of government themselves. By the same token the Commonwealth Secretariat might encourage official consultative bodies, such as the Commonwealth Education Liaison Committee, to invite NGO representatives to attend their meetings as observers. From this point it was only logical that the committee should move on to recommend that the Commonwealth Secretariat and Foundation, building on past performance, should hold regular consultations with NGOs, exchanging information and discussing matters of common concern. What had not been foreseen – and it was a proposal which at once caused misgivings iu the minds of Foundation staff and in those of many of its clients – was a further recommendation from the committee aimed at giving the Commonwealth Secretariat a more positive role in the official/unofficial relationship. On that issue the relevant passage from the report read as follows: 'To this end we recommend the setting up of an n.g.o. desk within the Secretariat. This would be initially for a trial period of three years. The desk would serve as a central point of contact with Commonwealth n.g.o. liaison units/centres that may be nominated by member governments.' As an annex to the committee's report, the Commonwealth Secretariat in fact presented a 'draft job description for officer in charge of the n.g.o. desk'. Among the tasks foreseen for this new, relatively senior staff member were the setting up of an information bank on the aims and activities of NGOs; close liaison with the Commonwealth Foundation; the preparation of a handbook on Commonwealth NGOs; and the co-ordination of advice to NGOs on development project activities through the relevant divisions of the secretariat. How and why such a proposal came eventually to grief will be described later in this chapter.

Meanwhile, turning from the role of the Secretariat to that of the Foundation, the committee recalled a suggestion in the final communiqué from the heads of government conference, 1977, that, given the Foundation's proven value in the professional field 'there might be further specific areas in which, in close consultation with non-governmental bodies, it could usefully be active on a regional or Commonwealth-wide basis'. In the light of the Foundation's work over the past twelve years the conclusion was that it should be encouraged to

189

extend its activities and that such expansion would not result
in any risk of the Foundation duplicating the work of the
Commonwealth Secretariat, and in particular of CFTC.

As to new areas into which the Foundation might now move,
the committee, with some slight misunderstanding of the work
on which that body was already engaged, recommended:

That the Foundation's mandate should be expanded so
that its Trustees may, subject to a continuing review of
priorities, embark on co-operative projects with a greater
range of NGOs. Initially we propose that the Foundation
might provide assistance in the following areas:

(i) Culture, Information and the Media: With particular
reference to the creation of Commonwealth-wide
associations for the arts; for practising journalists; and
in respect of films and broadcasting, as relating to
the more effective spread of knowledge about the
Commonwealth;

(ii) Social Welfare and the Handicapped, relating
particularly to NGOs of a voluntary rather than a
strictly professional character, which are concerned
with the improvement of the quality of life. Examples
submitted to us relate to the work of such Commonwealth-wide and regional bodies as those operating
in areas of blindness, deafness, the crippled, etc;

(iii) Rural Development, involving co-operation with
NGOs, universities, research centres, etc., turning on
such problems as the creation at village level of cottage
industries, and the transfer of appropriate agricultural
technology;

(iv) The Role of Women: The Foundation could usefully
support, through relevant NGOs, the contribution
that women can make.

In practice, the Foundation's trustees had for some time
been involved in support of the media and with aspects of
rural development. But, as their representative on the Committee, I saw some tactical advantage in allowing this particular
recommendation to go forward unabridged. On the other

hand I was less happy at my failure to persuade the chairman of the committee and his colleagues to make any firm recommendation as to the increased annual income which the Foundation would require, if its broadened mandate were eventually to be approved by heads of government. The furthest the committee would go was to recognise that 'if the Foundation is to receive the expanded mandate ... some substantial increase in its current annual income of £670,000 will be required. *In the view of the Foundation* a sum of the order of £200,000 would be needed ...'.

Despite that minor disappointment the report from the Advisory Committee was an encouragement to the Commonwealth Foundation and more importantly a challenge, albeit of small dimensions, to the official Commonwealth itself. Some account of the recommendations would clearly have to be taken by heads of government when next they met at Lusaka in the summer of 1979. Meanwhile one further effort would have to be made, at the now traditional meeting of senior officials preparatory to that conference, to persuade them to give a fair wind to the Wilson Committee report. The Foundation's trustees thus accepted that I should attend the meeting of officials, to be held on this occasion at Kuala Lumpur in November 1978, there to plead the further detailed financial case on which they had meanwhile agreed.

The Kuala Lumpur meeting proved to be the first occasion on which Commonwealth officials gave detailed and sympathetic attention not only to the importance of NGOs in general but to the role which, among others, the Foundation could play on their behalf. Opening the discussion on the report from the Advisory Committee Sridath Ramphal spoke warmly of the Foundation's efforts urging that, of all the committee's recommendations, priority should be given to that calling for an expanded mandate and for increased financial support. Invited to comment I referred to the growing cash-flow problems which the Foundation faced and to the fact that it had been thanks only to careful housekeeping in the early years that trustees still found it possible to respond to the most deserving among the growing calls upon their funds. If, as had been proposed, yet more responsibilities were to be placed on the shoulders of trustees, then more money must be found. Should that be agreed, then the Foundation might in the first place expand its work into the area of the arts and in support of a new pan-Commonwealth association geared to the training and education of journalists. On the Advisory Committee's more controversial proposal for the creation of an 'n.g.o. desk' within the Commonwealth Secretariat, I remained discreetly silent. But, as discussion developed, it became clear that this was, symbolically, to prove the dominant issue. As some insiders had from the first foreseen it was starkly to emphasise the conflict between those governments which respected (even if not always approving of) the complete autonomy of their national NGOs and those which, while appreciating their intentions, wished none the less to keep such activities under close control. In short, the 'adversary factor' was to the fore once more.

The cleavage of opinion was in almost all respects between the older and newer Commonwealth and the football, so to speak, the NGO desk itself. In favour of that proposition it was argued that a desk, located in the Commonwealth Secretariat, would greatly improve liaison between the official and the unofficial worlds. Even so, the post should be created on an experimental basis only and must prove its cost-effectiveness before it could be accepted as a permanent addition to the Secretariat machine.

Arguments against the desk, and by inference against any attempt to formalise links between Commonwealth governments and NGOs, whether nationally or internationally based, were however overwhelming. First, its opponents pointed to the additional and, in their view unnecessary, costs involved. Second, much antipathy was expressed at the idea of the Commonwealth Secretariat aping the behaviour of the United Nations by seeking to expand its operations into virtually every sphere of human activity. Third, there was considerable aversion to the implied 'bureaucratisation' of relationships between the official and the unofficial Commonwealth which the creation of such a desk would bring about. The fear was also expressed that, as and if such a recommendation were approved and NGOs were thereby assured of formal recognition, the unofficial world would then as of right demand an even fuller range of governmental services. NGOs would better flourish if allowed to develop on their own. By their very nature they operated most successfully when governments kept their distance. It would thus be unwise for the Secretariat to attempt to organise the unofficial Commonwealth or to monitor its activities. To sum up, the task of gathering and circulating information on NGOs active in the Commonwealth could as well be performed by the Commonwealth Foundation, whose role as a link between the official and unofficial worlds was highly commended by the meeting, as through the creation of new machinery at Marlborough House.

Given the weight of opinion against the creation of a desk within the Commonwealth Secretariat, it was not surprising that the majority of senior officials should also look with a jaundiced eye on a further suggestion from the Advisory Committee that greater efforts should be made by governments to attach NGOs to their official delegations to Commonwealth conferences. As one delegate put it, voluntary organisations tended to be highly protective of their own interests. Thus if a church synod frowned on the idea of the government of its country being invited to attend its proceedings, why should the government in turn invite members of that synod to be represented on its delegation to a Commonwealth meeting? Each government must of course have freedom to decide its own course of action. But, as proved to be the consensus on this issue, any blanket ruling in favour of the automatic admission of NGO representatives to meetings at the higher official level – let alone to those of heads of government themselves – would run counter to the intimate way in which the official Commonwealth conducted its own affairs.

As to the future of the Foundation itself, which one official was kind enough to describe as 'a spectacular success', the conclusion from the Kuala Lumpur meeting was that governments and their professions had benefited from its activities. A convincing case for an increased income had been made. Subject to heads of government being supplied with a more detailed analysis of the costs involved in expanding its mandate, it should in time develop into an even more 'essential element in the Commonwealth fabric'.

To sum up: if the debate at Kuala Lumpur on the unofficial Commonwealth had brought home one truth, it was that the 'adversary factor' still prevailed. Some governments, notably those in the older world, had as a matter of policy long since involved their NGOs at important stages of national programme development. They appreciated the freshness of approach and enthusiasm which NGOs could offer. Other governments, however, still held attitudes ranging from benign indifference through suspicion to outright hostility. But there was perhaps one bloc of pan-Commonwealth NGOs – the professional associations fostered by the Commonwealth Foundation – which had by now won the support of all. While, therefore, it might be premature to press the case for an NGO desk in the Secretariat, and thus for the formalisation of links between the official and unofficial Commonwealth it might, failing any such UN-type solution, be assumed that the Foundation was by now serving as a bridge between the NGO world and those governments whose views on the unofficial Commonwealth were still otherwise so sharply apprehensive.

In narrower terms there remained for the Foundation trustees 'one more river to cross' – not Jordan but Lusaka 1979. Once more papers to heads of government had to be prepared, analysing the Foundation's financial needs. Thus once again – and finally – I set forth to wait on the fringes of my last Commonwealth summit conference (not one of which, in one backroom capacity or another, I had missed since 1956).

Lusaka, of course, was dominated by the Zimbabwe issue. While fringemen such as I were privileged to attend the opening plenary session of the conference and to witness the British Prime Minister's dramatic and heartening U-turn, the security screws were later tightened even more effectively than in the past. Previously approachable heads of government met continuously in restricted session or, when not thus engaged, were either ensconced in some unapproachable inner sanctum of the meeting complex or whisked away to their nearby 'top peoples' village'. Meanwhile the official 'Committee of the Whole', somewhat easier of access, was day by day predigesting a number of the less glamorous items on the conference agenda. It was before this body that I was in due time bidden to appear to argue the Foundation's financial case, which by now had all the makings of a hardy biennial.

Trustees and staff had thought long and anxiously on a presentation to heads of government which would be crucial to the Foundation's mid-term future. Should advantage be taken of the favourable attitude of the Advisory Committee towards its efforts, to the point of seeking a truly substantial increase in the annual income? Or, given the many other claims on Commonwealth governments at a time of deepening recession, should modesty prevail? In the upshot the chairman and board decided on a middle course, retreating from an earlier target figure of £1.75 million per annum to one of £1.1 million. That latter sum they justified with an account of the Foundation's growing workload, its successful and cost-effective ventures in many fields, and by a detailed analysis of the additional expenditure involved in embarking on a widened remit. Their paper ended with an invitation to heads of government to reaffirm their support and encouragement for the Foundation in its efforts to promote and expand the activities of professions and professional bodies throughout the Commonwealth; to take account of the inroads made since 1976 by inflation on its current income, and to agree to the proposed broadening of its mandate.

Events proved trustees to have been right in their approach. My defence of their submission met with a sympathetic reaction from the 'Committee of the Whole'. Only one representative announced the inability of his government to subscribe one penny more to the Foundation's annual income (and this on political rather than financial grounds). The proposed new figure of £1.1 million per annum was accepted as reasonable, even if unlikely to be attained during the financial year on which most governments were by then embarked, while pledges of principle for future years were uttered by a number of those present. Considerable praise for the Foundation's work and for its good husbandry was expressed. I thus withdrew with the feeling that little further would be achieved by sitting on the sidelines until the last moments of the conference when Heads of Government would doubtless do no other, in a few rushed moments, than endorse the conclusions of their officials. In consequence I left Zambia for Kenya overnight, there to spend a few nostalgic days of farewell to one of the Foundation's most promising ventures, the Professional Centre of Nairobi.

Only on returning to London did I learn that, on the last morning of the Lusaka conference its chairman, Dr Kaunda, had summoned the Foundation Director to appear before the meeting to receive congratulations and good wishes on his impending retirement. It was a heartening gesture and a small experience missed. The more lasting satisfaction, however, was that of demitting office to the accompaniment of a heads of government communiqué which not only 'commended the cost-effectiveness and imaginative work of the Commonwealth Foundation', but also in principle accepted both its claim to the higher income sought and a sizeable expansion of its fields of operation.

Even though, by the close of 1980, that revised but still highly modest income had still to be achieved, it was a happy enough note on which to bid farewell.

Notes and References

1 Commonwealth Heads of Government Conference, London 1977, *Final Communiqué*.
2 *From Governments to Grassroots*, report of the Advisory Committee, Commonwealth Secretariat, July 1978.

14

The Arts, Youth and Voluntary Endeavour

> To avoid the risk of duplication with the activities
> of existing organisations concerned with cultural
> activities ... the Foundation should not initially
> seek to assume any functions in these fields.
> Agreed Memorandum, 1965

It was in March 1980, when I was coming to the close of a
final Commonwealth journey, that a group of trustees met in
London to interview short-listed candidates to succeed me as
Director of the Commonwealth Foundation. The post had
been widely canvassed through government channels, one
obvious understanding being that the successful candidate
could hardly come from Britain.

Considering the financial attractions of the appointment to
an incumbent from overseas, the response proved disappointingly small. But the few individuals invited to appear before
the selection committee, even though representing bureaucracies
to the exclusion of the private sector, were of high calibre.
With little hesitation, the trustees agreed to offer the appointment to a senior Australian diplomat, Ric Throssell, who was
at that time head of the Cultural Relations Branch of the
Department of Foreign Affairs in Canberra. Among his other
attainments, Throssell was a playwright and biographer. At a
time when the Foundation's involvement with the arts was
in the ascendant, the choice proved particularly apt.

197

Throssell duly accepted the appointment and, over the first fortnight of July, 1980, he and I enjoyed a harmonious transfer of both files and responsibilities.

As my successor was rapidly to find, he had entered on a somewhat challenging inheritance. The outcome of one full-scale evaluation of a major sector of the Foundation's activities to date had still to be digested. Others, relating to the future of professional centres, to a wide range of bursary schemes and publication programmes, were yet to be undertaken. Above all the financial future was obscure. To these quite daunting problems the new director would now have to add his own assessment of how and to what extent the trustees could reasonably involve themselves in cultural affairs and, as had been suggested at the Zambia Heads of Government Conference, in the activities of voluntary bodies falling outside the professional field.

It would be improper for me to comment on the conduct of Foundation business following my own departure from the scene. Indeed, all I can do is express my admiration for the speed and efficiency with which my successor mastered his numerous briefs and launched on the task of further evaluations. Among other achievements, he must be congratulated on having persuaded the trustees to add to the staff a Project Officer, Geoff Randal from New Zealand, who was clearly to fill a much felt gap.

But if comment from the departed might be seen as wanting in taste, I still feel at liberty to offer some reflections on the problems facing the Foundation in the cultural and allied fields at the time of my own retirement.

As has been mentioned in earlier chapters the trustees had already, at some slight risk of acting *ultra vires*, involved themselves in sporadic support of certain cultural activities. The Association for Commonwealth Literature and Language Studies had been one case in point. Another had been the role of the Foundation in promoting attendance from the developing Commonwealth of teams of performing artists who were to play so spectacular a part in the Carnival organised in parallel to the Commonwealth Games at Edmonton in 1978. In addition, a few small grants had been made to struggling theatre groups and, in one unusual case, to a gymnasium in south India where promoters of the ancient martial arts of Kerala were struggling to keep alive both the ethos of physical fitness and the ayurvedic treatment of broken bones and sprains. Token encouragement here was to lead indirectly to an invitation to a remarkable team of these 'dancer-warriors' to perform in 1980 at the Hong Kong Arts Festival, where both critics and public greeted them with rapturous applause. Until then the martial arts of Kerala had been barely known outside the state itself.

But it was above all the impact made by the dancers, singers, jugglers, musicians, painters, photographers and players at Edmonton which was to lead to a groundswell in favour of creating some permanent organisation through which the wealth of artistic talent throughout the Commonwealth could be better brought to public light and fostered. Thus, under the inspiration of the Commonwealth Arts Association, a London-based body on which Commonwealth artists living in Britain were represented, its members met at Edmonton with representatives of the Canadian Games Foundation, of the Government of Alberta which had so generously supported the 1978 Carnival and with delegates present from the Royal Commonwealth Society, the Commonwealth Institute and the Foundation.

There was no doubting the enthusiasm aroused at the thought of creating one overall controlling body through which, hopefully, exchange visits of artistic groups and individuals and of exhibitions could be organised and through which much-needed funds could be channelled for such purposes. But with so many conflicting interests at stake and so many prima donnas eager to promote the (to them) paramount interest of their own particular contribution to the world of culture the meetings were, to say the least, lively. Those like the Foundation trustee for Britain and I, who were called on to chair sessions of the conference, were often hard put to it to keep the peace or to prevail on many of those present to accept that the creation of a new organisation representative (as the existing Commonwealth Arts Association could not hope to be) of the interests of each and every Commonwealth country, would not automatically bring in its wake a ceaseless stream of silver.

Eventually, and not without some bitter rivalries left unappeased, it was decided at Edmonton to create a Commonwealth Arts Organisation (CAO), whose first chairman would be the distinguished Jamaican artist, the Hon. Rex Nettleford, OM and its first Secretary-General the Cultural Attaché at the Cyprus High Commission in London – and an eminent photographer to boot – George Lanitis. At the invitation of the Director of the Commonwealth Institute in London, James Porter, who had done much behind the scenes to bring the organisation to birth, it was decided to set up its secretariat temporarily at the institute's Kensington headquarters.

It was thanks largely to these developments that Commonwealth governments took their decision at the Lusaka conference of 1979 to include cultural activities within the Foundation's remit. This enabled the trustees both to make a small launching grant to cover the Arts Organisation's immediate administrative needs and, in timely fashion, to offer more substantial support for regional attendance at a Commonwealth Pacific Arts Festival which took place with marked success in Fiji late in 1980.

But, with the scant funds available, it was soon clear to the Foundation's trustees that there could be no open-ended commitment to the CAO, let alone to the arts in general. Thus one of the first tasks falling on the new director was to suggest to the board within what limits and in which areas it could best apply its expanded powers.

A policy paper presented to trustees at the close of 1980 started from a brief recital of projects supported in the cultural field since heads of government had met at Lusaka. Modest though the allocation of funds had been, it is interesting to note what a wide field they covered. To take a few examples: a Tanzanian artist had been helped to attend an Indian Ocean Festival of the Arts at Perth, Western Australia (a fine if minor example of cultural cross-fertilisation); representatives from Mysore, Banares, Malta and from the Africa Centre, London, had attended a Fiji-based conference of the Association for Commonwealth Literature. Funds had been provided for Commonwealth attendance at both a photography exhibition in Cyprus and at a traditional African drumming and dancing festival in Ghana. More substantial support had gone towards the promotion of *Arts Links*, a lively quarterly review published under the imprint of the London-based Commonwealth Arts Association. That journal's editorial opinion of the newly formed Commonwealth Arts Organisation was incidentally to suggest that culture could spark off controversy of no mean order.

Yet such disparate examples of what could be done served only to highlight the need for the Foundation to concentrate such funds as it could spare on projects likely to bring about a wider understanding of Commonwealth cultures, above all perhaps through education and the media. Desirable though world-wide and regional festivals might be, funds for attendance at such costly undertakings would generally have to be found from other sources. Nor did it seem likely that the trustees would be able further to support the somewhat grandiose administrative and programme ambitions of the new Arts Organisation.

By the close of 1980 the board had indeed endorsed new objectives as a guide to the further development of the Foundation's cultural activities. They were in brief aimed at providing stimulus and support for the introduction of the traditional and contemporary culture of Third World countries to more developed areas of the Commonwealth; to assist cultural exchanges between developing countries; to promote wider recognition and understanding of the indigenous cultures of more developed Commonwealth countries; and to provide limited support for the distinctive national cultures of the developed Commonwealth, in special cases, when other sources of aid were unavailable.

From this it followed that there must clearly be areas on which the Foundation could not, for the time being at least, embark, if only for want of funds. These would be likely to include the financing of travelling exhibitions and of strictly national arts organisations; routine cultural visits, or support for non-governmental bodies involved in promoting cultural activities among national ethnic minorities. Even less would help be envisaged towards the financing of national arts centres; extensive tours by performing groups, the commissioning of works of art or the subsidising of courses on behalf of individual students. As to the Commonwealth Arts

Organisation, that body would have to make its own case to heads of government at the Melbourne Conference late in 1981.

The broad concerns of youth had been another area of Commonwealth co-operation in which I personally would have wished to see the Foundation playing some role, however minor. That ugly phrase 'the younger element' did indeed find a place in the Agreed Memorandum of 1966 when trustees had, quite rightly, been urged to pay particular attention to the claims on their funds of young as opposed to well-established professionals. What I had had in mind was that the definition of 'young professionals' should be elastically interpreted and that the trustees should look for ways of collaborating with the lively Commonwealth Youth Exchange Council. This body, had, since 1968, worked in close co-operation with the Royal Commonwealth Society and other voluntary agencies. As its founder and chairman, Professor David Dilks, was to say in an address to the Royal Society of Arts in 1973,[1] the aims of the council had by then attracted the interest and financial support of both the British Council and of the Rhodes Trust. British government departments, local education authorities and such voluntary bodies as the English Speaking Union, the Standing Conference of National Voluntary Youth Organisations and the Central Bureau for Educational Visits and Exchanges also supported its endeavours.

As Dilks put it in his address: 'The CYEC ... discharges a whole range of functions. We organise or co-ordinate some exchanges on our own account. We have just said goodbye to a group of Zambian boys from Lusaka, we shall soon be receiving a group of girls from India ... and we shall as usual be responsible for this summer's official sponsored exchanges between Britain and Canada.' But, as he was at pains to add (and here comes the rub), 'the CYEC is careful not to pretend to speak as a Commonwealth-wide body. Its constituents are all British based ... the guide lines agreed between CYEC and the British Council distinguish exchanges of young workers, young agriculturists, young professionals and executives, students, youth leaders, the young disabled and hearing-impaired – and sports exchanges, cultural exchanges and voluntary special service – as broad categories into which assisted projects are likely to fall.' Thus, taking a few examples at random, physically handicapped young people had exchanged between Malta and the Borough of Lambeth; two Jamaicans had been financed to work in Liverpool community centres and there had been exchange visits between young farmers, youth club workers, sportsmen, and musicians.

Here, perhaps, lay the roots of the problem. First, was all such enthusiasm worthwhile and likely to produce lasting effects? If so, given the vast field to be covered, should it all be left to strictly voluntary endeavour? Or should youth exchanges be 'bureaucratised'? Secondly, who would come forward to finance such ventures? And thirdly, was 'youth' to be defined solely as young people in their own right – that is, unqualified individuals under some arbitrary age limit? Or was that definition to embrace young professionals and technicians or, even more to the point, those professionals and technicians involved with youth problems, for example, community officers, social workers, sports trainers, the police, probation officers and the like?

It was here perhaps that the CYEC became cramped by its own Achilles heels: those of financial insufficiency and of a strictly British as opposed to a Commonwealth-supported base. The funds available to the council were, in fact, ludicrously small, reflecting as they did the official lack of enthusiasm in Britain at that time (and later) for all things of the Commonwealth. Less than £30,000 was, in fact, made available in 1973 from British sources to cover the cost of youth exchanges involving 32 independent countries and dependent territories of the Commonwealth. Small wonder then that this admirably intentioned body was to retreat into the shadows when, at a meeting convened under Commonwealth Secretariat auspices at Lusaka in that same year of Commonwealth Ministers concerned with youth, it was decided to set up a Commonwealth Youth Programme with a launching three-year budget of well over £1 million.

That action, of course, virtually pre-empted any attempt by the Foundation to come to the support of CYEC. At the same time, the Secretariat's initiative gave a much needed and truly Commonwealth-based impetus to youth programmes in general, including awards for team as opposed to individual endeavour, exchanges of personnel between Third World countries and studies of youth unemployment problems. Unhappily, initial enthusiasm did not long survive the advent of bureaucratic control and the Commonwealth Youth Programme now justifies some, at least, of the criticism levelled at it for its administrative costs as against the practical results achieved.

Meanwhile voluntary endeavour continues, more often than not unpublicised. The Royal Commonwealth Society's CISGO operation is one such excellent example. Those of the Commonwealth Foundation itself in growing support of young professionals and medical students cannot be ignored. Nor should one forget the innumerable voluntary agencies which, frequently supported by airlines, banks, commerce and industry, make Commonwealth youth interchanges cheaper and more flexible than one would have dared to hope only two decades past.

What could be said of support for other forms of voluntary endeavour lying beyond the strictly professional field? Frankly there has been little of substance to record to date.

Certainly some effort was made by trustees from 1975 onwards to assist within that artificially defined area, 'the role of women' – artificial in my view at least in that in this age of his and hers women are active in their own right almost everywhere. (One has only to visit an African or West Indian market to appreciate which sex heads the entrepreneurial league.) However, some small efforts were made to promote women's voluntary organisations. Grants were thus sanctioned from time to time, particularly in the Caribbean area, to promote conferences of women university graduates and of those involved in service to the handicapped. But generally, and as it rightly should be, the claims of women for a travel or study award were to turn on individual merit rather than on some mysterious need to treat a woman applicant as a special case. In short, trustees found no need to differentiate between the sexes.

A few other examples of aid in the non-professional field have covered such varying activities as support to the Royal Commonwealth Society to keep its magazine *Commonwealth* afloat; study grants to technicians who, unable to afford a college education in their youth, had later acquired their skills 'in-house'; or a small range of directors' discretionary awards, generally of a topping-up nature, to promote worthwhile links in areas of research which would not normally have qualified in Foundation terms as forms of professional activity.

The fact that so little can be said of the trustees' involvement with voluntary bodies and with those working for them serves only to highlight the continuing need for the Foundation to concentrate scarce resources on its major task – that of promoting professional co-operation.

Notes and References

1 Paper delivered to the Commonwealth Section of the Royal Society of Arts in March 1973.

15

Conclusions

> Knowledge is power. Authority without knowledge
> is powerless. Power disassociated from knowledge
> is a revolutionary force. Unless the modern world
> works out a satisfactory relationship between expert
> knowledge and popular control the days of
> democracy are numbered.
>
> A. Zimmern, *Learning and Leadership*, 1928

In this book I have tried to trace the conception, birth pangs, growth and eventual blossoming of a small international organisation and to place the Foundation within the broader context of the unofficial Commonwealth. In no sense could this be described as a definitive history. The Commonwealth Foundation is still far too young and too experimental in its aims to merit such a claim. On the other hand, small and relatively unnoticed though its resources are, its birth and development do offer to the student of Commonwealth affairs the case history of a functional experiment and an example of the informal way in which the day-to-day business of the Commonwealth is done: often pragmatically, more often than not unpublicised.

Lusaka of course was but a further step along the road, though one important to those working for or associated with the Foundation. Funding would remain a problem, doubtless for years to come. Even the Commonwealth Secretariat, with its far greater persuasive powers with governments and its much vaster responsibilities, had at Lusaka felt the cold breath of recession. Yet it could be claimed that heads of government had at last taken official note of the richness and diversity of experience which the unofficial Commonwealth could place at their disposal. Even if links were not in the foreseeable future to be formalised through the creation of an NGO desk, the Lusaka communiqué had recognised that NGOs active in the Commonwealth, regarding which the Commonwealth Secretariat had recently issued a useful handbook,[1] were 'an under-utilised resource'. Governments and official Commonwealth bodies at all levels had been urged to make greater use of their energies and expertise. The special role of women in Commonwealth development; the reference to the Commonwealth's pressing communication and media problems, including 'the desirability of expanding media exchanges' through a voluntarily funded programme, in the co-ordination of which both the Commonwealth Secretariat and Foundation might find some role to play, all pointed to the growing responsibilities of the 'unofficial' Commonwealth.

Thus, whether or not its income materially increased, it was now clear that the 1980s would prove a busy and testing decade for the Foundation's board. Already the staff was being brought face to face with the myriad problems of the arts within the Commonwealth, and with the needs of other organisations and individuals working outside the strictly professional field. Since, at the same time, more strictly professional activities continued to expand, the need for self-discipline grew apace. Given the continuing likelihood of insufficient funds, where now would lie the future areas of greatest need? In recognised professional fields alone? With the ancillaries and technicians? With areas of NGO activity as yet barely touched? Or indeed with all?

As the chairman and board had insisted in their submission to the Lusaka Conference, all governments still needed to make maximum use of the talents of professional men and women in the nation-building process. As the professional base of developing countries broadened, so *pari passu* would grow the need to maintain and strengthen standards of competence and to encourage interaction between professionals themselves.

Help to those in new areas, as recommended at Lusaka, must certainly be attempted, yet, with funds in short supply, trustees would undoubtedly be driven to conclude that the continued strengthening of professional co-operation must remain the first priority – a conclusion leading back to the questions posed by Richard Symonds in his report (summarised in Chapter 9) on the role of the Commonwealth professional associations: namely, do the professions need the Commonwealth? or does the Commonwealth need them?

It was Symonds himself who, with much prescience, had first highlighted the problems facing the professions in the successor states of the Commonwealth during the flood-tide of independence from 1947 onwards. No one concerned with such matters should fail to ponder on his analysis of 'standards and prejudices'[2] as part of the legacy left by the departing colonial power to its emerging partners. As Symonds saw it, the British had left behind them an administrative heritage which, in the words of that great Ghanaian civil servant, A. L. Adu, offered such desirable features as 'integrity, impartiality, efficiency of service, loyalty to the government of the day and devotion to duty'.[3] But they had at the same time made a fetish of standards to a degree which, in the early years of independence, was to prove a grave handicap to both the administrative and professional machines – indeed to the whole educational philosophy of the newer states. In support of such criticism, far easier to admit now than twenty years ago, Symonds drew attention to a passage from a report published, eight years after its creation, by the Inter-University Council for Higher Education in the Colonies. This bluntly stated that

> there can be no compromise on this issue of standards ...
> The price for this fundamental decision of aiming at first
> class universities has been deliberately paid. It has meant
> that initially student numbers are small: that the staff/
> student ratio is high: that the institutions require very
> large funds ... that only a few of these university in-
> stitutions can be established at this stage. We do not
> doubt that this policy has justified itself.

But it also meant, given the inability of the authors of that report (and many others) to foresee the speed with which the British Empire was to plunge into voluntary liquidation, a headlong collision between two schools of thought. On the one side were ranged the perfectionists, represented by the Colonial Office and, with notable exceptions, their agents in the field from governors downwards. On the other, the politicians of the new states-to-be who now faced social and economic problems for the handling of which indigenously trained manpower remained in woefully short supply. It was now that the folly of the ivory tower approach which, in Symonds' words had 'restricted the output of graduates at a time when the [newly independent] governments were in desperate need of administrators and specialists to replace the British' came starkly to the fore. It had proved, as he bluntly put it, a policy which, whatever its good intentions, had taken 'virtually no account of manpower needs, and which drove the local youth to study abroad'. The same perfectionist attitudes had of course afflicted the majority of the professional bodies in Britain. Lying beyond the control of governments they had seen themselves as the arbiters of qualifications and standards for all those, expatriate or indigenous, who sought to practise in or to enter government service in the colonies. Thus had it come about that, for example, the Royal College of Veterinary Surgeons or the General Medical Council in London severally required either a British veterinary degree or stipulated that a locally obtained medical degree must be recognised by the GMC before any locally born candidate could be registered to practise in his country. It mattered little that the papers to be written by candidates bore scant relevance to the animal or human health problems which they would later face. Paradoxical situations thus came about where an African or Asian student sometimes found himself perforce trained to a higher standard for local service than that which would have been required from him if he were seeking employment in the United Kingdom. The same criticisms could be directed at the professions of dentistry, nursing, engineering, accountancy or the agricultural sciences.

It seemed in fact that both colonial officials and professionals had failed to take a leaf from the Indian book of experience and that, albeit with the best of intentions, they had allowed their fetish for standards to frustrate the national development of administrative and professional talent in the still dependent states of Africa and Asia. The fact that continuing insistence on the inviolability of British textbooks and examinations and on the British pupilage system were driving bright young students whose parents could afford the fees to study at American, Canadian or Australian universities led one eminent British teacher serving in East Africa to issue, as late as 1961, the following short-sighted warning: namely that 'the present inability of African students in engineering subjects had been interpreted and quoted as another aspect of British colonialism . . .' He and his colleagues feared a reduction, in due course, in the standard of the degree award towards that of the American first degree. The increasing availability of scholarships for study in America was a considerable embarrassment in this connection.[4]

As Symonds himself admitted, 'standards which may have been too high were far better than no standards at all. The professional associations, which were primarily concerned with conditions in the United Kingdom, cannot perhaps be blamed if their qualifications proved inappropriate in the colonies.' But as he presciently added:

only after independence could the issue be faced by setting up national professional associations as India had done much earlier, whose standards and curricula could be related to local needs and accepted by national governments. The Royal Institute of British Architects, which had previously controlled the development of the profession in the dependent territories found a formula after they became independent which might become a model for other professions. The function of assessing educational standards in schools of architecture, and of facilitating recognition of degrees, was transferred to a Commonwealth Association of Architects, which the RIBA joined as a member on an equal footing with national bodies of other countries.

Small wonder then that Symonds, already in 1965 so far ahead of others in this field and from whose penetrating analysis of the British heritage I have, with his agreement, quoted so extensively, should at a remove of fifteen years, have proved to be the ideal choice for the evaluation of the nexus of Commonwealth professional associations whose birth he had himself forecast.

It is with a retrospective look at the impact of those associations, and of the professional centres which have become their natural counterpart, that this survey can fittingly conclude, keeping in mind that both ventures, and indeed other Foundation initiatives, are now the subject of detailed evaluation by trustees.

In defence of the pan-Commonwealth Associations no better example of their practical and potential value to the newer Commonwealth could be found than in the report from an intra-disciplinary seminar held in November 1980, with the full support of the local government, at the Bangladesh Academy of Rural Development. The inspiration for this venture had come from a survey by the Asian Development Bank, published in 1978, on agricultural development and rural poverty in Asia. The report had cited Bangladesh as a country in which the lack of skilled manpower in certain professions was proving to be a serious impediment to progress. Thanks to an initiative, the credit for which goes largely to the secretary of the Commonwealth Association for Surveying and Land Economy, Robert Steel, the Foundation was persuaded to assist in mounting a seminar, the broad aim of which would be to investigate how Bangladesh might best be helped to acquire the skills it needed to handle its major programme of rural development.

In three senses this venture broke new ground. First, it attracted the wholehearted support of the government of Bangladesh, which seconded as many as fifty of its senior experts to attend the week-long meeting. Secondly, the seminar was the first multiprofessional project to be sponsored by the Foundation. Thirdly, and this underlined the importance of a concerted approach to major problems of national development, four of the Commonwealth professional associations most closely concerned with the physical aspects of rural development were invited to contribute papers and to take a full part in the discussions. They were, in addition to the surveyors and land economists themselves, the Commonwealth Planners, Engineers and Agricultural Scientists.

In all seventy delegates, drawn from five Commonwealth countries, took part in this experiment. Papers written for the meeting proved to be of a uniformly high standard and the report and summaries[5] subsequently published under the imprint of the Commonwealth Association of Surveyors suggest that the venture amply proved its worth.

In one sense the most important conclusion from the meeting was that the experience should be repeated in two years' time. As the report concluded: 'the four Commonwealth Associations exhibited a deep and sincere interest in the problems of Bangladesh – they pledged their intent to collaborate with the Government of Bangladesh and the national universities and other educational establishments in assisting the scale, quality and integrity of the professional services it requires'.

The breadth of the discussions may be briefly glimpsed from the topics covered in some of the papers submitted at the meeting. They included such basic issues as development organisation and administration; physical planning, infrastructures and construction resources for rural development; land administration and land reform, surveys and mapping and not least manpower needs and related educational requirements.

Based on the second Bangladesh Government five-year plan (1980–5) many practical recommendations were adopted. They related to such vital aspects of integrated rural planning for development as the creation of a satisfactory surveying and mapping service: the formulation of a co-ordinated rural housing policy: a nation-wide campaign to promote good sanitation: the importance of improving the surfacing of feeder roads and of preparing a national water resources plan: the need for more research into processing technology and crop marketing processes and the provision, as a matter of priority, of education in agricultural science and practice.

Of particular significance to the future of non-governmental professional relationships with governments of the newer Commonwealth – and as a happy example of the 'adversary factor' in reverse – were the final conclusions from the seminar relating to the educational contribution which the four Commonwealth professional associations present could make to the universities and other educational institutions in Bangladesh. Thus the Commonwealth Association of Scientific Agricultural Societies was in a position to advise on the extension or improvement of courses in farm management, to help with the formation of a local society covering the agricultural sciences as a whole and to serve as a means of communication between researchers, scientists and extension workers. For its part the Commonwealth Engineering Council stood ready to advise on any review which the universities might undertake into existing course standards and curricula. The Commonwealth Association of Planners in turn reported on current discussions with both the Bangladesh University of Engineering and Technology and with the local Institute of Planners on the development of existing courses to meet the immediate needs of the profession. Finally the Commonwealth Association of Surveying and Land Economy undertook, in the light of education and training needs which had come to notice in the course of the seminar, to help the government of Bangladesh to identify the tasks which should be undertaken by surveyors in the various disciplines of surveying and mapping, land economy and quantity surveying; to sponsor a manpower study to assess the number of professionals, sub-professionals and technicians required to undertake such duties; to appoint an advisory board to assist in creating appropriate courses; and finally to help 'in the formation of a professional society in Bangladesh to foster the development of an indigenous profession of surveying and land economy and ... to work with the government and the universities in producing surveying services of the scale, quality and integrity that the country requires'.

If I have dwelt so long on this one seminar it has been with the aim not only of underlining the growing role which the Commonwealth professional associations can play as exemplars of the unofficial Commonwealth but also to stress the fact that by tendering advice to governments through collective as opposed to national channels they can go far towards breaking down suspicions of neo-imperialism and can thus help in overcoming the twin bogys of 'élitism' and the 'adversary factor'.

213

Even if some of the associations now wither on the vine for want of funds, they already have much to their credit. The surveyors indeed have pointed the way to better things – to an interdisciplinary and thus more cost-effective approach to the problems of the modern Commonwealth.

Above all these associations, growing so rapidly in numbers in less than two decades, have proved three things; that a meeting of Commonwealth minds uninhibited by politics can by and large produce more results more quickly than an international Tower of Babel; that shared educational experiences, let alone a still largely comprehensible common language remain precious assets; and that membership of a professional 'club' brings comfort to the newer entrants while opening the eyes of its elders not only to the problems of the young but to new and sometimes better ways of problem-solving.

Nothing in fact stands more to the credit of this venture than the rapid growth in the number of new autonomous national professional societies which it has helped to bring to birth throughout the newer Commonwealth. For this, due tribute must be paid to bodies in the older world which, with a few notable exceptions, have had the wisdom and imagination to catch the tide of change.

As with the professional associations, so largely with the world-wide network of professional centres. As has been mentioned these too are currently the subject of critical review by the present director of the Foundation and his deputy. As official journeys take them to various regions of the Commonwealth, so they are able on the spot to assess the prospects for viability of earlier ventures. At the same time, as happened during a first visit by my successor to Zimbabwe early in 1981, it becomes clear that other newly independent countries are in turn anxious to benefit from an experiment which has already done much to fortify the ethos of national professional communities.

The dilemma thus remains, and indeed grows in dimension: namely, how to fit a quart of enthusiastic need into the available financial pint-pot.

All one can say, as a former Foundation director, is that the professional centre concept was worth the time, risk and money lavished on it. Looking back (and emphasising in passing that at one extreme even the Uganda centre has survived the horrors of the past few years, and that at the other a London Science Centre has finally seen the light of day), it can be said that a growing number of professional centres are now viable. While a small handful may never make the grade, all have done something to promote professional cohesion; to bring their governments to a realisation, however reluctantly in some cases, of the role which professional man can and must play in his own society, and to open the way to closer co-operation between the private and the public sectors.

There is indeed, greater hope of long-term success in this area than with the pan-Commonwealth associations. For unlike the latter each centre is a visible national asset: a building or grouping which has means of attracting government support, of influencing the community, and of co-operating in the nation-building process. There are thus more valid reasons for cutting short support for a centre which fails to make the grade within an approved time-scale than there are for abandoning some Commonwealth-wide association for which access to external funding must be infinitely more difficult.

It is worth recalling at this point that the old world, as much as the new, now faces its own professional dilemmas. What, as a former British scientific administrator wrote recently, should the professions contribute to society? They are not, as he put it from a national viewpoint,

identified with either capital or organised labour but are dedicated to every sector of society. Their members are bound by codes of conduct aimed at public advantage, rather than merely the advantage of the profession itself, and they contribute a sophisticated, educated, critical and independent-minded service to society. Indeed the professional man's unique contribution to society is his readiness to take a detached view, consider his problems in relation to the needs of society and then act with all the authority and influence of a professional institution. Most of those upon whose special skill the functioning of modern society depends are to be found within the ranks of the professions. No employer has the right to ask a professional worker to debase his professional judgement – and any such attempt to do so should be resisted by the appropriate professional association. The importance of learned and professional societies in fulfilling objectives in the public interest has been recognised by Government since the last century but the realisation of their full potential in this respect calls for co-operation and trust on the part of society on the one hand and the professions on the other.[6]

As the author of this paper went on to underline, the past century had seen, at least in the developed world, the emergence and spectacular growth in numbers of professional engineers, scientists and technologists as a major social and economic factor in society. There was now no escaping the pervasive and exhilarating effect on society at large of science and technology as mankind's most vital enterprises. At the same time, national social priorities were changing and the commercial professions including bankers, actuaries, management, insurance, architecture, surveying and accountancy were exercising a major influence upon the economy. Thus the current issue was not 'whether the common man is or is not to have a share in government' but 'whether his share is to be an unhelpful participation in a clumsy system of checks and balances, or an allocation corresponding to the special contribution he is fitted to make'.

I shall quote one further passage from Press's paper since it illumines not only the problems facing professions in a highly sophisticated society such as that of Britain, but those tormenting professional men and their governments throughout the newer world. As he put it:

Public appreciation of the importance, value and role of the professions can no longer be taken for granted. The professional bodies should examine whether they themselves have given any cause for this. If (they) . . . are to survive as effective instruments in modern society and to have a right, or even opportunity, to influence legislation or other national issues affecting their role, competence or ethos, they must be prepared to present and argue their raison d'être publicly. Their impact would be greatly enhanced by acting collectively or at least in a co-ordinated manner.

Furthermore, to gain acceptance in the public mind as an essential collective entity,

> societies should present their case not as a [science] interested pressure group but with the aim of preserving professional freedom in the demonstrable interest of society at large . . . Such a role need not necessarily require all the professions to contribute to a specific topic . . . but however grouped, such contributions should preferably be seen to emerge with the full blessing and authority of a collective professional 'Voice' in national affairs.

It is interesting to note how closely the aims set by this commentator for the professions in the oldest country of the Commonwealth now link in with those fixed for the growing range of centres and associations in the newer world.

Meanwhile, the scene shifts unceasingly. Already there are hints that the Foundation might forgo its charitable status under English law in favour of some more broadly recognised 'Commonwealth organisation' role. That in itself would be a logical development in that the fortuitous siting of its head-quarters in London is in practice immaterial to its Common-wealth-wide endeavours. The Foundation could, in theory, work equally well from Lesotho or Lilongwe. The one thing which counts is the autonomy and freedom of action of its chairman and trustees. It would be a sad day indeed if the imagination of those who first created it was to be smothered in the neat and tidy interests of bureaucracy. While the Commonwealth Secretariat properly exists to co-ordinate the behests of member governments, it has been the prime virtue of the Foundation to date that, with the support of those same governments but without their interference, a new means has been found of developing non-governmental co-operation. How much further the parameters of such action can be expanded, and with what if any increased funding may well have emerged, by the time this survey sees the light of day, from the Commonwealth Heads of Government Conference at Melbourne in September 1981.

What I hope to have conveyed, in this brief account of a non-governmental Commonwealth, is some sense of the continuing – indeed growing – importance of that Commonwealth as an association as much of peoples as of governments. Thanks to the imagination of the latter, the Foundation came into being at a critical point in time. Small though it was and small though it is likely to remain, it has already rewarded those who brought about its birth. Its successive chairmen and trustees have influenced not only professions, universities and learned bodies but also numerous individuals across the globe. They have, if modestly, stimulated other forms of voluntary endeavour. Not least, perhaps, in their continuing fight for a place in the financial sun, they have sown in the minds of Commonwealth leaders the need for a healthy spirit of 'creative friction'.

Notes and References

1   Commonwealth Secretariat, *Commonwealth Organisations: A Handbook of Official and Unofficial Organisations Active in the Commonwealth* (London, 1979).
2   Richard Symonds, *The British and Their Successors* (London, 1966), ch. 12.
3   A. L. Adu, *The Civil Service in New African States* (London, 1965).
4   Sir William Jackson, 'The Electrical Supervisor' (October, 1961), quoted in R. Symonds, op. cit.
5   *Integrated Rural Development in Bangladesh*, report on seminar, summary of report and recommendations (London, 1981).
6   Dr R. Press, CB, CBE, F. Inst. Phy., in a paper circulated in 1977 to a forum of presidents of British learned societies.

Epilogue

A meeting of the Board of Trustees, held at Marlborough House on 8 July 1981, proved to be one of the most important in the brief history of the Commonwealth Foundation. As the Chairman, Sir Adetokunbo Ademola, reported:

> We are beginning to see the results of policy decisions adopted in December 1980 and at our previous meetings. The new mandate given to us by the Commonwealth Heads of Government in Lusaka in 1979 is beginning to take shape. The results of the first major review of an area of the Foundation's activities are apparent in the submissions now presented by the Commonwealth Professional Associations, in accordance with policies adopted by Trustees in December 1980. We will have before us the first interim reports of the second major review of the Foundation's activities: the evaluation of Professional Centres being undertaken by the Director and the Deputy Director. Proposals are also before you for the evaluation of the remaining areas of the Foundation's activities, in accordance with the directive of the Heads of Government at Lusaka. The Director will report the results achieved on your behalf to the Heads of Government meeting in Melbourne. A draft report is submitted for your approval.

All of these matters, he continued, are of great interest,

but more sweeping in their general implications are the questions I shall submit to you on the future legal status of the Foundation. Heads of Government directed in 1965 that the Commonwealth Foundation should explore the possibilities of legal status as a charity in English law. There was at that time no alternative open to the Founda-

219

tion. Charitable status has served the Foundation well, although it has proved a limited incentive to private donors. There are, however, serious questions whether charitable status remains a suitable vehicle for the fulfilment of the Foundation's expanded mandate. You will be asked to examine the appropriateness of the draft Supplemental Deed prepared by the Foundation's lawyers and submitted to the Charity Commissioners. Should it seem to you that the response of the Charity Commission is not compatible with the directives of the Heads of Government, there remains the alternative of seeking status as an international organisation under the recently amended International Organisations Act adopted by the British Parliament and accorded Royal Assent on 15 April this year. This is a matter on which Trustees are asked to advise Heads of Government, with whom the final decision will lie.

The Chairman was also able to report on a much healthier financial position. The six major donor countries were now contributing to the Foundation's income at the new level recommended at the Lusaka Conference of 1979. Thus the mythical target of £1 million per annum was at last on the point of being hit. In addition the government of Brunei, anticipating its full membership of the Commonwealth in 1984, had now offered to make forthwith a substantial annual voluntary contribution.

During their day-long discussions, trustees agreed to refer the future status of the Foundation to Commonwealth heads of government at their meeting in Australia in the autumn and to recommend that they should approve an agreement 'establishing the Commonwealth Foundation as an international organisation, with the same objectives, autonomous character and organisational arrangements as at present'. Should such proposals be approved, the host government, Britain, would then be requested to extend to the Foundation as an international body, the privileges and immunities necessary for the performance of its functions.

Some other conclusions are worth recording. One was that outside experts should be selected to prepare evaluations of the Foundation's wide-ranging bursary schemes and of its publications and publication support programme. Another was that the holding of a further Foundation seminar, which I had myself proposed prior to my departure, on the theme 'skills and qualifications for small island states' should be held in Barbados in May of 1982. As regards the outcome of the present director's first visit to Zimbabwe, on which he had been accompanied by a small team representing the Commonwealth professional associations, a number of interesting recommendations were endorsed. They were in brief that existing Commonwealth associations should encourage and facilitate Zimbabwean membership of all appropriate pan-Commonwealth bodies; that the Foundation should itself be receptive to requests from Zimbabwe for project support in the professional field; and that the establishment of a professional centre in Zimbabwe should be looked upon as a matter of priority, subject only to a full local feasibility study being first undertaken with the support of a representative group of the professions in Zimbabwe.

For the rest, having heard reports from the director and his deputy on conclusions reached following their own recent Commonwealth journeys, the trustees agreed to offer continuing help over a limited period ahead to a number of existing professional centres, including those now in formation in Sierra Leone and Tanzania.

Finally, in continuation of the evaluation of professional associations, a number of further awards were made over the period 1981–4 to the majority of these bodies.

It remains only to add – and on that note this book can fittingly conclude – that in the final communiqué issuing from the Heads of Government Conference, Melbourne, in September 1981, the following passages appeared:

Heads of Government expressed satisfaction with the valuable work of the Commonwealth Foundation and approved the recommendation of its Board of Trustees that the Foundation be accorded the status of an international organisation by the host government. Noting with appreciation that the budgetary target approved in Lusaka in 1979 had almost been reached, they agreed that governments should endeavour to maintain this level of funding for the present.

Heads of Government expressed their warm appreciation to the retiring Chairman, Sir Adetokunbo Ademola of Nigeria, for his services to the Foundation over the last four years. They appointed Dr Muhammad Abdur Rashid of Bangladesh as the new Chairman.

Dr Rashid was unhappily killed in a car accident in Bangladesh early in November, 1981. A new chairman is unlikely to have been appointed in his stead before this book appears.

APPENDIX A

*Agreed Memorandum
on the Commonwealth Foundation*
(As published following the Commonwealth Prime Ministers'
Meeting of July 1965)

A Commonwealth Foundation will be established to administer a
fund for increasing interchanges between Commonwealth organizations in professional fields throughout the Commonwealth. It will
be the purpose of the Foundation to provide assistance where it is
needed in order to foster such interchanges.

2 The Foundation will be an autonomous body, although it will
develop and maintain a close liaison with the Commonwealth
Secretariat. Like the Secretariat, the Foundation will be accommodated at Marlborough House.

3 Within the broad purpose indicated above, the Foundation
will include among its aims the following objects:

(a) To encourage and support fuller representation at conferences
of professional bodies within the Commonwealth.
(b) To assist professional bodies within the Commonwealth to
hold more conferences between themselves.
(c) To facilitate the exchange of visits among professional people,
especially the younger element.
(d) To stimulate and increase the flow of professional information
exchanged between the organizations concerned.
(e) On request to assist with the setting up of national institutions
or associations in countries where these do not at present exist.
(f) To promote the growth of Commonwealth-wide associations
or regional Commonwealth associations in order to reduce the
present centralization in Britain.
(g) To consider exceptional requests for help from associations
and individuals whose activities lie outside the strictly professional field but fall within the general ambit of the
Foundation's operations as outlined above.

4 The Foundation could usefully develop informal contacts with

the Commonwealth Parliamentary Association. To avoid the risk of duplication with the activities of existing organizations concerned with cultural activities and the Press, the Foundation should not initially seek to assume any functions in these fields.

5 The policy of the Foundation will be directed by a Chairman, who will be a distinguished private citizen of a Commonwealth country appointed with the approval of all member Governments, and a Board of Trustees who should be expected to meet at least once a year. The Board of Trustees will consist of independent persons, each subscribing Government having the right to nominate one member of the Board. These nominees, even if officials, will be appointed in a personal capacity. The Commonwealth Secretariat will be represented on the Board of Trustees by the Secretary-General or an officer appointed by him.

6 There will be a full-time, salaried Director who will be appointed, initially for a period of not more than two years, by Commonwealth Heads of Government collectively acting through their representatives in London. He will be responsible to the Board of Trustees.

7 The Director will require a small personal staff: general office services will be provided by the Commonwealth Secretariat.

8 It is hoped that Commonwealth Governments will subscribe to the cost of the Foundation on an agreed scale. Payment of the first annual subscriptions will be made as soon as the Director has indicated that a bank account for the Foundation has been opened. It is hoped that, in addition, private sources may be willing to contribute to the funds of the Foundation.

9 The accounts of the Foundation will be audited annually by the British Comptroller and Auditor-General, whose report will be submitted to the Board of Trustees. The financial year of the Foundation will be from July 1st to June 30th.

10 The budget of the Foundation will be subject to the approval of the Board of Trustees.

11 The British Government will draw up the necessary documents to set up the Trust and take any further steps needed to constitute the Foundation as a legal charity.

APPENDIX B

*The Commonwealth Foundation Declaration of Trust**

THIS DECLARATION OF TRUST is made the fifteenth day of December One Thousand nine hundred and sixty-six BY His Excellency The Honourable Sir ALEXANDER DOWNER KBE, High Commissioner for Australia, GEOFFREY STUART MURRAY Deputy High Commissioner for Canada, ARTHUR BASNAYAKE of 6 Garway Road London W.2, acting on behalf of the Government of Ceylon, His Excellency COSTAS A. ASHIOTIS MBE, High Commissioner for Cyprus, His Excellency LOUIS FRANCIS VALANTINE CBE, High Commissioner for the Gambia, His Excellency SETH KOBLA ANTHONY, High Commissioner for Ghana, His Excellency Sir LIONEL ALFRED LUCKHOO CBE, QC, High Commissioner for Guyana, PARMESHWAR NARIAN HAKSAR, Acting High Commissioner for India, His Excellency HENRY LAURENCE LINDO High Commissioner for Jamaica, His Excellency NYEMBA WALES MBEKEANI High Commissioner for Malawi, His Excellency DATO SYED SHEH SHAHABUDIN PMN, High Commissioner for Malaysia, CONSTANTINE JOHN COLOMBOS QC of 8 Averfield House Park Lane London W.1, acting on behalf of the Government of Malta, RICHARD MITCHELSON CAMPBELL CMG of 36 Turners Mill Road Haywards Heath Sussex, acting on behalf of the Government of New Zealand, His Excellency Brigadier BABAFENII OLATUNDE OGUNDIPE, High Commissioner for Nigeria, His Excellency SAMIULLA KHAN DEHLAVI, High Commissioner for Pakistan, Doctor ALFRED MOSES KAMANDA, acting High Commissioner for Sierra Leone, His Excellency ARUMUGAM PONNU RAJAH, High Commissioner for Singapore, His Excellency WILFRED ANDREW ROSE, High Commissioner for Trinidad and Tobago, His Excellency Doctor SOLOMON BAYO ASEA, High Commissioner for Uganda, Doctor LESLIE FARRER-BROWN CBE of Dale House 18 Keere Street Lewes

*Registered with the Charity Commission of England and Wales, December 1966, as Charity no. 251161

Sussex, acting on behalf of the Government of the United Kingdom, His Excellency SIMON C KATILUNGU High Commissioner for Zambia

WHEREAS at the Commonwealth Prime Ministers' Meeting held during the month of July in the year One thousand nine hundred and sixty-five it was agreed that a Commonwealth Foundation should be established as set out in the Agreed Memorandum on the Commonwealth Foundation (Cmnd 2714) annexed to the Final Communiqué of the said Prime Ministers' Meeting and accordingly the parties hereto on behalf of the Commonwealth Governments concerned desire to establish the trust hereinafter set forth

NOW THEREFORE THIS DEED WITNESSETH as follows:

1 PURSUANT to the said agreement a trust is hereby established with the Constitution set out in the Schedule hereto to be known as THE COMMONWEALTH FOUNDATION (hereinafter referred to as 'the Foundation') and the capital and income of any money or other property received by the Foundation shall be held UPON TRUST that it may be applied in such manner as may from time to time be thought fit by the Trustees in order to maintain and improve (in the interests of the public) standards of knowledge attainment and conduct in the skilled or learned professions or skilled auxiliary occupations within the Commonwealth by promoting and facilitating the interchange of information through the medium of publications conferences seminars and visits and by the formation or support of Commonwealth regional or national institutions or associations for that purpose whether incorporated or unincorporated or by such other means whatsoever as may from time to time be thought fit by the Trustees The expression 'skilled or learned professions' shall mean and extend to any vocation in which a professed knowledge of some department of learning is used in its application to the affairs of or is imparted to others The expression 'skilled auxiliary occupations' shall mean and extend to any occupation in which a special skill is exercised for the purpose of furthering and assisting the professional work of a skilled or learned profession by persons trained for that purpose in such skill

2 THE Heads of the Commonwealth Governments which are for the time being Member Governments as defined by the said Constitution may at any time and from time to time by deed or deeds made by them or on their behalf wholly or partially revoke or alter all or any of the trusts powers and

provisions herein contained and at their discretion in lieu thereof declare such new or altered charitable trusts with and subject to such new or altered powers or provisions as they shall think proper

3   REFERENCES to the Commonwealth shall be deemed to be references to the Commonwealth as it may be established for the time being Reference to the Trustees shall refer to the Board of Trustees constituted in accordance with the Schedule hereto or other the governing body for the time being of the Foundation

4   THE Trustees shall out of the capital or income of the Foundation pay all costs and expenses of or incidental to the creation and management of the Foundation and the income thereof and the execution of the trusts or powers of these presents and save harmless and keep indemnified the Trustees and any persons appointed as alternates or members of committees in accordance with the Schedule hereto or who are officers of the Foundation and each of them and their respective executors administrators and assigns estates and effects from and against all actions proceedings claims and demands costs damages and expenses arising out of any act deed matter or thing whatsoever made done executed omitted or neglected by the Trustees or any such person as aforesaid in the execution or purported execution of the trusts hereof or otherwise howsoever in relation to the premises save only any breach of trust or duty arising from the wilful default of the person who is sought to be made liable The expenses of and incidental to the establishment and maintenance of offices for the purpose of the Foundation and any activity undertaken by or on behalf of the persons named in clauses 14 and 15 of the said Constitution for the said purpose (including the payment of honorarium and salaries) between the First day of March in the year One thousand nine hundred and sixty-six and the date of this deed shall to the extent that they are confirmed by the Trustees be deemed to be expenses of the Foundation and shall be paid accordingly

5   THIS Deed shall be interpreted in accordance with the laws of England and any question dispute or difference arising thereunder shall be subject to the jurisdiction of the Supreme Court of Judicature in England

IN WITNESS whereof the said parties to these presents have hereunto set their respective hands and seals the day and year first above written

THE SCHEDULE above referred to:

THE CONSTITUTION OF THE COMMONWEALTH FOUNDATION

1   In this Constitution:
    'Commonwealth' means the Commonwealth as it may be
    established for the time being. 'Member Government' means
    the Government of a member country of the Commonwealth
    which:

  (a) (i)   either appears in the first column of the Schedule
            hereto (the governments so appearing being called
            'Founding Member Governments')
      (ii) or hereafter notifies in writing to the Foundation its
            decision to become a member of the Foundation and
  (b) in either case is not in arrear in payment of the whole or
      part of its subscription payable pursuant to clause 2 for
      twelve months after the same became due.

    'The Board' means the Board of Trustees constituted as
    hereinafter provided. 'The Chairman' means the Chairman
    appointed in accordance with clause 14. 'The Director' means
    the Director appointed in accordance with clause 15. Any
    written communication requiring to be sent to the Foundation
    or to the Director shall be addressed to the Director at
    Marlborough House, London, or other the office of the
    Foundation.
    Any notification of its decision to become a member of the
    Foundation by the Government of a member country of the
    Commonwealth or any appointment or termination of an
    appointment by a Member Government shall be made in
    writing signed, by a person qualified so to do, on behalf of
    the Government and sent to the Foundation.

2   The Member Governments shall subscribe to the Foundation
    at such respective annual rates as may from time to time be
    fixed by agreement between all the Member Governments
    and until other rates shall be so fixed at the following rates
    namely:

  (a) In the case of Founding Member Governments, the
      respective rates agreed by them before the establishment
      of the Foundation.
  (b) In the case of a Member Government admitted after the
      establishment of the Foundation, the lowest rate which
      at the date of such Government's admission is payable
      by any other Member Government.

Any agreement fixing the respective annual rates of subscription may be made, in the absence of any other means accepted by the Trustees, by letters from all the Member Governments, signed, by persons qualified so to do, on behalf of the respective Member Governments and sent to the Foundation.

3 The subscriptions in respect of each financial year shall become payable on the first day of that financial year and any subscription in arrear may be paid up at any time.

4 The Foundation shall be administered by the Board of Trustees consisting of one Trustee appointed by each Member Government and the ex-officio Trustee referred to in clause 7.

5 The Trustee appointed by a Member Government may be appointed either for a fixed term, after which if he is to remain a Trustee he will require re-appointment or without limitation of term. Each of the persons named in the second column of the Schedule hereto shall, in the absence of any express limitation by the relevant Founding Member Government, be deemed to have been appointed a Trustee without limitation of term by the Founding Member Government which appears opposite his name, and those persons together with the ex-officio Trustee shall constitute the first Board.

6 A Trustee appointed or deemed to have been appointed by a Member Government shall cease to hold office when:

(a) he dies,
    or
(b) he resigns by notice in writing to the Foundation,
    or
(c) if appointed for a fixed term, the term expires,
    or
(d) the Member Government terminates his appointment, which it may do at any time whether he was appointed for a fixed term or not,
    or
(e) the Member Government ceases to be a Member Government.

And in any such event (save where sub-paragraph (e) applies) the Member Government may appoint a person to be Trustee in his place.

7 The Commonwealth Secretary-General for the time being, or an officer of the Commonwealth Secretariat appointed by him, shall be an ex-officio Trustee. Any appointment or removal of any such officer shall be made in writing, signed by such Secretary-General and sent to the Foundation.

8 The Chairman and Director shall be entitled to attend and speak at all meetings of the Board, but shall not be members of the Board or vote except as provided by clause 11.

9 The Board shall meet at such times and places as it may decide and the Director shall summon a meeting of the Board as and when requested by the Chairman or any six members of the Board. The Board shall meet at least once in every calendar year.

10 The proceedings of the Board shall not be invalidated by any vacancy therein.

11 The quorum for a meeting of the Board shall be eleven or such other number as may from time to time be fixed by the Board and the Board shall have power from time to time to settle its own procedure, except that every question which comes before the Board shall, in the absence of unanimous agreement, be decided by the vote of the majority of the members voting and except that the Chairman, if present, shall preside at any meeting. If the Chairman is not present at the time appointed for holding any meeting the members present shall choose one of their number to preside. In the case of an equality of votes but not otherwise, the Chairman shall, except on a question relating to the terms and conditions of his appointment, have a vote, which if he be absent from the meeting, he may exercise by letter addressed to the director.

12 Any member of the Board may in writing given to the Director appoint any person to be his alternate to act in his place at a specified meeting of the Board at which he expects to be unable to be present. Every such alternate shall be entitled to attend and vote thereat and shall be counted in a quorum, if the person appointing him is not personally present. A Member of the Board may at any time in writing given to the Director revoke the appointment of an alternate appointed by him and may appoint another alternate in his place.

13 The Board may appoint committees, which may include persons who are not members of the Board, for the purpose of making recommendations as to the application of the funds of the Foundation, as to its administration or as to any other subject referred to them by the Board.

14 There shall be a Chairman of the Foundation, who shall subject to the control of the Board, be generally responsible for directing the policy of the Foundation. The Chairman shall be a citizen of a member country of the Commonwealth appointed (initially for a period of not more than two years) by all the Member Governments and the Chairman may,

notwithstanding the terms of any agreement entered into in any particular case, be removed by all the Member Governments. Any such appointment or removal may be made, in the absence of any other means accepted by the Trustees, by letters from all the Member Governments, signed, by persons qualified so to do, on behalf of the respective Member Governments and sent to the Foundation. The Chairman, not being a member of the Board, shall receive from the Foundation an honorarium at the rate of ONE THOUSAND POUNDS ($£1,000$) per annum, or at such other rate as may be fixed by the Board, for his services as such; and in addition his travelling, hotel and other expenses reasonably incurred by him in attending and returning from meetings of the Board or in connection with the performance of his duties may be charged to the Foundation. Sir Macfarlane Burnet, OM, shall be deemed to have been appointed the first Chairman pursuant to the foregoing provision for a period of two years from the 1st March, 1966.

15 There shall be a full time salaried Director of the Foundation appointed (initially for a period of not more than two years) by all the Member Governments and the Director may, notwithstanding the terms of any agreement entered into in any particular case, be removed by all the Member Governments. Any such appointment or removal may be made, in the absence of any other means accepted by the Trustees, by letters from all the Member Governments, signed by persons qualified so to do, on behalf of the respective Member Governments and sent to the Foundation. The terms and conditions of his service except as to his removal shall be fixed by the Board. The Director shall have such powers as may be conferred by, and shall be responsible to, the Board and, subject to the directions of the Board, and subject thereto, of the Chairman, he shall be responsible for the day to day conduct of the affairs of the Foundation. The Director may engage such staff as the Board may authorise on such terms and conditions as, subject to any directions given by the Board, he may think fit. Gerald William St John Chadwick CMG shall be deemed to have been appointed the first Director pursuant to the foregoing provision for a period of two years from the 1st March, 1966.

16 No Member of the Board shall receive any remuneration from the Foundation, but he shall be entitled to be repaid all expenses reasonably incurred by him within the United Kingdom in attending and returning from meetings of the

Board and in connection with the performance of any duties carried out by him at the request of the Board.

17 Within the limits prescribed by this Constitution the Board shall have full power from time to time to make regulations for the management of the Foundation and for the conduct of its business, including the summoning of meetings, the deposit of money at a Bank, the custody of documents and the carrying out of the duties of Director if there is no Director, and shall have power to vary or rescind any regulations so made.

18 The Board shall cause minutes to be kept of all their decisions in relation to the Foundation and shall cause accounts to be kept of the capital and income of the Foundation.

19 The financial year of the Foundation will be from the 1st July to the 30th June and the Board shall cause accounts to be prepared annually and submit them for audit by the Comptroller and Auditor-General of the United Kingdom, who shall be requested to make a report to the Board. A budget for the Foundation will be prepared for each financial year by the Director for the approval of the Board. The period from the 1st March, 1966 to the 30th June, 1966 shall be deemed to be a financial year and next financial year of the Foundation shall be deemed to have commenced on the 1st July, 1966.

20 Any moneys of the Foundation may be invested in the purchase of, or at interest upon, the security of such stocks, funds, shares, securities, or other investments of whatsoever nature and wheresoever, and whether involving liability or not, or upon such personal credit, with or without security, as the Board may in its absolute discretion authorize, to the intent that there shall be the same full and unrestricted power of investing and transposing investments in all respects as if it were absolutely entitled thereto beneficially.

21 The Board shall not be bound to expend in any year the whole of the income, which may be available in that year, and, in the event of the income or the whole of the income in any year not being expended, any income not so expended may be utilised in any succeeding year.

22 The Foundation may hold any investment in the name of a nominee or nominees and in the case of a corporate nominee remunerate such nominee.

23 Every discretion hereby conferred upon the Board shall be an absolute discretion.

24 The Board may at any time and from time to time by deed or deeds executed by all its members wholly or partially

revoke or alter all or any of the provisions in this Constitution contained and may in like manner prescribe such new provisions as it shall think proper, provided always that no such revocation, alteration or new provision shall

(a) revoke, alter or add to the definition of Member Government or to provisions relating to subscriptions by Member Governments; or

(b) be such as would impair the charitable status of the Foundation.

THE SCHEDULE to the Constitution:

Column 1	Column 2
Founding Member Government	
AUSTRALIA	
CANADA	
CEYLON	
CYPRUS	
GAMBIA, The	
GHANA	
GUYANA	
INDIA	
JAMAICA	
MALAWI	
MALAYSIA	
MALTA	
NEW ZEALAND	
NIGERIA	
PAKISTAN	
SIERRA LEONE	
SINGAPORE	
TANZANIA	
TRINIDAD AND TOBAGO	
UGANDA	
UNITED KINGDOM	
ZAMBIA	

SUPPLEMENTAL DEED is made the twenty fourth day of September One thousand nine hundred and sixty-nine BETWEEN His Excellency The Honourable Sir ALEXANDER DOWNER KBE, High Commissioner for and the representative of the Head of the Government of the Commonwealth of Australia, Sir LIONEL LUCKHOO, the representative

233

of the Head of the Government of Barbados, His Excellency
CHARLES STEWART ALMON RICHIE, High Commissioner for and the
representative of the Head of the Government of Canada, APPIAH
PATHMARAJAH, Acting High Commissioner for and the representative
of the Head of the Government of Ceylon, His Excellency COSTAS
ASHIOTIS MBE, High Commissioner for and the representative of the
Head of the Government of Cyprus, His Excellency HORACE
REGINALD MONDAY CBE High Commissioner for and the representative
of the Head of the Government of The Gambia, His Excellency
SETH KOBLA ANTHONY High Commissioner for and the representative
of the Head of the Government of Ghana, His Excellency Sir LIONEL
LUCKHOO KCMG, CBE, QC High Commissioner for and the representa-
tive of the Head of the Government of Guyana, His Excellency
Mr APA B. PANT, High Commissioner for India and the repre-
sentative of the Head of the Government of India, His Excellency
Sir LAURENCE LINDO CMG, High Commissioner for and the representative of the Head of the Government of Jamaica, His Excellency
Doctor JOSPHAT NJUGUNA KARANJA, High Commissioner for and
the representative of the Head of the Government of Kenya, His
Excellency TIMON SAM MANGWAZU, High Commissioner for and the
representative of the Head of the Government of Malawi, His
Excellency Tan Sri ABDUL JAMAL BIN ABDUL RAIS, High Commissioner for and the representative of the Head of the Government
of Malaysia, His Excellency JOHN FRANCIS AXISA MBE High Commissioner for and the representative of the Head of the Government
of Malta, His Excellency Doctor LECKRAZ TEELOCK CBE, High
Commissioner for and the representative of the Head of the
Government of Mauritius, His Excellency Sir DENIS BLUNDELL KBE,
the representative of the Head of the Government of New Zealand,
His Excellency Brigadier BABAFEMI OLATUNDE OGUNDIPE, the
representative of the Head of the Government of Nigeria, His
Excellency MAHMOUD HAROON, High Commissioner for and the
representative of the Head of the Government of Pakistan, His
Excellency Mr VICTOR S. KANU, High Commissioner for and the
representative of the Head of the Government of Sierra Leone,
His Excellency ARUMUGAM PONNU RAJAH, High Commissioner for
and the representative of the Head of the Government of Singapore,
His Excellency DONALD CASIMIR GRANADO, High Commissioner for
and the representative of the Head of the Government of Trinidad
and Tobago, His Excellency PHILEMON PAUL MURO, High Commissioner for and the representative of the Head of the Government
of Tanzania, His Excellency SWAIB MATUMBWE MUSOKE, High
Commissioner for and the representative of the Head of the
Government of Uganda, Doctor LESLIE FARRER BROWN CBE of

Dale House, 18 Keere Street, Lewes, Sussex, the representative of the Head of the Government of the United Kingdom, His Excellency Mr HOSEA JOSIAS SOKO, High Commissioner for and the representative of the Head of the Government of Zambia.

WHEREAS this Deed is supplemental to a Declaration of Trust dated the Fifteenth day of December One thousand nine hundred and sixty-six establishing a trust with the Constitution set out in the Schedule thereto to be known as the Commonwealth Foundation

AND WHEREAS by Clause 2 the Declaration of Trust provides that the Heads of the Commonwealth Governments which are for the time being Member Governments as defined by the Constitution of the Commonwealth Foundation may by deed or deeds made by them or on their behalf wholly or partly revoke or alter all or any of the trusts powers and provisions contained in the said Declaration of Trust and at their discretion in lieu thereof declare such new or altered charitable trusts with and subject to such new or altered powers or provisions as they shall think proper

AND WHEREAS the parties hereto are the representatives of the Heads of all the Commonwealth Governments which are at the present time such Member Governments and each of them is duly authorised by the Head of the Commonwealth Government whom he represents to execute this Deed on behalf of such Head of Government and does so execute this Deed

NOW THEREFORE THIS DEED made in exercise of the power conferred by Clause 2 of the said Declaration of Trust WITNESSETH AND IT IS HEREBY DECLARED that Clause 1 of the said Declaration of Trust shall be altered by the addition thereto at the end thereof of a provision in the following terms namely:

'PROVIDED THAT:

(1) The Trustees may accept and administer any gift legacy or other donation for the foregoing purposes of the trust or for any one or more of such purposes whether or not the donation is given subject to any limitation or trust as to the manner in which or the particular area within which it is to be applied for such purposes or purpose so long as such limitation or trust shall not adversely affect the charitable nature of the donation

(2) The Trustees may accept and administer any gift legacy or other donation for any purpose (being a wholly charitable purpose) which is not within or not wholly within the foregoing purposes of the trust if the trustees are satisfied that the purpose of the donation is sufficiently near to or associated with the forgoing purposes for it to be expedient and proper that the Trustees should administer it and may so accept and

administer whether or not the donation is given subject to any limitation or trust as to the manner in which or the particular area within which it is to be applied for the purpose for which it is given so long as such limitation or trust shall not adversely affect the charitable nature of the donation

(3) Where any charitable trust has been constituted for a purpose for which under either of the two last mentioned powers the Trustees could otherwise accept a donation the Trustees may either accept trusteeship of such charitable trust and administer the same accordingly or may without becoming trustees assist in the administration of such charitable trust in such manner as the Trustees think fit'

IN WITNESS whereof the said parties to these presents have hereunto set their respective hands and seals the day and year first above written

APPENDIX C

Chairmen and Senior Staff of the Commonwealth Foundation

CHAIRMEN

1966–9	Sir Macfarlane Burnet, OM, KBE (Australia)
1970–3	Dr Robert Gardiner (Ghana)
1974–7	Sir Hugh Springer, KCMG, CBE (Barbados)
1978–81	Rt Hon. Sir Adetokunbo Ademola, GCON, KBE, CFR, PC (Nigeria)

STAFF

Directors

1966–80	John Chadwick (Britain)
1980–	Ric Throssell (Australia)

Deputy Directors

1969–72	U. A. Ansari (Pakistan)
1973–8	Paul Scoon (Grenada)
1978–	S. Mahendra (Sri Lanka)

Project Officer

1981–	G. J. Randal (New Zealand)

Administration Officer/ Accountant

1966–76	R. N. Dawson, MBE (Britain)
1976–	E. Trewhitt (Britain)

APPENDIX D

Governments in membership of the Commonwealth Foundation

Africa
Botswana
The Gambia
Ghana
Kenya
Lesotho
Malawi
Mauritius
Nigeria
Seychelles
Sierra Leone
Swaziland
Tanzania
Uganda
Zambia
Zimbabwe

America
The Bahamas
Barbados
Canada
Grenada
Guyana
Jamaica
St Lucia
Trinidad and Tobago

Asia/Oceania
Australia
Bangladesh
Fiji
India
Kiribati
Malaysia
New Zealand
Papua New Guinea
Singapore
Solomons
Sri Lanka
Tonga
Western Samoa

Europe
Britain
Cyprus
Malta

Voluntary Contributors
Hong Kong
Brunei

APPENDIX E

Commonwealth professional associations

The broad aims of the associations listed below are briefly:

(1) To promote co-operation between relevant national societies within the Commonwealth.
(2) To assist each country to achieve the skills, quality and integrity of the professional services it requires.
(3) To foster the creation and development of national societies and to promote their usefulness to the public benefit.
(4) To promote the status of professional men and women in the community; to encourage training and retraining to the improvement of professional standards.
(5) To organise Commonwealth-wide and regional conferences, seminars and workshops on matters of common concern, for example, codes of ethics, reciprocity and recognition, educational standards.
(6) To promote advisory services; to disseminate through publications, conference reports, news-letters and by other means, knowledge and information relating to a particular profession and to foster the development of research and technical information services.
(7) To facilitate personal contacts within the professions and to encourage the interchange of specialist advisers and students.
(8) To provide a central secretariat to act as a focal point and clearing house for the achievement of such goals.

The following pan-Commonwealth professional associations and non-governmental organisations currently subscribe towards these aims.*

Commonwealth Association of Scientific Agricultural Societies
Founded 1978. Address: c/o Agricultural Institute of Canada, 151 Slater Street, Ottawa.

* Their activities are described in greater detail in a Commonwealth Foundation booklet published in 1979, *Guide to Pan-Commonwealth Professional Associations*.

Membership is primarily institutional and covers 32 Commonwealth countries in 17 of which there are corresponding members.

Commonwealth Association of Architects

Founded 1965. Address: The Building Centre, 26 Store Street, London WC1E 7BT.

There are 25 member institutes. Training and qualification problems are handled through a Commonwealth Board of Architectural Education. The association has convened numerous pan-Commonwealth and regional meetings. It publishes a news-letter and occasional training manuals. Its most recent publication, *Architectural Education in the Commonwealth*, provides a comprehensive survey of over 100 schools of architecture.

Commonwealth Society for the Deaf

Founded 1959. Address: 105 Gower Street, London WC1.

The society has organised numerous seminars and research and advisory projects. It publishes news-sheets and a magazine for deaf children.

Commonwealth Human Ecology Council

Founded 1969 as a charitable trust. Address: c/o Mrs Z. Daysh, 63 Cromwell Road, London SW7.

Membership includes corporate bodies, national units and university departments. The council has promoted a number of interdisciplinary workshops and seminars and has published research reports and guides to university courses.

Commonwealth Council for Educational Administration

Founded 1970. Address: c/o Faculty of Education, University of New England, Armidale, Australia.

Membership includes 10 national societies and individuals in 20 other countries. Numerous regional meetings have been held and publications include a quarterly news-letter and a directory of relevant courses organised throughout the Commonwealth.

Commonwealth Association of Science and Mathematics Educators

Founded 1974. Address: Benjamin Franklin House, 36 Craven Street, London WC2N 5NG.

The present membership of about 100 is institutional. The association publishes *The Science Teacher* and has fostered an awards scheme to encourage teachers in science and mathematics in the newer Commonwealth.

Commonwealth Engineers' Council

Founded 1946 (as the Commonwealth Engineering Conference). Address: 2 Little Smith Street, London SW1.

The council controls a Commonwealth Board on Engineering Education and Training and has recently set up a Commonwealth Assessment Board to assess qualifications in engineering awarded by any educational body in the Commonwealth requesting such advice. The council, which has organised a series of pan-Commonwealth and regional meetings, also issues registration cards to engineers for use in Commonwealth countries other than their own.

Commonwealth Geographical Bureau

Founded 1968. Address: c/o Department of Geography, University of Canterbury, Christchurch, New Zealand.

The bureau, in co-operation with the Royal Geographical Society and Commonwealth Foundation, operates a bursary scheme for young geographers and publishes a news-letter and research directory. It has also organised a number of seminars.

Commonwealth Journalists' Association

Founded 1978. Address: 1st Floor, 63 Carter Lane, London EC4V 5DY.

There are to date founder members from 12 Commonwealth countries. The first project undertaken by the association was to advise local journalists on the resumption of publication by the *Uganda Times*.

Commonwealth Legal Bureau

Founded 1969. Address: c/o PO Box 4006, Auckland, New Zealand.

Membership covers law and bar associations throughout the Commonwealth. One of the bureau's many tasks has been to help in the preparation of the quinquennial Commonwealth law conferences. Particular efforts have been made to strengthen co-operation between national bodies in Africa and the Caribbean. In 1972 an independent study was commissioned into the problems of the legal profession in the Commonwealth countries of Africa.

Commonwealth Legal Education Association

Founded 1972. Address: c/o Legal Director, Commonwealth

Secretariat, Marlborough House, Pall Mall, London SW1.

Present membership, made up mainly of university law faculties and institutes teaching law, is now upwards of 200. The association assists research projects related to teaching, education and the publication of legal literature. It has organised seminars and publishes a journal and news-letter.

Commonwealth Library Association

Founded 1972. Interim address: c/o The Library Association, 7 Ridgmount Street, London WC1E 7AE.

Forty-eight Commonwealth countries are represented on the council of the association which has held a series of Commonwealth-wide conferences. Exchanges, attachments and internships have been financed and workshops held on such problems as reciprocity of qualifications, training for librarianship and research methodology. Proposals exist for the development of rural library services in Africa, the development of bibliographic services and a regional library association in the South Pacific. Publications to date include a quarterly news-letter and reports on workshops relating to national bibliographies, reciprocity and training.

Association for Commonwealth Literature and Language Studies

Founded 1966. Address: c/o The Department of English, University of Guelph, Ontario, Canada N1G 2WI.

Membership is made up of some 600 higher education institutes and individuals. The association has formed nine regional groups which organise their own conferences and seminars. It helps schools and universities to establish courses in Commonwealth literature and to arrange scholar and student exchange schemes.

Publications other than a news-letter include a bibliography of Commonwealth literature and a handbook of Commonwealth holdings in British and European universities.

Commonwealth Magistrates Association

Founded 1970. Address: 28 Fitzroy Square, London W1.

Some 40 national associations are in membership. Apart from its regular Commonwealth-wide conferences, the association has held a number of regional seminars dealing with such problems as the administration of justice, the treatment of offenders and the training of adjudicators in lower courts. *The Commonwealth Judicial Journal* is published bi-annually and has achieved a wide circulation. The association is now developing a technical and professional information service and can arrange visits to courts and penal institutions throughout the Commonwealth.

Commonwealth Medical Association

Founded 1962. Address: c/o BMA House, Tavistock Square, London WC1.

There are national associations in some 30 countries. Among the projects undertaken have been the study of the equivalence of medical qualifications and of codes of ethics in all Commonwealth member countries; the gathering of data on the movement of medical manpower and on the role of the physician in primary health care in the newer world. Travelling fellowships have also been financed to enable eminent doctors from the older Commonwealth to visit developing countries.

Commonwealth Association of Museums

Founded 1974. Address: c/o The Science Museum, South Kensington, London SW7.

Membership extends to some 25 Commonwealth countries. Apart from the holding of seminars on problems of mutual concern, two main aims of the association have been to develop regional training for in-service personnel and to promote individual secondments. A number of travel study grants have been awarded in the latter context.

Commonwealth Nurses' Federation

Founded 1973. Address: c/o The Royal Commonwealth Society, 18 Northumberland Avenue, London WC2.

There are close on 50 national bodies in membership. Since its creation, the Federation has helped to set up 23 new nursing associations in the developing Commonwealth. It operates a comprehensive advisory service on professional problems including education, scholarships, specialist courses and employment. It also plans orientation programmes for overseas nurses attending post-basic and post-graduate courses in Britain and has particularly encouraged regional co-operation with others working in the field of health. Apart from organising regular regional and Commonwealth-wide meetings, it also arranges for national nursing associations from throughout the Commonwealth to foregather in the course of the biennial conferences of the International Council of Nurses. Twice yearly the federation publishes an eight-page Commonwealth supplement for inclusion in the *Nursing Times*. In addition the Federation publishes directories, reports and information documents at low cost to the benefit of its members.

Commonwealth Pharmaceutical Association

Founded 1969. Address: c/o Pharmaceutical Society of Great Britain, 1 Lambeth High Street, London SE1.

Over 30 national societies in membership. Principally through Commonwealth-wide meetings, the association has aimed to foster a high standard of control over the quality and distribution of drugs, at the same time encouraging the implementation of appropriate legislation. Apart from a news-letter, publications have included reports on education for pharmacists and on pharmaceutical services in rural areas.

Commonwealth Association of Planners

Founded 1971. Address: c/o Royal Institute of Town Planners, 26 Portland Place, London W1.

There are some 20 national societies in membership. The association has convened a number of Commonwealth-wide and regional meetings and has adopted policy guide-lines for action regarding planning in the machinery of governments: education and training, professional practice and regional co-operation. A number of studies of national manpower requirements have been made. Publications have included periodic news-letters and reports on education for planning and rural–urban drift in Africa.

Commonwealth Association of Surveying and Land Economy

Founded 1969. Address: c/o Royal Institute of Chartered Surveyors, 12 Great George Street, London SW1.

There are 41 national societies in membership covering the disciplines of land economy, land surveying and quantity surveying in 30 Commonwealth countries. Correspondents have also been appointed in 20 other countries which do not yet have national societies. The association has promoted a vigorous programme of Commonwealth-wide and regional conferences and made studies of the development of its constituent professions in all Commonwealth states. These have included analyses of patent and latent manpower requirements; of existing educational facilities and of further facilities needed to achieve a desired expansion of professional resources.

The introduction of new degree and correspondence courses has also been a major aim. A model code of conduct for the guidance of member societies has been produced, together with a report on matters to be taken into account when individual societies consider the advantages and disadvantages of registering the profession. Numerous reports have been published, including a handbook of surveying societies in the Commonwealth; a manual on surveying and land economy, and a brochure on education in these fields. The association also publishes bi-annually a newspaper, *Commonwealth Surveying and Land Economy*, of which 10,000 copies are distributed free to member societies. The association is now concentrating its efforts on regional collaboration, including the development of local facilities for education and training.

Commonwealth Veterinary Association

Founded 1968. Address: c/o Canadian Medical Veterinary Association, 360 Bronson Avenue, Ottawa.

Close on 30 national societies are in membership. The activities of the association to date have included the provision of travel grants to encourage the interchange of veterinarians; aid, financial and otherwise, towards the creation of national societies; and the provision of libraries and journals, audio-visual equipment and other material to smaller bodies. A number of regional meetings have been held. The association also sponsors seminars, lectures and demonstrations on subjects of Commonwealth-wide concern.

APPENDIX F

Professional Centres

The Professional Centre of the Northern Territory Incorporated
Mr G. K. Lindsay, Chairman, The Master Builders' Association Building, 191 Stuart Highway, Darwin, NT 5790, Australia.
Professions in membership: 20. Overall membership:* 960.

Sydney Science Centre
Mrs Ruth Inall, General Manager, 35–43 Clarence Street, Sydney 2000, Australia. Tel: 29–7747.

The Barbados Association of Professional Organisations
Mr C. A. Blackman, Honorary Secretary, Lucas Street, Bridgetown, Barbados.
Professions in membership: 9. Overall membership: 737.

Fiji Professional Centre
Mr Mumtaz F. Ali, Manager, 21 Des Voeux Road, PO Box 1015, Suva, Fiji. Tel: 25376.
Professions in membership: 10. Overall membership: 576.

Guyana Society
Mr Norris Mitchell, President, 169 New Market Street, Georgetown, Guyana.
Professions in membership: 16. Overall membership: 903.

Professional Societies Association of Jamaica
Mr Lascelles Dixon, Chairman, The Professional Centre, 2¾ Ruthven Road, PO Box 122, Kingston 10, Jamaica. Tel: 926–2434.
Professions in membership: 20. Overall membership: 7,649.

* All membership totals are variable. Membership of a national association does not in all cases include the right of personal membership of the centre.

Professional Centre of Kenya
Colonel A. J. Danvers, Administrator, St John's Gate, PO Box 72643, Nairobi, Kenya. Tel: 336146.
Professions in membership: 18. Overall membership: 4,150.

Malawi Professional Centre
Dr J. Chiphangwi, Chairman, c/o Medical Association of Malawi, Kamazu Central Hospital, PO Box 149, Lilongwe, Malawi.
Professions in membership: 10. Overall membership: 402.

Malaysian Professional Centre
Mr John M. Ambrose, Director, PO Box 109, Kuala Lumpur, Malaysia. Tel: 03-787171.
Professions in membership: 15. Overall membership: 8,000.

Malta Federation of Professional Bodies
Mr E. F. Bencini, President, 1 Wilga Street, Paceville, Malta. Tel: 38851.
Professions in membership: 9. Overall membership: 803.

Sierra Leone Association of Professional Organizations
Dr W. S. Marcus Jones, PO Box 53, Fourah Bay College, Mount Aureal, Sierra Leone.
Professions in membership: 9. Overall membership: not available.

Singapore Professional Centre
Mr Fong Chan Yoon, Centre Director, BLK 23, 129-B, Outram Park, Singapore 3. Tel: 2205877.
Professions in membership: 21. Overall membership: 5,473.

Organization of Professional Associations of Sri Lanka
Mr W. B. A. Jayasekera, General Secretary, 'Seevalie Mandirya', 179 Sir James Peiris Mawatha, Colombo, 2, Sri Lanka. Tel: 33763.
Professions in membership: 16. Overall membership: 7,000.

The Tanzania Professional Centre
Prof. J. K. Shija, Chairman, PO Box 7235, Dar-es-Salaam, Tanzania.
Professions in membership: 12. Overall membership: 2,830.

Professional Centre of Trinidad and Tobago
Mr A. C. Lutchman, Hon. Secretary, 19 Stanmore Avenue, Port of Spain, Trinidad. Tel: 62-54651.
Professions in membership: 13. Overall membership: 2,638.

Professional Centre of Uganda
Mr G. W. Katatumba, Hon. Secretary, 24 Lumumba Road, PO Box 3216, Kampala, Uganda. Tel: 63010.
Professions in membership: 15. Overall membership: 1,300.

London Science Centre
Colonel D. Hall, Director, 18 Adam Street, London, WC2. Tel: 01-839-4902.

Professional Centre of Zambia
Mr A. W. Anderson, Chairman, Chadwick House, 733 Chachacha Road South, PO Box 3730, Lusaka, Zambia. Tel: 75751.
Professions in membership: 8. Overall membership: 1,241.

Centre in Formation:
Mauritius Professional Centre

APPENDIX G

Commonwealth Foundation Lectureships

1968
Dr V. M. Hamilton, Director, New Zealand Scientific and Industrial Research Organization – to East and Central Africa; subjects: scientific organization and animal husbandry.

1969
Dr J. L. Sumption, (then) University of Alberta, Canada – to Tanzania and West Africa; subject: animal genetics.

1970
Professor R. L. Huckstep, (then) Professor of Orthopaedic Surgery, Makerere University, Uganda – to Kenya, Malawi, Mauritius, Australasia, the Pacific Islands, Hong Kong, Singapore, Malaysia and Canada; subject: orthopaedic problems in the newer world.

1971–2
Sir Frederick Warner, past-president of the British Society of Chemical Engineers and Visiting Professor, Imperial College, London – to India and Australia; subjects: chemical engineering and problems of pollution.

1973
Dr R. Tupper, formerly Vice-President, Canadian National Research Council – to Jamaica, Trinidad and Tobago, Barbados and Guyana; subject: science and technology in the newer world.

Professor S. R. A. Dodu, University of Ghana Medical School – to The Gambia, Sierra Leone, Nigeria and to universities in Ghana outside Accra; subject: meeting the health needs of our developing countries – past, present and future.

1974
Dr Guy Hunter, Visiting Professor, University of Reading and

249

Overseas Development Institute, London – to Ghana, Nigeria, Kenya and India; subject: rural–urban migration in Tropical Africa.

Dr R. N. Gonzalez, formerly technical director, Scientific Research Council, Jamaica – to Sri Lanka and India; subject: problems confronting the industrial scientist.

Lord (then **Dr David**) **Pitt** (of Grenada), formerly Chairman, Greater London Council – to East and West Africa; subject: the problems of the big city.

1975
Mr K. C. Harrison, President, Commonwealth Library Association and City Librarian of Westminster – to Zambia, Malawi, Tanzania, Kenya and Uganda; subject: the importance and relevance of librarianship for developing countries.

1976
Professor N. R. E. Fendall, Liverpool School of Tropical Medicine – to Fiji, Tonga, Niue, Western Samoa, Nauru, New Caledonia, New Zealand; subject: the training of ancilliary health personnel.

Professor L. Neville Brown, formerly Dean, Faculty of Law, University of Birmingham – to Barbados, St Lucia, Trinidad and Tobago, Guyana, Jamaica and the Bahamas; subject: legal education and public law.

Dr D. Linstrum, Radcliffe Lecturer and Director of Conservation Studies, University of York – to Nigeria, Ghana, Zambia and Kenya; subject: the conservation of historic towns and monuments.

1977
Professor D. Hinton, Department of Architectural Planning and Urban Studies, University of Aston in Birmingham – to India, Bangladesh, Sri Lanka, Malaysia, Singapore, Hong Kong; subject: interdisciplinary approach to environmental development.

Dr N. A. Myers, Chairman, Department of Surgery, Royal Children's Hospital, Melbourne, Australia – to India, Sri Lanka and Bangladesh; subject: paediatric surgery.

1979
Professor D. G. Howell, Dean, Ontario Veterinary College, Guelph, Canada – to India, Sri Lanka, Malaysia, Australia and

New Zealand; subject: the interrelationship between animal production and animal health.

1980

Mr D. Jackson, lately Consultant Surgeon, Birmingham Accident Hospital – to Sri Lanka and India; subject: the treatment of burns.

Professor Shamsul Haque, University of Dacca, Bangladesh – to Solomon Islands, Fiji, Tonga, Western Samoa and Papua New Guinea; subject: educational administration.

1981

Dr Helen Mussalem, Executive Director, Canadian Nurses Association – to Nigeria, Ghana, Sierra Leone, The Gambia, Malta and Cyprus; subject: nursing education.

Mr D. Ingram, President Commonwealth Journalists' Association (London) – to Australia, Bangladesh, Malaysia, Singapore, New Zealand; subject: training in journalism.

Dr L. S. Chandrakant, Bangalore, India, formerly Director, Colombo Plan Staff College for Technician Education – to Kenya, Tanzania, Zambia, Uganda; subject: technical education and training.

APPENDIX H

Non-Governmental Bodies Active in the Commonwealth

Any attempt at definition in this field must defy logic. Numerous efforts have been made to categorise such organisations. However admirably intentioned all have in some way failed, in that many such bodies are international in compass though with a pronounced bias towards the Commonwealth: others work from a national (and not necessarily Commonwealth country) base in the interests of the world at large, or of a particular continent or region. Only a few are concerned with the Commonwealth alone.

Thus the following list of (non-professional) NGOs can be no more than illustrative. It will, however, give some idea of the weight of the iceberg below the surface.

A Commonwealth-wide NGOs

Association of Commonwealth Universities
Commonwealth Broadcasting Association
Commonwealth Press Union
Commonwealth Parliamentary Association
Royal Commonwealth Society for the Blind
Royal Commonwealth Society
Royal Overseas League
English Speaking Union of the Commonwealth
Commonwealth Forestry Association
Standing Committee of Commonwealth Forestry
Commonwealth Legal Advisory Service
Royal Agricultural Society of the Commonwealth
Commonwealth Advisory Aeronautical Research Council
Victoria League for Commonwealth Friendship
Commonwealth War Graves Commission
Commonwealth Medical Advisory Bureau
Commonwealth Games Federation

B Internationally Operating NGOs with a Preponderant Commonwealth Interest

Oxfam
War on Want
Christian Aid
Help the Aged
Save the Children Fund
World University Service
International Red Cross
World Council of Churches
International Council of Women
World Scout Movement
World YMCA and YWCA
International Voluntary Service
International Council for Adult Education
United World Colleges

C National NGOs Active in the Commonwealth

(1) *Britain*
National Council for Voluntary Organisations
Institutes of Commonwealth Studies, London and Oxford
Queen Elizabeth House, Oxford
Commonwealth Institutes, London and Edinburgh
Barclays Development Fund
British Executive Service Overseas
City and Guilds of London Overseas
Commonwealth Youth Exchange Council
Commonwealth (Educational) Linking Trust
League for the Exchange of Commonwealth Teachers
Leonard Cheshire Foundation
Confederation of British Industry
British Producers' Association
Industrial Society
Royal Society of Arts
Intermediate Technology Development Group
LEPRA
St John's Ambulance Association and Brigade
Nuffield Foundation
Gulbenkian Foundation (UK Branch)
Overseas Development Institute
Duke of Edinburgh's Award Scheme
Ranfurly Library Service

Commonwealth Expedition (COMEX)
Thomson Foundation
Voluntary Service Overseas
British Commonwealth Ex-Service League
Centre for International Briefing
Council for Education in the Commonwealth
Diplomatic and Commonwealth Writers' Association of Britain
Scout, Girl Guide and Boys' Brigade Movements

(2) *Canada*
Canadian Council for International Co-operation
Canadian Executive Service Overseas
International Development Research Centre
Canadian University Services Overseas
North–South Institute

(3) *Australasia*
Australian Council for Overseas Aid
Foundation for the Peoples of the South Pacific
Australian Overseas Service Bureau
New Zealand Council of Organisations for International Relief,
    Rehabilitation and Development
New Zealand Volunteer Service Abroad

(4) *Caribbean*
Christian Action for Development in the Caribbean
Caribbean Conservation Association

(5) *Africa*
Association of African Universities
Pan-African Institute for Development
African Centre for Educational Exchange
African Adult Education Association

Numerous religious and other voluntary bodies – international, regional and national – also support relief, social and development programmes in the Commonwealth: as do other agencies based in the US and countries of the EEC. Further information on their activities can be found in a series of regional directories published by the Commonwealth Foundation between 1978 and 1980, and in *Commonwealth Organisations*, a handbook issued by the Commonwealth Secretariat in 1979.

Select Bibliography

Adu, A. L., *The Civil Service in New African States* (London, 1965).
Ashby, Sir Eric, *African Universities and Western Traditions* (London, 1964).
Ball, M. M., *The 'Open' Commonwealth* (Durham, NC, 1971).
Casey, Rt Hon. Lord, *The Future of the Commonwealth* (London, 1963).
Currie, Sir James, *Professional Organizations in the Commonwealth* (London, 1970).
Garner, Rt Hon. Lord, *The Commonwealth Office 1925–1968* (London, 1978).
Gordon-Walker, Rt Hon. Lord, *The Commonwealth* (London, 1962).
Hall, H. D., *Commonwealth: A History of the British Commonwealth of Nations* (London, 1971).
Hamilton, W. B. et al. (eds), *A Decade of the Commonwealth, 1955–1964* (Durham, NC, 1965).
Hornby, Richard, *The Changing Commonwealth* (London, 1965).
Ingram, Derek, *The Commonwealth at Work* (London, 1969).
Ingram, Derek, *The Imperfect Commonwealth* (London, 1977).
Kirkman, W. P., *Unscrambling an Empire: A Critique of British Colonial Policy, 1955–1966* (London, 1966).
Mansergh, Professor Nicholas, *The Commonwealth Experience* (London, 1969).
Miller, Professor J. D. B., *The Commonwealth in the World*, 3rd edn (London, 1965).
Miller, Professor J. D. B., *Survey of Commonwealth Affairs: Problems of Expansion and Attrition, 1959–1969* (London, 1974).
Nathan, Lord, *The Charities Act 1960* (London, 1962).
Perham, Dame Margery, *Colonial Sequence, 1949–1969* (London, 1969).
Ramphal, Sridath, *One World to Share: Selected Speeches of the Commonwealth Secretary-General* (London, 1979).
Rees, Trevor R., *The History of the Royal Commonwealth Society 1868–1968* (London, 1968).
Sandys, Rt Hon. Lord Duncan, *The Modern Commonwealth* (London, 1962).
Smith, Arnold C., *A Stitch in Time* (London, 1981).
Soper, T. P. (Rapporteur), *The Future of the Commonwealth: A British View*, report on the Ditchley Park Conference (London, 1963).
Symonds, Richard, *The British and Their Successors* (London, 1966).
Tett, N. and Chadwick, J., *Professional Organizations in the Commonwealth*, 2nd edn (London, 1976).
Walker, Andrew, *The Modern Commonwealth* (London, 1975).
Wheare, K. C., *The Constitutional Structure of the Commonwealth* (Oxford, 1960).

Other Specialist Publications

Yearbook of the Commonwealth, British Foreign and Commonwealth Office, London.

Yearbook of International Organisations, Union of International Associations, Brussels.

Development Guide, 3rd edn, 1978, Overseas Development Institute, London.

Commonwealth Universities Yearbook, Association of Commonwealth Universities, London.

Directory of Grant-making Trusts, 6th edn, 1978, Charities Aid Foundation, Tonbridge, Kent.

The International Foundation Directory (Europa Publications, London: 1974).

Relevant Commonwealth Secretariat Publications

Annual Reports of Commonwealth Secretary–General: from 1966 onwards.

Report of the Review Committee on Intra-Commonwealth Organisations (London, 1966).

From Governments to Grassroots, report of the Advisory Committee on non-governmental organisations in the Commonwealth (1978).

Commonwealth Organisations: a Handbook of Official and Unofficial Organisations Active in the Commonwealth, 2nd edn (1979).

International Activities in Science and Technology (1976).

Training for Agricultural Development (1976).

Appropriate Technology in the Commonwealth (1977).

Health Training Facilities in the Commonwealth (1979).

Commonwealth Foundation Publications

Biennial Progress Reports (eight to date) covering the period 1966–81.

Fifty papers in the Foundation's 'Occasional Paper' series, of which the following are relevant to this study.

(a) *General*

Paper no. 13, *The Role of the Professions in a Changing World*, report on a Foundation seminar held at the Professional Centre of Singapore, 1971.

Paper no. 19, *Commonwealth University Co-operation*, report on a Foundation seminar held at the Institute of Development Studies, 1973.

Paper no. 28, *Commonwealth Co-operation: The Role of the Commonwealth Professional Associations*, report on a Foundation-sponsored meeting held at Marlborough House, London, October 1974.

Paper no. 32, *The Professions, Universities and the Civil Service*, report on a Foundation seminar held at the Professional Centre of Jamaica, 1975.

Paper no. 42, *Professional Centres in the Commonwealth*, report on a Foundation seminar held at the Professional Centre of Kenya, 1977.

Paper no. 46, *The Professional in the Wider Community*, report on a Foundation seminar held at the Professional Centres of Malaysia and Singapore, 1979.

(b) *Specialist*

Paper no. 5, *Quality in Education*, report on a conference of inspectors of schools from the Asia/Pacific area, Singapore, 1969.

Paper no. 8, *Report on a Conference of Librarians from Commonwealth Universities in Africa*, Zambia, 1969.

Paper no. 20, *Report on a Team Visit from the Universities of the West Indies and Guyana to Universities in Commonwealth West Africa*, 1973.

Paper no. 23, *Orthopaedic Training in Developing Countries*, report on a conference held at Oxford, 1973.

Paper no. 24, *Adult education and National Development*, report on an Asian regional seminar held in New Delhi, 1974.

Paper no. 34, *Problems of Deafness in the Newer World*, report from a seminar at the University of Sussex, 1974.

Paper no. 40, *Problems Facing the Medical Laboratory Professions in the Commonwealth*, report on a seminar held in London, 1976.

Paper no. 41, *The Disabled in Developing Countries*, report on a seminar held at Oxford, 1976.

Paper no. 45, *Engineers for the 21st Century*, report on a Commonwealth Engineers' Council seminar held in London, 1977.

(c) *Other publications*

A Guide to Pan-Commonwealth Professional Associations (London, 1979).

A Commonwealth Caribbean Directory of Aid Agencies (London, 1978).

A Commonwealth African Directory of Aid Agencies (London, 1979).

A Guide to Aid Agencies Active in Commonwealth Countries of Asia and Oceania (London, 1981).

Index

Ademola, Adetokunbo, Rt Hon. Sir, chairman xii, 162, 219–20, 222, 237
Adu, A. L., civil servant 208
adversary factor 7, 192, 194, 212, 213
Advisory Committee on relationships between Official and Unofficial Commonwealth 162, 185–90
Africa, agriculture research stations, duplication in 165
regional guide for 163
Africa Education Trust 24
Agreed Memorandum for Commonwealth Foundation 53–4, 223–4
and duplication of activities 141
and the younger element 202
Agricultural Institute of Canada bursary 83
Alberta Government support 199
American–British Group of US Congress 31
ancillary medical professions assisted 76
Anglican Church education machinery 14
Anglo–Francophone scientific conference, Dakar 164, 165–6
Ansari, U. A., first deputy director 88, 237
architectural societies, work of 109, 110, 113
Art(s) 35, 207
interchange of students 24
Asia trusts 66
Asian Development Bank, survey of 211
Asquith Report on universities 16
Association for Commonwealth Literature and Language Studies 118, 127–8, 198, 200, 242
Association of Commonwealth Universities 15, 16, 21, 83, 146, 181, 252
Association of Faculties of Agriculture 164
Attlee administration and trusts 6
Auchmuty, Professor J. J., first holder of Commonwealth chair 164

Australia, bursary scheme 168
co-operation of 166
nurses of on British register 27
professional centre in 104–5
Australia Academy of Science 29
Australian Big Brother Movement 36

Bandury Pact 45
Bangladesh Academy of Rural Development 211–13
Bangladesh University of Engineering and Technology 213
Banks and the Commonwealth 31
Barbados Association of Professional Organisations, The 246
Barclays International Development Fund, research assistance 106, 126
Barwick, Sir Garfield 59
Beveridge, Lord 6
Board of Charities Commissioners 5
Board of Trustees 162, 219
Bottomley, Rt. Hon. Arthur 59
Boys' Brigade 36, 254
Boy Scout Movement 36, 254
brain-drain syndrome 77
Brayton, Miss Margaret 126
Britain, chooses Europe for Commonwealth 19
church and missionary societies, and Commonwealth education 23
Commonwealth student population 20–1
problem of professional bodies 102
British Academy 102
British Association for the Advancement of Science 29
British Association of Malaysia 35
British Broadcasting Corporation links with Commonwealth 33–4
Reith lectures (1980) 164
staff training school 34
British Chest and Heart Association scholarship 27–8
British Commonwealth Relations Office, list of organisations 20

British Community Relations Commission, award of 85
British Council 35, 202
British Dental Council 27
British doctors recognised by Commonwealth 26
firms and industrial training 23–4
foundation and trusts, financial aid for Commonwealth 23
Government assists annual income 154
policies affecting Commonwealth 46
professional bodies, meeting 47–8
trust directors, attitude of 68
universities and development in Commonwealth countries 21
British Empire 12, 13, 14, 209
British Institute of Hospital Administrators training courses 28
British Institute of International and Comparative Law 25
British Institute of Radio Engineers training courses 30
British Leprosy Relief Association 28
British Medical Association 109
links with Commonwealth 27
British–Nigeria Association 35
British Red Cross Society scholarships 27–8
British Veterinary Association forms Commonwealth Association 110
links with member countries 27
Brown, Dr Farrer, trustee 57, 148
Brunei assists Foundation 220
Bureau of Information for universities of the Empire 15, 16
Burnet, Sir Macfarlane, chairman of trustees 56, 59, 63–4, 75, 86, 257
bursary schemes 71, 79, 83, 136, 198, 221, 241
Bury, Viscount 11
business world links with Commonwealth 31–3

Campbell, Richard, Trustee 57
Canada, Government of 162, 175
universities 15
Canadian Games Foundation 199
Canadian International Development Agency 167, 186
Canadian proposal for advisory Committee 186

Canadian University Services Overseas 84
Canadian Veterinary Association 110
Canadians, study projects assisted 84
Caribbean regional co-operation 167
CARICOM 167
Carnegie trust 66
Casey, Lord, Governor-General of Australia 43, 44
Catholic Institute for International Relations 23
Central Africa, professional co-operation 166
Central Bureau for Educational Visits and Exchanges 202
Centre Council 99
Centre for Educational Television Overseas 24, 34
Ceylon Commercial Association 32
Chadwick, G. W. St. J., first Director of Foundation 56, 57, 58–9, 60, 237
chair, 'rotating' in Modern Commonwealth Studies, holders of 163–4
charitable purposes defined 4, 8
Charitable Trusts Act (1853) 4, 5
Charities Act (1960) 3, 4–5, 6, 7
charities, empire-minded 9
registration of 8
Charity Commission 5, 8
Chartered Institute of Secretaries Commonwealth divisions 30
Chartered Insurance Institute 30
Christian Aid 38, 253
Church bodies, work of 3–4, 36
Clegg, Dr Hugh 82
Clunies Ross Memorial Foundation 102
College of General Practitioners Commonwealth faculties 27
Colombus, Dr C. J. Trustee 58
Colonial Development and Welfare Act (1940) 16
Colonial Institute 10
COMEX (Commonwealth Expedition) 37
Committee of Vice-Chancellors and Principals of Commonwealth universities 21
'Committee of the Whole' 184, 194, 195
Commonwealth, difficulties in 45–7, 48, 174
education in 20f.
governments and benefits of the associations 123; income assistance